NEO-IMPERIALISM IN CHILDREN'S LITERATURE ABOUT AFRICA

Children's Literature and Culture
Jack Zipes, Series Editor

Little Women and the
Feminist Imagination
Criticism, Controversy, Personal Essays
edited by Janice M. Alberghene and
Beverly Lyon Clark

The Presence of the Past
*Memory, Heritage, and Childhood
in Postwar Britain*
by Valerie Krips

The Case of Peter Rabbit
*Changing Conditions of Literature
for Children*
by Margaret Mackey

The Feminine Subject in Children's
Literature
by Christine Wilkie-Stibbs

Ideologies of Identity in
Adolescent Fiction
by Robyn McCallum

Recycling Red Riding Hood
by Sandra Beckett

The Poetics of Childhood
by Roni Natov

Voices of the Other
*Children's Literature and the
Postcolonial Context*
edited by Roderick McGillis

Narrating Africa
George Henty and the Fiction of Empire
by Mawuena Kossi Logan

Reimagining Shakespeare for Children
and Young Adults
edited by Naomi J. Miller

Representing the Holocaust in
Youth Literature
by Lydia Kokkola

Translating for Children
by Riitta Oittinen

Beatrix Potter
Writing in Code
by M. Daphne Kutzer

Children's Films
History, Ideology, Pedagogy, Theory
by Ian Wojcik-Andrews

Utopian and Dystopian Writing for
Children and Young Adults
edited by Carrie Hintz and Elaine Ostry

Transcending Boundaries
*Writing for a Dual Audience of
Children and Adults*
edited by Sandra L. Beckett

The Making of the Modern Child
*Children's Literature and Childhood in the
Late Eighteenth Century*
by Andrew O'Malley

How Picturebooks Work
by Maria Nikolajeva and Carole Scott

Brown Gold
*Milestones of African American Children's
Picture Books, 1845-2002*
by Michelle H. Martin

Russell Hoban/Forty Years
Essays on His Writing for Children
by Alida Allison

Apartheid and Racism in South African
Children's Literature
by Donnarae MacCann and
Amadu Maddy

Empire's Children
*Empire and Imperialism in Classic British
Children's Books*
by M. Daphne Kutzer

Constructing the Canon of
Children's Literature
Beyond Library Walls and Ivory Towers
by Anne Lundin

Youth of Darkest England
*Working Class Children at the Heart of
Victorian Empire*
by Troy Boone

Ursula K. Leguin Beyond Genre
Literature for Children and Adults
by Mike Cadden

Twice-Told Children's Tales
edited by Betty Greenway

Diana Wynne Jones
The Fantastic Tradition and Children's Literature
by Farah Mendlesohn

Childhood and Children's Books in Early Modern Europe, 1550-1800
edited by Andrea Immel and Michael Witmore

Voracious Children
Who Eats Whom in Children's Literature
by Carolyn Daniel

National Character in South African Children's Literature
by Elwyn Jenkins

Myth, Symbol, and Meaning in Mary Poppins
The Governess as Provocateur
by Georgia Grilli

A Critical History of French Children's Literature, Vol. 1 & 2
by Penny Brown

Once Upon a Time in a Different World
Issues and Ideas in African American Children's Literature
By Neal A. Lester

The Gothic in Children's Literature
Haunting the Borders
Edited by Anna Jackson, Karen Coats, and Roderick McGillis

Reading Victorian Schoolrooms
Childhood and Education in Nineteenth-Century Fiction
by Elizabeth Gargano

Soon Come Home to This Island
West Indians in British Children's Literature
by Karen Sands-O'Connor

Boys in Children's Literature and Popular Culture
Masculinity, Abjection, and the Fictional Child
by Annette Wannamaker

Into the Closet
Cross-dressing and the Gendered Body in Children's Literature
by Victoria Flanagan

Russian Children's Literature and Culture
edited by Marina Balina and Larissa Rudova

The Outside Child In and Out of the Book
Christine Wilkie-Stibbs

Representing Africa in Children's Literature
Old and New Ways of Seeing
by Vivian Yenika-Agbaw

The Fantasy of Family
Nineteenth-Century Children's Literature and the Myth of the Domestic Ideal
by Liz Thiel

From Nursery Rhymes to Nationhood
Children's Literature and the Construction of Canadian Identity
Elizabeth A. Galway

The Family in English Children's Literature
Ann Alston

Enterprising Youth
Social Values and Acculturation in Nineteenth-Century American Children's Literature
Monika Elbert

Constructing Adolescence in Fantastic Realism
Alison Waller

Crossover Fiction
Global and Historical Perspectives
Sandra L. Beckett

The Crossover Novel
Contemporary Children's Fiction and Its Adult Readership
Rachel Falconer

Shakespeare in Children's Literature
Gender and Cultural Capital
Erica Hateley

Critical Approaches to Food in Children's Literature
Edited by Kara K. Keeling and Scott T. Pollard

Neo-Imperialism in Children's Literature About Africa
A Study of Contemporary Fiction
by Yulisa Amadu Maddy and Donnarae MacCann

NEO-IMPERIALISM IN CHILDREN'S LITERATURE ABOUT AFRICA

A Study of Contemporary Fiction

YULISA AMADU MADDY
AND DONNARAE MACCANN

First published 2009
by Routledge
270 Madison Ave, New York, NY 10016

Simultaneously published in the UK
by Routledge
2 Park Square, Milton Park, Abingdon, Oxon OX14 4RN

Routledge is an imprint of the Taylor & Francis Group, an informa business

© 2009 Taylor & Francis

Typeset in by Minion by IBT Global.
Printed and bound in the United States of America on acid-free paper by IBT Global.

All rights reserved. No part of this book may be reprinted or reproduced or utilised in any form or by any electronic, mechanical, or other means, now known or hereafter invented, including photocopying and recording, or in any information storage or retrieval system, without permission in writing from the publishers.

Trademark Notice: Product or corporate names may be trademarks or registered trademarks, and are used only for identification and explanation without intent to infringe.

Library of Congress Cataloging in Publication Data
Maddy, Yulisa Amadu, 1936-
  Neo-imperialism in children's literature about Africa : a study of contemporary fiction / by Yulisa Amadu Maddy and Donnarae MacCann.
    p. cm. — (Children's literature and culture; 60)
  Includes bibliographical references and index.
  ISBN 978-0-415-99390-6
  1. Children's stories—History and criticism. 2. Africa—In literature. 3. Africans in literature. 4. Racism in literature. I. MacCann, Donnarae. II. Title.
  PN1009.5.A47M34 2009
  809.3'93586—dc22
                                              2008023900

ISBN10: 0-415-99390-3 (hbk)
ISBN10: 0-203-88649-6 (ebk)

ISBN13: 978-0-415-99390-6 (hbk)
ISBN13: 978-0-203-88649-6 (ebk)

If you are in one boat, you have to row together.

✶ ✶ ✶ ✶ ✶ ✶

Not all lovely houses are for passing the night.

✶ ✶ ✶ ✶ ✶ ✶

At the tribunal of the foxes, the chickens are always guilty.

—African Proverbs

Contents

Series Editor's Foreword ... xi

Acknowledgments ... xiii

Introduction ... 1

PART I
Background

Chapter 1 "Darkest Africa": A Persistent Western Fantasy ... 13

Chapter 2 Feminism in Africa: Complexities and Activism ... 21

Chapter 3 Institutional Racism ... 29

PART II
Neo-Imperialist Stories, 1994–2008

Chapter 4 Eurocentric Feminism in *The Shadows of Ghadames* and *Our Secret, Siri Aang* ... 39

Chapter 5 White Supremacy in Isabel Allende's *Forest of the Pygmies* ... 55

Chapter 6 Anti-African Themes in "Liberal" Young Adult Novels ... 65

Chapter 7	Crime and Crime Syndicates in *Many Stones* and *Zulu Dog*	79
Chapter 8	"Doomed Races" in Elana Bregin's "Ella's Dunes"	91
Chapter 9	Disease and the "Darkest Africa" Myth: Novels About AIDS and Smallpox	101
Chapter 10	When the West Talks to Itself: Ethnocentricity in Nancy Farmer's "African" Novels	113
Chapter 11	Child Soldiers and Survivors in *Chanda's Wars*	125

PART III
Rewarding the Best

| Chapter 12 | *Out of Bounds* and the Legacy of
South African Child Martyrs | 135 |
| | Epilogue | 147 |

Notes	151
Selected Bibliography	165
Index	169

Series Editor's Foreword

Dedicated to furthering original research in children's literature and culture, the Children's Literature and Culture series includes monographs on individual authors and illustrators, historical examinations of different periods, literary analyses of genres, and comparative studies on literature and the mass media. The series is international in scope and is intended to encourage innovative research in children's literature with a focus on interdisciplinary methodology.

Children's literature and culture are understood in the broadest sense of the term children to encompass the period of childhood up through adolescence. Owing to the fact that the notion of childhood has changed so much since the origination of children's literature, this Routledge series is particularly concerned with transformations in children's culture and how they have affected the representation and socialization of children. While the emphasis of the series is on children's literature, all types of studies that deal with children's radio, film, television, and art are included in an endeavor to grasp the aesthetics and values of children's culture. Not only have there been momentous changes in children's culture in the last fifty years, but there have been radical shifts in the scholarship that deals with these changes. In this regard, the goal of the Children's Literature and Culture series is to enhance research in this field and, at the same time, point to new directions that bring together the best scholarly work throughout the world.

Jack Zipes

Acknowledgments

We extend our deep appreciation to three journal editors who have given us permission to reprint articles from their journals: Dean Roberta Trites, who accepted and edited our essay "Anti-African Themes in 'Liberal' Young Adult Novels" (reprinted by permission of the Children's Literature Association and originally appearing in *The Children's Literature Association Quarterly*, Summer, 2002, Vol. 27:2, pp. 92–99); Dr. Osayimwense Osa for permission to reprint "White Supremacy in Isabel Allende's *Forest of the Pygmies*," published in *JACYL (Journal of African Children's and Youth Literature*, 2007–2009, Vol. 17–18, pp. 60–75); Dr. Meena Khorana for permission to reprint "When the West Talks to Itself: Ethnocentricity in Nancy Farmer's 'African' Novels" (in *Sankofa: A Journal of African Children's and Young Adult Literature*, 2004, Vol. 3, pp. 6–15).

Also in the preparation of this book we are greatly indebted to Ian Noah and Mahoumbah Klobah for help with typing chores, and to Mahoumbah for his thoughtful observations and suggestions about "When the West Talks to Itself." Jill Blaine was indispensable in unraveling computer complexities, and Lucille Hernández Gregory was always at hand with much generous friendship and hospitality. We are grateful for such dependable, joy-inspiring helpers.

A Note About Terminology

We have added quotation marks around terms that are widely used, but that constitute the colonizer's invention of names for African people (e.g., "Pygmies," "Kaffirs," "Bushmen," and "Hottentots," as well as "Colored" or "Coloured"). We will capitalize the terms White and Black when they imply an ethnic population, but use a lowercase letter when we speak of "white supremacy" or other concepts that have a color line connotation. In particular in books dealing with South Africa, names often represented a hierarchy that deeply influenced the freedoms and oppressions allotted to a group.

Introduction

> Imperialism is by its nature bombastic; it has to suppress the memory of the violence it commits to perpetuate its power, or it would lose faith in its own goodness.
> —Johann Hari (11)

> Juvenile literature . . . is steeped in every aspect of imperialism.
> —Jeffrey Richards (3)

Children's literature is a useful instrument for imperialists as they preserve their faith in their imperial agendas. Stories for the young appear innocent, unconnected with the violence of political and cultural domination. However, these stories are largely improvisations on the Western notion that there exists a "white man's burden,"[1] a concept reinforced when fictional African characters are depicted in children's books as incapable of self-determination. White children absorb this myth easily from educational professionals and see no reason to doubt their own alleged superiority. By keeping the white supremacy myth alive in children's books, the inequalities experienced in real life by children of color are supported. Even a belief in the *inevitability* of inequality may take hold in young minds (Cashmore and Troyna, 189). One thing is certain: following a colonial conquest, "patterns of inequality persisted for generation after generation" (Cashmore, 85).[2]

Definitions

Colonialism, as we use the term, involves the domination of one group over culturally dissimilar groups. And the domination works on many levels, as when colonizers proclaim a great moral and physiological chasm between themselves and the colonized. This insistence on dissimilarity is echoed by children's book authors who overemphasize physical characteristics (both bodily and cultural), suggesting an inescapable distance between Westerners and non-Westerners.

Understanding children's literature and its ongoing links with myths about Africa becomes easier if we realize that colonialism "constitutes an epochal era in Africa" (Samuel-Mbaekwe, 36). That means that it has importance beyond the period in which it initially developed. Colonialism has shaken off extant social formations and instituted ones that are more permanent. It is epochal in the way lives are so forcefully affected that there is "no room for individuals to choose to participate or not to participate" (36). From Iheanyi Samuel-Mbaekwe's sociological perspective, this puts colonialism in Africa on a scale equivalent to such epochs as the Industrial Revolution and the French Revolution.

Similarly, historians attribute this enormous scope to *imperialism*. As John MacKenzie defines the term, imperialism also connotes an epochal movement. It reaches beyond specific individual ramifications. He writes: "Imperialism was more than a set of economic, political, and military phenomena. It was a habit of mind, a dominant idea in the era of European world supremacy which had widespread intellectual, cultural, and technical expressions" (qtd. in Mangan, ix). MacKenzie treats empires as networks with practically unlimited scope, as entities in which developments of every imaginable sort are aligned with the aspirations of the colonial power. Referring to Great Britain, Ellis Cashmore and Barry Troyna note that although the British Empire has been essentially declining for centuries, "the consciousness associated with that empire has been transmitted through generations and remains largely intact. . . . [T]he idea that being white denotes superiority is . . . a remnant of the colonial mentality" (53).[3] Edward Said makes a similar point about the difference between nominal colonialism and what has followed. He comments: "In our time, direct colonialism has largely ended; imperialism . . . lingers where it has always been, in a kind of general cultural sphere, as well as in specific political, ideological, economic, and social practices" (9). Children's literature illustrates such cultural tenacity when its practitioners claim that literary art is neutral and inclusive, while at the same time they have in mind a narrowly defined child population. In this way, the Western book establishment can talk the talk of universalism while still operating within its own cultural cocoon.

Ngũgĩ wa Thiong'o, a Kenyan novelist and playwright, makes the following observation as he links imperialism, colonialism, and education:

> The aim of imperialism whether in its colonial or neocolonial stage is to steal the wealth generated by the people: that is, generated by the labor power of the workers and peasants of the colonial world. . . . The aim of

colonial education is to bring up a partly developed native . . . who has internalized a consciousness that blinds him into not seeing the loot and the plunder going on around him. . . . Education and culture are in fact class education and culture. (97, 95, 91)[4]

Education and Current Imperialist Literature

We have critiqued thirteen novels and one short story that bear out the ongoing persistence of cultural imperialism. These works were published from 1994 to 2008 and they include African settings from Libya to South Africa, from Sierra Leone to Kenya. In remarkably similar ways they contain these earmarks of imperialist literature:

- They do not take account of cultural or historical processes among the colonized.
- They discourage close interactions among races.
- They presume the right of colonizers to take charge of land and other resources.
- They condone the displacement of one population on behalf of benefits for another.
- They serve to develop for Westerners a mirror of themselves, whether through self-congratulatory projects concerned with reforming the "heathen" or projects designed to ennoble the "savage."

What the literature amounts to is a symbolic system for affirming human inequality. Or put differently, the undercurrents in both plot and characterization separate groups in relation to a racial or cultural hierarchy. Whatever the intentions may be, the storylines reveal a politically motivated justification for containing Africans. As for the *resistance* to Western incursions on the part of indigenes, Western-based fiction for the young is conspicuously silent on this point.

Why does this mis-education persist? We critiqued books about Africa in 1996 (*African Images in Juvenile Literature*) and again in 2001 (*Apartheid and Racism in South African Children's Literature, 1985–1995*), but there has been no appreciable improvement.[5] Cultural relativism would suggest that perceptions of some people at the "center" (White) versus other people at the "margin" (Black) would ultimately give way to cultural inclusiveness—to multicultural ideals and programs. But instead, contemporary stories about Africa sustain the idea that Whites constitute a superior class of persons. There is rarely a hint of post-colonial influences, if we mean by "post-colonial" a shift from "race purity" to racial "hybridity." The hybrid ideal can take form when people no longer seek to maintain a "purist" attitude within their homeland environment, and when they also reject assimilation in another nation. Instead they are embracing the idea of a racial and/or cultural mixture.

A more culturally diverse fiction about Africa can be an indirect means for promoting the socialization of children in the direction of hybridization. Socialization is the transference of a community's culture (including its political perceptions and attitudes) from one generation to the next. In many Western societies, imperial and ethnocentric values have been part of this transfer. Speaking of the British example, Martin Kaplan explains that "when a culture builds the content and regulations of its schools and universities, it institutionalizes and thereby legitimizes a particular myth or vision of itself" (qtd. in Mangan, 5). Maintaining the formal political control of a region has not been critical to the perpetuation of British influence since the myth has gained an intractable, internal logic of its own.

This connection of myth and institution points to the dilemma of the child in school. What difference does it make if children are consistently presented with prejudiced images of themselves? What does it matter if one is told that he or she belongs to an innately inferior group? How can children receive even the slightest hint of their own potential if they are placed in a hostile educational setting? Ngũgĩ has noted that education should give people knowledge about "how the world shapes them and how they shape the world." He sees a complex chain of outcomes: "How people look at themselves affects the way they look at their values which in turn affects the way they look at the culture, at their political and economic life and ultimately at their relations with nature" (95).

While contemporary fiction writers have been interested in political, economic, and cultural themes (as the books in this study illustrate), they have been less concerned with stereotypical characterizations and their negative impact on the young. The stories in our sample reveal authors' perspectives on such timely subjects as coming-of-age rites (especially circumcision for girls), environmental protection, pandemic diseases, Islam's relation to sexism, educational deprivation, urban crime, the placement of Africans in game park exhibitions, and the use of "child soldiers" as weapons of war. As these topics are imaginatively explored, they are nonetheless presented in ways reminiscent of an earlier age. We have found that while book critics have pointed to cultural and geographical information as an educational advantage, the actual "information" in the books has been about the same as the "exotic" material from the past. The florid pulp fiction and travelogues of earlier eras are not strikingly different from the novels of today that are mistakenly called "authoritative."

Teachers and Theories

Teachers of children's literature often direct their students' attention to multiculturalism, essentialism, social history, and other topics of interest to literary critics. What our book urges is greater attention to the African context and meaning of these ideas.

Multiculturalism, like so many subjects in the educational establishment, is being largely interpreted by antagonistic intellectual camps. It is seen as a liberationist project, or contrariwise, as a mischievous means for pushing affirmative action (Fourny and Ha, 1). Both perspectives are ultimately about power. Which societies are to be included and which ones excluded in relation to full citizenship rights for its members?

In Western-derived fiction about Africa, the question is usually put to rest in the opening pages: African characters are depicted as primarily "primitive." They are not portrayed as excluded from "civilization" because Europeans want their resources and labor, but because these imagined Africans are inherently Stone Age beings. "Culture" is hard to pin down in exact terms, given its subjective component. But although contrasting cultures have been recognized over the centuries, this awareness has not resulted in perceptions of diverse groups as being equally human or equally reputable.[6] In children's book circles, literature has been traditionally associated with values deemed universal, even though research tells a different story, pointing to a failure to actually achieve cultural inclusiveness. Kenneth Kidd's study of Newbery Medal history, for example, reveals the way multiculturalism has been undermined by institutions reflecting notions of American superiority.

History shows evolving power relationships as among the reasons for this failure. We can scan over time the progressive change from separate political and cultural units in Europe, to their eventual unification, and then to the need to sustain that unity through the creation of nation-states. Unfortunately, the unified national culture "has often meant the imposition of high culture on society at the exclusion of other existing cultures that find themselves thereby marginalized or devalued" (Fourny and Ha, 3).

For our purposes, it is also useful to note that "the legitimation of what is presented as the national culture is carried out most effectively through schooling" (Fourny and Ha, 3). The indoctrination of children has been a powerful hegemonic instrument in earlier epochs, as it also is today. Children's novels about Africa bear witness to this phenomenon. So who benefits? What is at stake? The basic issue is grounded in "what one does with it [multiculturalism], and how it is used or manipulated, by whom, for whose benefits, and to whose detriment" (Fourny and Ha, 6).

Essentialism has much to do with whose voices will be allowed to enter a debate that is essentially about benefits. Not surprisingly, essentialism is therefore viewed differently by colonized and non-colonized people. To the colonized, charges made against an essentialist may be a colonizer's attempt to gloss over a less than admirable history—a condition that subjugated people are still living with every day; a history that has much to do with current experience. Essentialism, writes Ellis Cashmore, pertains to sets of characteristics that "not only work to distinguish one group from others, but remains largely unchanged over time and exerts decisive influences over other facets of the group" (133). This describes the problem exactly. Colonialism *has* remained intact for a long time, and its influence remains destructive to specific cultures and to self-determination on the part of certain groups.

On the other hand, to the non-colonized the world contains no absolutes, and it is therefore pointless to dwell upon what is rendered fair or unfair by historical and other intractable influences. The non-colonized would likely disagree with this comment about essentialism by an indigene:

> The significance of place, of land, of landscape, of other things in the universe, in defining the very essence of a people, makes for a very different rendering of the term essentialism as used by indigenous peoples. (Smith, 74)

Details about identity, group interests, and shared experience are largely a distraction to the non-colonized. Or worse, they are viewed as "cultural schizophrenia" and become self-defeating in the way they turn both identity and nationalism into obsessions (Ashcroft, Griffiths, Tiffin, 24). The main issue, as we see it, is not whether we treat culture and history in all their particularity. It is about recognizing the importance of specific cultural histories if we are to understand the power disparities that impact daily living. African women have been analyzing these power issues, and they have not perceived their efforts as the egoistic obsession that Ashcroft and his collaborators would attach to them. In exploring essentialism, it could be argued (says Filomina Chioma Steady) that "given the hegemonic and universalizing nature of corporate globalization, essentialist and modernist realities continue to be relevant" (174). Such a statement does not imply a lack of intellectual balance. Steady knows full well that just as people can oppose empires, so can they build them. But to infer that in Africa the *colonized* have been basically like the *colonizer* is to either suffer from amnesia or resort to means for clouding the issues that affect daily life.[7] In short, essentialism as a form of cultural racism deserves criticism (i.e., when differences are treated as immutable traits). But condemning it out of hand is also a mistake when that criticism is used to cover up rampant color-consciousness—even using someone else's cultural practices as an excuse to abhor, repel, attack, insult, and exclude them.

Social history is also tied to our ideas about power. The point is made explicit by Anne McClintock. She sees historical specificity as crucial. She alerts us to how the scanning of the "panorama of the horizon [can] become . . . so expansive that international imbalances in power remain effectively blurred" (86). Children's books retain their usefulness to the imperialist because they greatly oversimplify some information and at the same time make it easy for children to internalize a well-dramatized, well-crafted set of ideas. "Fiction," says Joan Rockwell, "plays a large part in the socialization of infants . . . " (4).[8] The self-colonization that children undergo by means of imperialist curriculums—this is no trivial form of abuse.⁹ Ngũgĩ notes that "to control a people's culture is to control their tools of self-definition in relationship to others" (16). Child culture can be shaped through the social control that is so characteristic of early schooling. Both fiction and nonfiction are selected with predetermined ideas about society in mind. Schoolbooks pertaining to Africa can be positive aids to self-definition, or instruments for justifying race and class inequities.

The critical vocabulary of literature suffers if it is dismissive of history and its vast documentation. It can be argued that distortions of history, reinforced over generations, have helped form implacable national psyches. White supremacy, for example, was successfully foisted upon children over long periods during fascist and Apartheid eras. Needless to say, the tools of educators warrant reassessment if they discount the lessons of history.

This Book: Organization and Content

In the following pages, Part I contains background material, as in Chapter 1 where we discuss the way terms such as "primitive" and "darkness" represent the same basic idea—an idea rooted in the myth of white superiority. In children's books, references to "Darkest Africa" are consistently coupled with the "savage" stereotype. This is true now, as it was in the nineteenth century, when anthropological studies became largely centered in Africa and were aligned with the colonial administrations of the conquering nations: Great Britain, France, Germany, Belgium, Portugal, Spain, and Italy. The precise impact of colonialism is widely debated, but Steven Feierman has captured the basic power relationship when he refers to "a macrohistorical narrative grounded in Europe." Moreover, while "the local and global interact, . . . the African is always local, and the global always originates outside Africa" (qtd. in Tilley, 3).

In Chapter 2 we examine feminism as an African concept, one that simultaneously affirms and criticizes aspects of Western feminism. Since many Western women are using Africa for settings and characters in their novels, and since their narratives highlight glaring deficiencies in African societies, background information on this subject has been necessary as a prelude to critiques of their fiction.

In Chapter 3 literary prizes in the children's book field are shown to be frequently contradictory. That is, multicultural goals are claimed as the initial impulse behind some prizes, but in practice the prize-winning books are more Eurocentric than culturally inclusive. And when literary criteria have been cited by prize jurors as exclusively aesthetic, the results have been about the same: the prize-winning book over-generalizes the characteristics of particular groups. South African poet and novelist, Es'kia Mphahlele, cautions critics about aesthetic absolutism: "Just as an ideology is a *historical* moment, so are art products also *historical* items—i.e., fashioned by historical moments. . . . To try to sound transcendental about our aesthetics, about literature itself . . . is to be romantic" (*Es'kia* . . . , 388).

In Part II we include eight chapters in which we critique specific neo-imperialist novels (plus one short story). We discuss those that project images of "Darkest Africa." We look at how misplaced Western feminism enters into Western-produced children's fiction, and how environmentalism has been used as an anti-African weapon. We examine the way urban crime is misrepresented, as well as pandemic diseases and the kidnapping of children for combat in wartime. In short, we pinpoint neo-imperialism in its many masks.

For a contrasting treatment of Africans and the anti-colonial resistance movement, we conclude our study in Part III with a selection of stories about Apartheid from Beverley Naidoo's *Out of Bounds: Seven Stories About Conflict and Hope* (2001). Naidoo is a native-born White South African who was imprisoned and sent into exile for being a supporter of the resistance movement. She knows the social history of which she speaks. She knows how to use the short story form to convey that history in ways that engage children.

* * *

Fiction is a two-sided art, calling for a double vision in those who critique it. We want fiction to communicate and reenact the life of the people (either in symbolic or realistic terms), or as Ruth Obee comments about the work of Es'kia Mphahlele, to offer "a realistic documentation of community history" as well as a clear sense of the Black aesthetic (117). Fiction needs to be understood as an artistic performance, an aesthetic event that deepens portrayals of character and encourages masterful treatments of imagery. Thus content and form coincide. But considering fiction as a group of literary canons, it is impossible to forget the role of imperial power. This point is brought to the foreground by Obioma Nnaemeka: "Free speech becomes meaningful when it is heard, but unequal power relations determine who is heard and what is heard" (86). In the world of childhood education, children are a *captive audience* for large chunks of their day. Their "unequal power relations" are obvious. Imperialist indoctrination is not within their power to change.

Works Cited

Ashcroft, Bill, Gareth Griffiths, and Helen Tiffin. 1998. *Key Concepts in Post-Colonial Studies.* London: Routledge.
Cashmore, Ellis. 2005. "Colonialism." In *Encyclopedia of Race and Ethnic Studies,* ed. Ellis Cashmore, 85–87. London: Routledge.
———. 2005. "Essentialism." In *Encyclopedia of Race and Ethnic Studies,* ed. Ellis Cashmore, 135–139. London: Routledge.
Cashmore, Ellis and Barry Troyna. 1990. *Introduction to Race Relations,* 2nd ed. London: Falmer Press.
Fourny, Jean-François and Marie-Paule Ha. 1997. "Introduction: The History of an Idea." *Research in African Literatures* 28:4 (Winter): 1–7.

Hari, Johann. 2007. "Oceanic World Orders." *New York Times Book Review* (November 18): 11.
Kidd, Kenneth. 2007. "Prizing Children's Literature: The Case of Newbery Gold." *Children's Literature* 35: 166–190.
McClintock, Anne. 1992. "The Angel of Progress: Pitfalls of the Term 'Post-Colonial.'" *Social Text* 31–32: 84–98.
Mangan, J. A., ed. 1988. *'Benefits bestowed'? Education and British Imperialism*. Manchester, UK: Manchester UP.
Mphahlele, Es'kia. 2002. *Es'kia: Education, African Humanism and Culture, Social Consciousness, Literary Appreciation*. Cape Town, South Africa: Kwela Books.
———, Ezekial. 1976. "The African Critic Today: Toward a Definition." In *Reading Black: Essays in the Criticism of African, Caribbean, and the Black American Literature*, ed. Houston A. Baker, Jr., 13–19. Philadelphia: University of Pennsylvania.
Naidoo, Beverley. 2001, 2003. *Out of Bounds: Seven Stories of Conflict and Hope*. London: Puffin Books; New York: HarperCollins.
Ngũgĩ wa Thiong'o. 1983. *Barrel of the Pen: Resistance to Repression in Neo-Colonial Kenya*. Trenton, NJ: Africa World Press.
———. 1986. *Decolonizing the Mind: The Politics of Language in African Literature*. London: James Currey.
———. 1986. *Writing Against Neocolonialism*. Middlesex, UK: Vita.
Nnaemeka, Obioma. 1995. "Feminism, Rebellious Women, and Cultural Boundaries: Rereading Flora Nwapa and Her Compatriots." *Research in African Literatures* 26:2: 80–113.
Obee, Ruth. 1999. *Es'kia Mphahlele: Themes of Alienation and African Humanism*. Athens: Ohio UP.
Richards, Jeffrey, ed. 1989. *Imperialism and Juvenile Literature*. Manchester, UK: Manchester UP.
Rockwell, Joan. 1974. *Fact in Fiction: The Use of Literature in the Systematic Study of Society*. London: Routledge and Kegan Paul.
Said, Edward. 1993. *Culture and Imperialism*. New York: Knopf.
Samuel-Mbaekwe, Iheanyi J. 1993. "Colonialism and Social Structure." In *The Colonial Epoch in Africa*, vol. 2, ed. Gregory Maddox, 33–47. New York: Garland.
Smith, Linda Ruhiwai. 2002. *Decolonizing Methodologies: Research and Indigenous Peoples*. London: Zed books.
Spencer, Nick. 1990. "The African Tale." *English Journal* 79:8: 36–37.
Steady, Filomina Chioma. 2006. *Women and Collective Action in Africa: Development, Democratization, and Empowerment, with Special Focus on Sierra Leone*. New York: Palgrave Macmillan.
Tiffin, Chris and Alan Lawson. 1994. *De-Scribing Empire: Post-Colonialism and Textuality*. London: Routledge.
Tilley, Helen. 2007. "Introduction: Africa, Imperialism, and Anthropology." In *Ordering Africa: Anthropology, European Imperialism, and the Politics of Knowledge*, ed. Helen Tilley, with Robert J. Gordon, 1–45. Manchester, UK: Manchester UP.

Part I
Background

Chapter One
"Darkest Africa":
A Persistent Western Fantasy

[There] is a desire—one might indeed say a need—in Western psychology to set Africa up as a foil to Europe, as a place of negations... in comparison with which Europe's own state of spiritual grace will be manifest.
—Chinua Achebe (2–3)

The image of Africa, in short, was largely created in Europe to suit European needs—sometimes material needs—more often intellectual needs.
—Philip D. Curtin (480)

We examine in this book the specific ways Africa is set up as a foil, "as a place of negations" within highly touted children's books. There are few exceptions to this type of negative image-making. Today's fictional works for the young extend centuries of myth-making about Africa as a "dark place." Typically an author selects an African community, and then places its members in an unfavorable light in comparison with the Western characters. Jan Nederveen Pieterse's terse comment on colonialism applies equally to colonialist content in children's books: "Europe's light shone brighter by virtue of the darkening of other continents" (75).

The American and European network of gatekeepers share the "Darkest African" myth, thereby creating a system that abuses both Western and Black African children. Students of race relations have diligently traced the myths that define Africans as stunted children[1] or a "White man's burden." Kwaku Asante-Darko explains the importance of such studies in the education of the young:

> The Black African child is a member of a racial group whose maturity, humanity, and equality have been dishonestly and assiduously denied.... [T]he theme of race relations remains largely unexplored, thereby stifling children's understanding of racial stereotyping and insight into how to handle such issues. (2, 4)

How do children handle a work published in 2005 with this inscription on the cover: "Journey into the heart of darkest Africa" (Isabel Allende's *Forest of the Pygmies*)? Does "dark" suggest intellectual darkness, a limited capacity to think rationally? So it seems given the way Africans have been stereotyped for centuries as endlessly childish, superstitious, and immoral. For example, George A. Henty's *By Sheer Pluck: A Tale of the Ashanti War* (1884, 1890) is a novel in which Africans are said to stop maturing mentally at the age of ten:

> "They are just like children," Mr. Goodenough said. "They are . . . clever up to a certain point, densely stupid beyond. The intelligence of an average negro is about equal to that of a European child of ten years old." (117–118)

Kathryn Castle's study of schoolbooks and juvenile magazines analyzes the way Africans were supposedly unable to grasp such a concept as freedom, and some African leaders therefore offered their support to the slave-raids conducted by Europeans. In relation to religious thought, Castle shows how the spiritual leaders ("witch doctors") have been portrayed in children's magazines as "the force of 'darkness' incarnate," as designers of "repulsive," "hideous," "horrifying" rituals (108).

"Dark" also means something explicitly immoral, as when Africans are called "degenerates" and as they wage war as the result of sheer savagery, never in relation to self-defense or national self-determination. Any group resisting territorial incursions is automatically in the "ignoble savage" category. In the 1920s and 1930s, Hugh Lofting's "Doctor Dolittle" series presented Africans as dangerous as well as ridiculous: "Oh, Bumpo! Stop, stop, for heaven's sake! . . . You're not in Africa, now, Bumpo. Put him down . . . ." Bumpo must be restrained from dumping his opponents overboard, eating them, of bashing their "brains out on his own doorstep" (*Doctor Dolittle's Zoo*, 1925).

Given such images in the most "entertaining" novels, child readers would not necessarily find colonization unjust (especially as it was touted as a way to share "civilization"). But in any case, their schoolbooks left no room for doubt about the importance of European incursions: "No one could have expected that the Dark Continent of Africa would not be explored, largely by British men, but also portioned out among Europeans, among whom the British would be not the least successful" (qtd. in Castle, 65). It would appear that morality for Europeans meant successful intervention in Africa and, above all, seizing one's rightful "portion" of the continent. Assumptions about any conceivable African morality must be set aside: "We must lay aside all thought of reverence and morality—all that we call feeling—if we would rightly comprehend [the Negro]" (Hegel, 93).

Although the stereotypes reach back to antiquity, anti-African images became institutionalized within the larger framework of colonization. To the colonizer, African people lacked even a history. This aspect of the "Dark Continent" myth is not only ahistorical. It is insidious since a people that is attributed no history is a people that is afforded no humanity (Samuel-Mbaekwe, 37–38). Such dehumanization was the mainstay of a social structure that Iheanyi Samuel-Mbaekwe calls a "volcano-sized social change" (35).

Foundations of Colonialism: What Sustains Them?

"Dark Continent" terminology expanded as Africa's interior became the main focus of explorers. After the formal renunciation of slavery in England in 1807, the British congratulated themselves on being abolitionists and turned inland to the central part of Africa they called "dark." "The myth of the Dark Continent," writes Jan Nederveen Pieterse, "came into being only in the nineteenth century as an appropriate stage décor for European exploration" (64).

Colonizers did not create a systematic colonialism which then shifted mysteriously to "neo-colonialism." Documents could be signed and "independent" statehood proclaimed, but colonialism remained basically secure in the institutions that made it formidable in the first place.[2] Colonial administrators, backed by European power, integrated their notions of race and culture, and thereby found a means to conceptualize their own self-proclaimed leadership in the world (Curtin, 480). Distinctions drawn between Westerners and colonized peoples were invidious formulations having one overriding objective: "to effect the imposition of one human group upon another" (Onwubu, 80).

From this groundwork there evolved a mythical African who was allegedly "primitive," "barbarous," "tribal," and antithetical to "civilization" (Samuel-Mbaekwe, 37). As noted above, "darkness" becomes the word of choice. In the mid-twentieth century, an "eminent" history professor claimed that Africa *still* lacked history: "[A]t present," he said, "there is none; there is only the history of Europeans in Africa. The rest is darkness . . . and darkness is not a subject of history" (qtd. in Onwubu, 80). This echoes Hegel's comments from a hundred and fifty years earlier: "Africa . . . is no historical part of the world. . . . The Negro exhibits the natural man in his completely wild and untamed state" (Hegel, 99).

The institutions of colonialism were dynamic enough to set these ideas in concrete, so to speak. Colonization became "a phenomenon in its own right." Its forces "act[ed] in terms of [their] own totality"; they became predictable, enduring, massive, consolidated, and connected to everyone within the colonial epoch and region (Samuel-Mbaekwe, 34–37). Western-published children's books, with few exceptions, have perpetuated the storyline that treats colonial settlers, travelers, and "scientists" as Africa's saving grace. Some introduce a "clash of cultures," but European and American cultures always appear in a superior light, and the very existence of colonialism is disclaimed or concealed. From the way Western writers generally *make up* pseudo-Africans, it is not surprising that children's novelists are unreliable portrayers of African characters. Aimé Césaire's assessment of Westerners in Africa would have undoubtedly mystified the well-intentioned children's authors. He writes that the motives of colonizers were

> neither evangelization, nor a philanthropic enterprise, nor a desire to push back the frontiers of ignorance and tyranny, nor a project undertaken for the greater glory of God, nor an attempt to extend the rule of law. (qtd. in Samuel-Mbaekwe, 34)

While colonizers were pursuing none of these goals, they *were* facilitating the use of Africa as a fictional backdrop for writers of all sorts. The continent served well as a symbol of colonial expansionist aims. A historian specializing in dynamic cultural images states unequivocally: "[T]he European *Afrikaanschauung* was part of a European *weltanschauung,* and it was warped as necessary to make it fit into the larger whole" (Curtin, 480).

Social Darwinism and Other Pseudo-Sciences

Africans and their descendents have been treated for centuries as the *natural* subordinates of Whites. They were, according to social Darwinism, created with that in mind! In their book *The Science of Society* (1927), William Graham Sumner and Albert Galloway Keller declared that "[a]ny interference to prevent the survival of the fittest" would tend "only to promote the survival of the unfittest" (qtd. in Newby, 173). Sumner and Keller saw this "fit"–"unfit" equation as a matter of natural law. Certainly it was a convenient concept for racist politicians, since even if Blacks "evolved," their unfitness remained intact alongside the concurrently "evolving" White population. In Isabel Allende's *Forest of the Pygmies* (2005), the author's depiction of the Central African Aka people emphasizes such a permanent gap. And Allende's vivid contrasts between Western "saviors" and this short-statured people may well lead readers to believe there is scientific support for Allende's claim. In the minds of Western children, thanks to children's authors, thousands of years may indeed separate Africans from their Western privileged selves.

When political history "has been explicitly structured on the assumption of racial differences," writes Saul Dubow, "ideas of race are *ipso facto* related to social existence" (10). Educational practices have been and remain builders of a young person's social existence, whether negative or positive. In the early twentieth century, the many "Negro problem" commentators vigorously promoted restrictions on the education of Blacks. William P. Calhoun took this position and even invoked the will of God in support of it:

> [Y]ou cannot by cultivating the mind of the ass make a horse out of him; nor can the negro be made a white man by cultivating his brain, since they [sic] are what God made them and will remain so. (qtd. in Newby, 176)

Calhoun's perspective coincided with Howard W. Odum's belief that "[t]he young educated negroes are not a force for good in the community but for evil.... They love only the show of apparent results.... They have not rejected vicious practices in their own lives ... ." (qtd. in Newby, 41–42).[3]

Shifting our gaze to the twenty-first century, we discover in Cristina Kessler's *Our Secret, Siri Aang* (2004) that education is firmly rejected by a present-day Maasai community, with the exception of one teacher. And Kessler belittles both teacher and parents as she indicts a whole village for its supposed primitivism and mistreatment of children. In another recent novel, Joëlle Stolz's *The Shadows of Ghadames* (1999, 2004), readers are told that Islamic law forbids the education of girls,[4] but this is Stolz's own invention. Sharia laws explicitly require equal education for boys and girls. And in Nancy Farmer's *A Girl Named Disaster* (1996), African customs are broadly condemned, while the protagonist succeeds in escaping an unmistakably dangerous marriage through the help of Western-trained educators.

Following World War II, social anthropology gained ground with its emphasis upon the "plasticity of culture," but nineteenth-century evolutionist ideas remain in many children's books.[5] Authors describe African education as if it must, inevitably, be connected to the African's so-called racial "peculiarities," echoing the white supremacist beliefs of the late nineteenth-century American sociologist, Franklin Henry Giddings. From Giddings' perspective, "The same educational effort does not yield equal results when applied to different stocks" (qtd. in Newby, 175).

Eugenics, another pseudo-science, was instrumental in embedding this fiction of white racial superiority even more intractably in Western thought. The term "eugenics" refers to the belief that humans can breed selectively to produce desired racial "stocks" or stamp out those deemed undesirable. So-called race hygiene societies were established throughout the world to encourage the management of "fit" and "unfit" groups. "Racism," according to Nancy Stepan, "was not inherent in the science of human heredity, but gradually became associated with it" (124). Francis Galton[6] first used the term "eugenics" in 1883, and like his peers began his "scientific" efforts from the premise that certain races were self-evidently inferior. Accordingly, they saw no problem in putting eugenics to work on behalf of race-based purposes, including racial discrimination. "One is struck by the extraordinary durability of racial ideas in biology in the era of eugenics . . . "—an era that only Nazi atrocities in the name of science brought to the point of partial (but not total) repudiation (Stepan, 139). A eugenics mind-set was again visible at the time of the *Brown v. Board of Education* court ruling against school segregation in the United States. That Supreme Court decision was a "deep, dark plot which would lead to . . . miscegenation," said a Yale-educated circuit court judge. "When a law transgresses the moral and ethical sanctions and standards of the mores, invariably strife, bloodshed and revolution follow . . ." (qtd. in Bennett, 312).

In children's fiction, racism and colonialism are complementary. Cultural imperialism is expressed as cultural racism, as when skin color is not presented as the issue but African adults are depicted as immutably "Others" (e.g., as being childish or incapable of rational thought). Cultural racism will be discussed in *Zulu Dog* (Chapter 7) when a grandmother performs her tasks as a traditional healer.

* * *

African novelist Ama Ata Aidoo has observed the way people in a traditional village are fully aware of colonialist retentions in their midst: "Ask any village woman how post-colonial her life is. Colonialism has not been 'posted' anywhere at all" (qtd. in Osundare, 205). Children's novels have a long history of sustaining prejudiced impressions of Africa. In the early twentieth century George A. Henty wrote seven such novels, and in the last decade Eric Campbell's novels about East Africa are prime examples. As we comment in Chapter 6, Africans in Campbell's *Papa Tembo* (1998) are portrayed as a danger to the planet, as well as to viable African statehood. In Nancy Farmer's futuristic science fiction novel, *The Ear, the Eye, and the Arm* (1994), environmental destruction comes into play as the result of African misrule (see Chapter 10).

In a word, Africa as a "dark place" has been combined with contemporary Western interests such as environmental protection, Western feminism, disease prevention, law and order, and ethnic-based wars. But the "darkness" theme has remained in place with only a few notable exceptions. Countering that myth is the novel about urban South Africa by Beverley Naidoo, *Chain of Fire* (1989), and the historical novel about slave-raids by Jamaican author James Berry, *Ajeemah and His Son* (1992, 1994).

The resurgence of overt imperial enterprises has spurred new studies of imperialism as both "a habit of mind"[7] and a series of public policies. In Harilaos Stecopoulos' "Putting an Old Africa on Our Map: British Imperial Legacies and Contemporary US Culture," the "Dark Africa" myth is referred to as the same vital imperialist tool that it proved itself to be in earlier centuries. The author writes:

> The new imperial nostalgia speaks to more than the global range of white American racism; it speaks to a growing desire . . . to relegitimate empire through recourse to "dark" Africanist fictions. (226–227)

In children's literature, Kathryn Castle's research on schoolbooks and children's magazines remains broadly applicable in a discussion of current children's fiction. African images, she says, are "a vehicle for securing a consensus around race, hierarchy, and nationality" (115).

Works Cited

Achebe, Chinua. 1989. *Hopes and Impediments: Selected Essays*. New York: Doubleday.
Allende, Isabel. 2005. *Forest of the Pygmies*. Translated by Margaret Sayers Peden. New York: HarperCollins.
Asante-Darko, Kwaku. 2002. "Towards a Post-Colonial Children's Literature for Black Africa." *Mots Pluriels* 22 (September); reprinted online: http://motspluriels.arts.uwa.edu.au/MP2202kad.html
Baba, A. M. 1972, 1981. "Postscript." in *How Europe Underdeveloped Africa* by Walter Rodney, 311–316. Washington, DC: Howard UP.
Bennett, Lerone, Jr. 1964. *Before the Mayflower: A History of the Negro in America, 1679–1964*. Chicago: Johnson.
Berry, James. 1992, 1994. *Ajeemah and His Son*. New York: HarperCollins.
Campbell, Eric. 1998. *Papa Tembo*. New York: Harcourt.
Castle, Kathryn. 1996. *Britannia's Children: Reading Colonialism Through Children's Books and Magazines*. Manchester, UK: Manchester UP.
Curtin, Philip D. 1964. *The Image of Africa: British Ideas and Action, 1780–1850*. Madison: University of Wisconsin Press.
Dubow, Saul. 1995. *Scientific Racism in Modern South Africa*. Cambridge, UK: Cambridge UP.
Davidson, Basil. 1955. *Awakening Africa*. London: Jonathan Cape.
Farmer, Nancy. 1994. *The Ear, the Eye, and the Arm*. New York: Orchard Books.
———. 1996. *A Girl Named Disaster*. New York: Orchard Books.
Hegel, Georg Wilhelm Friedrich. 1956. *The Philosophy of History*. With prefaces by Charles Hegel and Translator J. Sibree, and a New Introduction by C. J. Friedrich. New York: Dover. (Original posthumous manuscript published 1840)
Henty, George A. 1884, 1890. *By Sheer Pluck: A Tale of the Ashanti War*. London: Blackie and Son; New York: A. L. Burg.
Kessler, Cristina. 2004. *Our Secret, Siri Aang*. New York: Philomel.
Lofting, Hugh. 1925, 1967. *Doctor Dolittle's Zoo*. New York: Frederick A. Stokes. Reissued, New York: Lippincott, 1967.
Naidoo, Beverley. 1989, 1990. *Chain of Fire*. London: Collins; New York: Harper.
Newby, I. A. 1965. *Jim Crow's Defense: Anti-Negro Thought in America, 1900–1930*. Baton Rouge: Louisiana State UP.
Onwubu, Chukwuemaka. 1990. "The Intellectual Foundations of Racism." In *Black Studies: Theory, Method, and Cultural Perspectives*, ed. Talmadge Anderson, 77–88. Pullman: Washington State UP.
Osundare, Nyi. 1994. "How Post-Colonial Is African Literature?" *Matatu* 12: 203–216.
Pakenham, Thomas. 1991. *The Scramble for Africa, 1876–1912*. London: Weidenfeld and Nicolson.
Pieterse, Jan Nederveen. 1992. *White on Black: Images of Africa and Blacks in Western Popular Culture*. New Haven, CT: Yale UP.
Richards, Jeffrey, ed. 1989. *Imperialism and Juvenile Literature*. Manchester, UK: Manchester UP.
Rodney, Walter. 1972, 1981. *How Europe Underdeveloped Africa*. Washington, DC: Howard UP.
Sada, Ibrahim N., Fatima L. Adamu and Ali Ahmad. 2006. *Promoting Women's Rights Through Sharia in Northern Nigeria*. Centre for Islamic Studies, Ahmadu Bello University, Zaria, Nigeria. http://www.dfid.gov.uk/pubs/files/promoting-women-sharia.pdf
Samuel-Mbaekwe, Iheanyi J. 1993. "Colonialism and Social Structure." In *The Colonial Epoch in Africa*, vol. 2, ed. Gregory Maddox, 33–47. New York: Garland.
Stecopoulos, Harilaos. 2007. "Putting an Old Africa on Our Map: British Imperial Legacies and Contemporary US Culture." In *Exceptional State: Contemporary U.S. Culture and the New Imperialism*, eds. Ashley Dawson and Malini Johar Schueller, 221–227. Durham, NC: Duke UP.
Stepan, Nancy. 1982. *The Idea of Race in Science: Great Britain, 1800–1960*. London: Macmillan.
Stolz, Joëlle. 1999, 2006. *The Shadows of Ghadames*. Translated by Catherine Temerson. New York: Random House.

Chapter Two
Feminism in Africa: Complexities and Activism

While Western feminism exists within a structure which had successfully broken away from fetters of tradition, African feminism operates within a framework that sees tradition as inherently part of the present.

—Olabisi Aina (72)

The sky is vast enough for all birds to fly without colliding.

—African proverb[1]

Differences among the world's feminisms are rooted in diverse historical experiences. For the most part, Western feminism (excluding Black American feminism) reflects European and Euro-American history, while African women are affected by their historical (but quite dissimilar) experience: slavery, colonialism, neo-colonialism, imperialism, debt crises, and food crises, to name a few struggles (Aina, 68, 69).[2] These widely separate experiences usually show up in English language children's books from the Western perspective exclusively. That is, we have found in many cases that novels with African characters are essentially Western feminist narratives unloaded on African terrain. Examples examined in upcoming chapters include Cristina Kessler's two novels, *No Condition Is Permanent* and *Our Secret, Siri Aang*; Joëlle Stolz's *The Shadows of Ghadames*; Isabel Allende's *Forest of the Pygmies*; and Nancy Farmer's *A Girl Named Disaster* and *The Ear, the Eye, and the Arm*. The question arises, therefore, will an expanded background in African feminism serve to reduce cultural (and often race-based) biases?

Feminism (Islamic and Otherwise)

International feminist coalitions and conferences have thrown light on specific regional histories, pointing the path to a potentially expansive feminist activism. In 2005, an Islamic perspective was presented at a Nigerian conference by Professor Fatima L. Adamu. She spoke at the session titled "Extolling Women's Rights in Sharia," and commented on the way Islamic sharia laws contain tenets specifically supporting the rights of women. But in the book about Libya in our sample (Joëlle Stolz's *The Shadows of Ghadames*) readers encounter various violations of those laws, as if the Muslim community rejects its own legal history and values.

Stolz's silence about sharia rules causes cultural distortion in her novel because Western Libya is made to serve as the primary reference point for violations of women's rights, even as the *existence* of such rights goes unmentioned. Although sharia laws are not always obeyed, as Islamic scholars have emphasized, they do contain important child-related content:

- Girl children as well as adult women are not to marry without their consent.
- Girls are ensured, alongside boys, an equal education.
- Girls are to be protected from harassment and assault (a serious dilemma in impoverished families where girls are sent out to advertise ["hawk"] the products in their mother's market stalls and where girls are sent away to join a child labor force).
- "Necessary provision for the decent development of children" is required, as well as provision for the special care of orphans and other needy children (Sada, Adamu, Ahmad: 9–13).

Stolz makes much of forced child marriages and educational deprivation, while her silence about sharia principles wrongly implies that these negatives are in accord with Islam.

Another source of confusion in children's novels is the author's construction of small rural communities without an understanding of how domestic life, education, and employment operate as essentially one unit. The practices connected with each part are not independent of activities in the others. Western-oriented novelists have often contrived plots that contradict this unity. Cristina Kessler's *Our Secret, Siri Aang* is a case in point. Professor Olabisi Aina's description of grassroots communities should alert novelists who plunk down girl-children in the bush, while isolating them psychologically from the closely knit spheres of work, education, and household duties. Dr. Aina writes: "A theoretical scheme which separates home and work undermines the complex nature of household economies in the Third World ..." (74). Individual family members function within such complex units, and at least in some communities, members' "rights and privileges [have been] accorded without reference to gender" (qtd. in Aina, 71). In such an integrated system, it is not surprising when "the individual sees himself or herself as a member of a group and possesses more loyalty to the group than to self . . ." (Aina, 77).

Writers of children's novels seem to start automatically with a Western conception of individualism. Obioma Nnaemeka believes a winner-take-all philosophy pervades Western feminism, whereas African feminists view power as "relative," as a matter of "power-sharing and power ebb and flow." This approach emphasizes the power of community and is expressed in the Igbo proverb: "When something stands, something stands *beside* it" (11). On the other hand, Western individualism tends to be absolutist, shaped by independence at the expense of interdependence. Not having the typical African's communal standpoint, it is not surprising that Western children's novelists see only a trivial, petty life for an African woman, a life utterly powerless and disconnected from her community's public sphere. (Cases in point include all the novels listed above.) We are given no glimpses of problem-solving strategies among rural women—their creation of cooperatives and other economic-political means for combating ill-conceived "Development" programs.

Religious Practices, "Secret" Societies, Initiation Rituals

Western feminists have used children's books to condemn genital surgery (circumcision, clitoridectomy), as well as alleged secret organizations, perhaps unaware of their religious implications. As in Western religions where some icons are visible to the general public and some are not, in traditional African belief systems one finds ideas about the appropriate treatment of sacred practices and objects. In initiation rituals in particular (as, for example, in the Poro and Sande societies in Sierra Leone) certain features in the ritual remain private.

Given increasing Western campaigns against clitoridectomy, Kenyan President Moi banned the practice in 1982 on the grounds that it signaled "backwardness." But he was soon informed that under no circumstances would the Maasai obey such a law—an order that "strikes at the very heart of their culture" (Talle, 122, n12). In fact, without circumcision, a girl is "not considered fully fertile" (229), an idea that is also tied to a religious precept. From a spiritual perspective, the practice involves an agreement sacredly entered into with God. Nigerian anthropologist E. Babatunde explains: "The logic of clitoridectomy is that by taking a tiny bit of the sacred instrument of fertility as an offering, the god of fertility will bless you with more children" (qtd. in Steady, 108). Babatunde's research shows that this emphasis on bearing many children weakens with the achievement of improved health care and its results: especially fewer child deaths.

What Westerners call secret, child-abusing organizations are basically organizations seen by most African women as spiritually constructive and essential. And, in fact, these women's organizations fulfill many functions. For example, the Sande Society in Sierra Leone is a women's organization with multiple functions. It is a networking system that enhances opportunities for women in the political sphere; it is an educational institution with well-established and flexible curricula; it is an instrument of integration for different ethnic groups; and with its emphasis on motherhood and fertility, it is a means for strengthening Sierra Leone's health delivery system (Steady, 108–109).

But the picture is quite different in Cristina Kessler's *No Condition Is Permanent*. In this novel, a California teenager refuses to respect the request that she refrain from observing her Sierra Leonean friend's initiation events. And once she disobeys, her anthropologist mother has no option but to grab daughter and passport and flee post haste. Readers are led to believe (like the California narrator) that the young Sierra Leonean could die from infected circumcision wounds, and that the mother–daughter breach of protocol had threatened them with imminent execution. Kessler's zeal about abolishing female circumcision is shared by many, but her misrepresentation of nearly every detail in African beliefs and routines only discredits her Western feminist credentials, as well as her identity as artist rather than propagandist. Moreover, she does not extend her anger to cover male circumcision, although here also the risk from infection is a possibility.

Given the increasing force of international opposition, "it seems clear that female circumcision will soon be a thing of the past," notes Filomina Chioma Steady (an Africana Studies professor) (108). But meanwhile risks are reduced through the use of antibiotics, tetanus shots, tranquilizers, and well-trained performers of the operation.

Polygamy

It is typical for children's novelists to attack polygamy on all fronts: on the number of wives, on their youthfulness and early child-bearing, on their squabbles and rivalries over controlling children, and on the likelihood of jealousy and its accompanying intrigues. In 1995, however, researchers in Kenya found Maasai women reluctant to shift from semi-nomadic dwellings to communally run ranches, since closeness with their co-wives would be reduced. The research "findings" included this comment: "Maasai women form, as wives of the same husband or as women living in the same settlement, sisterhoods. There is a togetherness that makes life easier for everybody involved" (*Our Life*, 53).

In her studies of polygamous colonial cultures, Anne McClintock has uncovered labor and profit concerns among the rural European settlers. She makes this comment:

> Colonial documents readily reveal that the assault on polygyny was an assault on African habits of labor that withheld from the resentful farmers the work of black men and women ... [This was] a direct and deadly threat to the profits of the settlers. As Governor Pine complained: "How can an Englishman with one pair of hands compete with a native with five to twenty slave wives"? (qtd. in Okonkwo, 15)

Without realizing the complexities of family life in relation to neo-colonialist profits, the Westerner will fail to recognize survival strategies of families in nomadic, pastoral, and ranch-style economies.

Polygamous family structures are an integral part of that African story. In the novels covered in this book, however, this domestic arrangement is abusive or even downright dangerous. In Nancy Farmer's *The Ear, the Eye, and the Arm*, adolescent girls live miserable, unhealthy, unfair lives, and if they are unlucky enough to bear no children, they can be labeled witches and face execution. In her book *A Girl Named Disaster*, the young protagonist, Nhamo, is about to be forced into a fourth wife position—a place on the marital ladder in which her very life is endangered. That is, according to Nhamo's grandmother, the three co-wives will poison her. "You will not last a year," warns grandmother (85). In Joëlle Stolz's *The Shadows of Ghadames*, the rivalry between the co-wives and the rivalry between the wives' offspring reduce the happiness of everyone. In short, a positive, functional home life is not apt to be combined, in Western-derived children's fiction, with polygamy.

Traditional Healers as "Witch Doctors"

Western images of African healers have been consistently and grossly inaccurate. Perhaps this is due to the long-standing practice of inserting traditional healers into novels as the primary villains. In our era they continue to be offered to young audiences as cunning con artists and/or people who use religion to conceal their crimes. In Nancy Farmer's *The Ear, the Eye, and the Arm* and in Isabel Allende's *Forest of the Pygmies* spiritually prepared African healers have been supplanted by dangerously malicious, power-hungry "witch doctors." Less complicated but no less grotesque are the spiritist performances in Nancy Farmer's *A Girl Named Disaster*, Eric Campbell's *Papa Tembo*, and Allan Stratton's *Chanda's Secrets* and *Chanda's Wars*. Books advertised as serious artistic creations contain "witch doctor" scenes that could have been pulled from Tarzan melodramas. Western societies often discount the spirituality of non-Western peoples, but this bias reaches huge proportions when directed at Africa. Perhaps this is because the "witch doctor" has been such a ubiquitous figure in the fantasies conjured up in pulp fiction, and because it is an essential element in the "Dark Africa" myth.

So what is the role and status of contemporary spiritual healers? In earlier decades, diviners were usually women who diagnosed an ailment while herbalists were men who prescribed the methods to be used in the treatment. They worked as a team (Gort, 298). Studies based in Swaziland have explained how the two separate functions became combined and are now practiced by individual men or women. Training lasts from one to three years and today the profession is often combined with agricultural or "cottage industry" occupations. Additionally, some spiritual healers have had professional training as nurses and others are eclectic in their choice of healing methods (including, for example, the use of over-the-counter drugs and the call for assistance at a local hospital if signs of improvement are not as expected).[3]

The terrain of entrepreneurial healers has been changing and expanding in recent times. In fact, Enid Gort claims that spiritual healing is a growth industry in Africa. For women this profession continues to be an especially important means for income, status, autonomy, and occupational development. At the same time, its spiritual foundation remains constant.[4]

Debt Crises and International Programs

The monumental debt crises in sub-Saharan Africa have as one of their root causes the practice of Western lenders in the 1970s and 1980s to use loans to Africa as a foreign policy strategy. Even the most repressive African governments needed merely to assert their support for U.S. interests in the Cold War and they were rewarded with millions. Such monetary aid seldom reached communities to bolster internal development programs. This is what Salih Booker has called an "odious debt." People paid "for their own repression" by an externally financed tyrant (qtd. in Hunter-Gault, 102). And on top of this system of bribes for gaining increased leverage over the Soviet Union, loans from the World Bank and the International Monetary Fund placed conditions on the loans that could only result in massive cuts in education, health care, and other vital social services. If we exclude South Africa, we find that more than $2.5 billion was spent on debt servicing in contrast to much less received in new long-term loans and credits (Hunter-Gault, 102).

Not surprisingly, African scholars (and especially women) are serving as whistle-blowers since the debt-derived deprivations are placing even the lowest subsistence existence on shaky ground. Children feel the greatest impact, the greatest increase in malnutrition, and ill health generally. And young men can be mobilized to engage in the looting and conquests of "child soldiers," since other options for them are practically nonexistent. "Poverty fuels conflict," writes Michael Kevane, "especially when riches [diamonds, oil, etc.] are within grasp" (10). There is a vicious cycle: the "relative persistence and rise in conflict probably lies in the vicious circle of economic decline leading to war, leading to further economic decline" (10).

Ironically, poor survival conditions only exacerbate over-population, since children are one form of insurance for the care of the elderly. For example, according to William S. Ellis the Niger village people "have contributed to a smothering population growth of 2.7 per cent annually (while food production increases, by comparison, reach only 1.5 per cent)" (qtd. in Okediran, 248). Poverty in the Delta Region of Nigeria is a classic neo-colonial case, with national revenue from this rich oil-producing district being unfairly distributed. Consequently, people suffer displacement from their homes, deprivation of education for the children, and "unquantifiable psychological disadvantage" (Okediran, 252). International institutions have been manipulating the exploitation of African resources, as Gloria Emeagwali explains in *Women Pay the Price: Structural Adjustment in Africa and the Caribbean*:

> "New protectionism" philosophies appear to operate against third world interests through a series of import quotas, custom procedures, etc. . . . . . Furthermore, natural resources of the developing countries are not purchased at their true values . . . so the developing countries, especially African nations, remain in the economic doldrums. (qtd. in Okediran, 253)[5]

Given the many interrelated forces at work, African women have been bringing the connections between gender, race, and public policy into the foreground at international conferences. Kum-Kum Bhavnani has emphasized the importance of locating "women in public and private spheres" and including them as agents of public policy transformations. Jane Bennett has noted the risks to impoverished Black women when "liberal" policy makers insist upon the de-linking of gender from race. In sexual harassment cases, for example, a low-income woman does not have the luxury of reporting the offense because her job (as well as the jobs of family members) is often at stake. Race-blind gender policies have mainly benefitted White women, as case studies in South Africa clearly show (Bangura, 17–18).

Put briefly then, Western feminists could make a greater contribution by broadening their concerns. Filomina Steady urges them to take note of the exploitation and "inhumane global economic policies emanating from their own [Western] countries" (108–109). She urges solidarity in the battle against human devastation (lack of sanitation, housing, water supplies, food).[6] From a position of both necessity and commitment, feminism in Africa confronts colonialism, racism, and economic exploitation, as well as sexism. Making "feminism relevant to the reality of African social formations"—this is the immediate task (Aina, 84). Novelists would do well to tap that reality.

Works Cited

Aina, Olabisi. 1998. "African Women at the Grassroots: The Silent Partners of the Women's Movement." In *Sisterhood, Feminisms & Power: From Africa to the Diaspora*, ed. Obioma Nnaemeka, 65–88. Trenton, NJ: African World Press.

Allende, Isabel. 2005. *Forest of the Pygmies*. Translated from the Spanish by Margaret Sayers Peden. New York: HarperCollins.

Bangura, Yusef, with Thomas Ansorg and Anita Tombez. 2002. "UNRISD Conference News: Racism and Public Policy" (International Conference Report 3–5 September 2001, Durban, South Africa). *The Black Scholar* 32: 3–4 (Fall/Winter): 2–25.

Farmer, Nancy. 1994. *The Ear, the Eye, and the Arm*. New York: Orchard Books.

———. 1996. *A Girl Named Disaster*. New York: Orchard Books.

Gort, Enid. 1997. "Swazi Traditional Healers, Role Transformation, and Gender." In *African Feminism: The Politics of Survival in Sub-Saharan Africa*, ed. by Gwendolyn Mikell, 298–309. Philadelphia: University of Pennsylvania Press.

Hunter-Gault, Charlayne. 2006. *New News Out of Africa: Uncovering Africa's Renaissance*. Oxford, UK: Oxford University Press.

Kessler, Cristina. 2000. *No Condition Is Permanent*. New York: Philomel.

———. 2004. *Our Secret, Siri Aang*. New York: Puffin Books.

Kevane, Michael. 2004. *Women and Development in Africa: How Gender Works*. Boulder, CO: Lynne Rienner.

Moraga, Cherríe. 1981. "La Güera." In *This Bridge Called My Back, Writings by Radical Women of Color*. eds. Cherríe Moraga and Gloria Anzaldúa, 24–33 Watertown, MA: Persephone Press.

Nnaemeka, Obioma, ed. 1998. "Introduction: Reading the Rainbow." *Sisterhood, Feminisms, and Power: From Africa to the Diaspora*, 1–35. Trenton, NJ: Africa World Press.

Okediran, Adefolake Y. 1998. "Bonds That Bind, Bondages That Burden—Women and Environmental Sustainability in Africa." In *Gender Perceptions and Development in Africa: A Socio-Cultural Approach*, ed. Mary E. Modupe Kolawole, 243–259. Lagos, Nigeria: Arrabon Academic.

Okonkwo, Chidi. 1999. *Decolonization Agonistics in Postcolonial Fiction*. London: Macmillan.

Our Life: A View of Maasai Women. 1995. Programme Co-ordinator: Matthijs de Vreede. Nairobi: Centre of Biodiversity of the National Museums of Kenya.

Russo, Ann. 1991. "We Cannot Live Without Our Lives." In *Third World Women and the Politics of Feminism*, eds. Chandra Talpade Mohanty, Ann Russo, and Lourdes Torres, 297–313. Bloomington: Indiana University Press.

Sada, Ibrahim N., Fatima L. Adamu, and Ali Ahmad. 2006. *Promoting Women's Rights Through Sharia in Northern Nigeria*. Centre for Islamic Studies, Ahmadu Bello University, Zaria, Nigeria. http://www.dfid.gov.uk/pubs/files/promoting-woman-sharia.pdf

Steady, Filomina Chioma. 2005. *Women and Collective Action in Africa*. New York: Palgrave Macmillan.

Stolz, Joëlle. 1999, 2006. *The Shadows of Ghadames/Les Ombres de Ghadamès*. Translated from the French by Catherine Temerson. Originally published in France by Bayard Editions Jeunesse; New York: Random House.

Talle, Aud. 1988. *Women at a Loss: Changes in Maasai Pastoralism and Their Effects on Gender Relations*. Stockholm: University of Stockholm.

Chapter Three
Institutional Racism

[Individual racism] consists of overt acts by individuals, which cause death, injury or the violent destruction of property. . . . [Institutional racism is] far more subtle . . . but no less destructive of human life. [It] originates in the operation of established and respected forces in the society.
—**Stokely Carmichael and Charles V. Hamilton (4)**

More interesting [than exchanging one domination for another] is what makes intellectual domination possible; how knowledge is transformed from invasion and conquest to revelation and choice; . . . and what forces help establish the parameters of criticism.
—**Toni Morrison (8)**

Children's books are perceived as well-meant offerings and therefore surely unconnected with institutions deserving close scrutiny. But stories for the young have been important to social history for centuries and each new generation experiences their influence. We could call this chapter "institutional paternalism," but paternalism as practiced by Europeans in Africa rests on the same premise as racism: Whites are "better" than Blacks.

European colonial administrations were replete with racially biased institutions, and contemporary children's books about Africa carry forward some of the same colonialist assumptions.

What are publishers, teachers, librarians, and English professors thinking when they allow books to define Africa for children by misrepresenting it? We usually find a heroic African child at the center of a children's novel, but this appealing character is surrounded by an adult African world that is incapable of caring for the young. African officialdom is corrupt and inept, African religious leaders are downright dangerous in their manipulations of so-called witchcraft, and communities are full of con artists who rob and abuse people of all ages. Thus the gist of the story is to substitute this unacceptable "family" with a stand-in European "family" or its lackeys. The white supremacist and exploitative nature of institutional paternalism is obscured by the friendly scenario apparently directed at the Black child's best interests. As the works of fiction in this study indicate, persons in the adult African world are presented as unable to manage their own affairs, and neo-colonial interventions are the only humane solution.

Sociologist Stephen Small has presented in broad strokes the way the system works: "[Non-Blacks] have demarcated the acceptable terrain (political, economic, social) which could be traversed by Black people, while keeping all terrains open to non-Blacks" (15). Racist and paternalist institutions constitute a very large terrain, but are nonetheless not easily uncovered. Joe Feagin and Hernán Vera explain how hard it is for a legal system to deal with them: "A significant number [of institutionalized racist acts] may be so embedded in the way U.S. institutions operate or so subtle or covert that it may be difficult for a white-controlled legal system ever to deal effectively with them" (7–8). For those in the fields of children's literature and education, the challenge is to study not only the books placed in the hands of children, but the institutions that sponsor and back up those publications. As we consider this literature in the upcoming pages, we see how choosers of "best books" and literary canon–builders are at work. And behind these choosers and builders, a less than obvious mixture of commercial, political, and educational interests are actively in play.

National Interests and Education

How knowledge becomes legitimatized is the issue underlying what educational institutions actually do. Educational historican Michael Apple writes that knowledge "is always part of a *selective tradition*, . . . some group's vision of legitimate knowledge. It is produced out of . . . tensions and compromises that organize and disorganize a society" (345, emphasis in the original). "Neo-colonialist literary critics," according to Wole Soyinka, have the habit of projecting "*their* history [and] *their* social neuroses" on their subjects (qtd. in Okonkwo, 14). Kenneth Kidd's research on Newbery Medalists has revealed a similar pattern. He shows how authors and critics could talk the talk of internationalism, while making sure that the intellectual territory placed before children was *their own* version of American values. The American Library Association, says Kidd, "gave priority to American work, defined not by setting but by authorship, theme, and values." As for the setting, "what was American was established through and against contact with the cultural other, usually safely removed across time and/or space" (177). To be able to define knowledge per se on behalf of one group and downgrade the ideas of a less powerful group—this represents raw power.

Choosing "best books" sometimes rests in a committee or jury within a professional or non-professional organization (e.g., the American Library Association or the online service, Parents' Choice). Sometimes that power rests in government (e.g., the Apartheid regime and its policies about childhood education). And sometimes an industry is exercising its power of control (as when publishers kowtowed to "Jim Crowism" and its discriminatory rules for the sake of maintaining sales). In today's children's book business, works of white supremacist fiction about Africa win major American book prizes, a process that begins with an inadequate knowledge of Africa on the part of the author, and from that point feeds upon itself. From the first book review to the bestowal of a coveted prize, the gap between African reality and misinformation about Africa only widens. A system is at work that reflects widely accepted stereotypes about Africa, and a top prize can extend a book's life span enormously, as well as exercise a noticeable impact on other aspiring authors. When there is a totalitarian government, this system becomes even more formidable, as in South Africa under the Apartheid regime. Here books and their prizes were screened to make sure they supported rigid white supremacist policies. Throughout half a century of National Party control, the White-over-Black ideology was the only permissible doctrine. In the United States, the inclusion of authentic images of Blacks in mainstream children's fiction was for centuries disallowed. But it was the publishing industry that regulated this discriminatory practice until the door was forced open as a result of the expanding Black Revolution in the 1960s. The social history of both South Africa and the United States connects children's books, prizes for children's books, and a record of unabashed institutional racism.[1]

The socialization of the child through literature has been largely for the purpose of stabilizing the ruling group's social assumptions. R. Gordon Kelly has described the process: "We may properly regard a group's children's literature as constituting . . . [reaffirmations] of that body of knowledge and belief regarded as essential to the continued existence of the group, for not only must children be convinced of the validity of the truths being presented to them, 'but so must be their teachers'" (xvi). As in the past, African realities are not part of the body of knowledge deemed essential to the American mainstream and its nationalistic "truths." This seems clear when considering the prizes that are awarded to fiction with anti-African biases.

Multiculturalism and the American Library Association's Batchelder Award

Mildred L. Batchelder's professional contributions had international effects for more than three decades. The prize in her honor encourages "interchange of children's books between countries ... [and] communication between the peoples of those countries" (Wheeler, 180). But the goal and the practice have not been in sync when it comes to books with African settings. Book prizes begin with high ideals, but key questions are overlooked in their implementation. How are specific social groups affected when praise is showered on works that misrepresent them? How well do prize jurors understand a prize's ties to money, power, and other non-art issues? In discussing commercial and literary connections in the prize-awarding business, James F. English alerts the adult book world to take account of the complexities. "What's left out," he says, "is the whole middle-zone of cultural space, a space crowded not just with artists and consumers but with bureaucrats, functionaries, patrons, and administrators of culture ... " (14). He urges attention to the historical and ethnographic details of the "middle-zone"—an important hint for publishers, critics, and prize jurors (not just authors) when Western children's books about Africa have contained such a long and ignoble imperialist slant.

Given the history of colonialism in Africa, the criteria most relevant to Batchelder jurors include "interpretation of the theme or concept," "presentation of information, including accuracy," and "delineation of characters."[2] Noticing these features in a work of fiction brings the critic closer to Batchelder's desire to "eliminate barriers to understanding between people of different cultures, races, nations, and languages" (American Library Association, www.ala...). The extensive scope of the imperialistic tradition is illustrated in poorly selected award winners since both an American institution and a non-American author and publisher are involved in the support of the novel's content. A misplaced award is an instance of wide-ranging institutional failure, as in the award given to *The Baboon King*.

Malawian author and critic Steve Sharra has critiqued Anton Quintana's *The Baboon King* (1999) in "*The Baboon King*: Institutionalizing Anti-African Bias in Children's Literature." Sharra illustrates how Quintana is in the business of "discrediting the core systems of the [Kikuyu] culture" (98). Whether in financial, legal, religious, or interpersonal matters, the Kikuyu people are treated as a hopeless case, even to the point where "the novel seems to suggest that baboon society does not have far to reach to surpass the African community that Moreng'aru [the protagonist] has escaped" (98). "Quintana's hero," writes Sharra, "is not white, but Moreng'aru is nevertheless portrayed as someone who has rejected African society and culture as he has observed and suffered its unmitigated flaws" (97). These conclusions are explained as Sharra connects readers with the early twentieth century and especially with Edgar Rice Burroughs' "Tarzan" novels. He takes note of Burroughs' racism as it has been well-documented by "Tarzan" scholars.[3] Finally Sharra adds further context by alluding to multicultural initiatives in education, the fulfillment of which *The Baboon King* so thoroughly interrupts (97–99).

The Batchelder Award for 1999 could not have been more misplaced, given the stated desire of jurors to honor an ALA leader and fulfill her aim to "eliminate barriers... between people." And the same can be said about the award bestowed on a French novel: Joëlle Stolz's *The Shadows of Ghadames* (1999, 2006). This book is critiqued in Chapter 4, where we pinpoint how this blend of good writing and feminist issues is marred by the inclusion of "primitive" caricatures and by a disregard for historical accuracy.

More Misplaced Awards: The "Phoenix" and the "Henry Bergh"

As its name suggests, the Phoenix Award calls attention to something of beauty that rises from ashes, from a burial it did not deserve. Thus the Children's Literature Association resurrects a "best book" and several "honor books" after twenty years have elapsed since their dates of publication. Clayton Bess' *Story for a Black Night* (1982, 2004) was selected as an "Honor Book" in 2002. Bess had been a member of the Peace Corps in Liberia, and his story depicts what is essentially Black-on-Black manslaughter when a character intentionally removes a smallpox victim from her own town to her sister's farm. In Africa, it seems, transferring a contagious disease to other households was one's only means of coping. The trick was to send the disease to people who were still unaware of the danger. By means of this scenario, Bess indicts a whole African town. Having been a volunteer in Africa, he undoubtedly engaged in humanitarian work, but does he occupy any common ground with his imagined African population? We explore this issue and critique the novel in Chapter 9.

One of the most serious misjudgments in relation to prizes occurred when the American Society for the Prevention of Cruelty to Animals (ASPCA) gave its children's book prize to Cristina Kessler's *Our Secret, Siri Aang* (2004). This "best book" honor, the Henry Bergh Award, is bestowed on a work that makes a contribution to "humane children's literature." But Kessler's book is about a Maasai community in Kenya, and to offer a humane portrayal the writer would need to avoid the stereotypes and misinformation that characterize *Our Secret, Siri Aang*. The narrative includes a mother rhinoceros and her newborn, but the Bergh prize is designed to "respect all living things," and Kessler's work is far from an expression of respect for the Maasai. Environmental conservation is one of the criteria on which jurors must base their selection, and the award process includes a "first stage" when the nominated manuscript is read by ASPCA members. Apparently this initial reading is treated as the most essential, even when the setting is Africa and a large cast of characters consists of Africans. It can be argued that the organizational details in managing the prize invite institutional racism since even the last stage in the process is in the hands of librarians, animal welfare professionals, or both, who may be unacquainted with the book's central subject—in this case, Maasai culture and community life. If opposition to mistreatment of animals is not coupled with opposition to mistreatment of ethnic groups, then the professed goal of the prize cannot be taken seriously. (Our full critique of *Our Secret, Siri Aang* can be found in Chapter 4.)

Poor Award Choices on the Internet

Not surprisingly, child advocacy groups are often created by people engaged in making educational products. Mis-education is not their intention, but their treatment of Africa, as seen in reviews of Anton Ferreira's *Zulu Dog* (2002), produces this result. *Zulu Dog* has satisfied the expectations and standards of both Parents' Choice[4] and KidsPOD[5] in relation to Black–White friendships, and in one part of the plot, child protagonists do indeed act like friends. What has been missed is the need for some informed commentary about the novelist's treatment of indigenous culture and South African history. In developing a post-Apartheid context, Ferreira has been called "authoritative," but the reviewers seem to be accepting this on faith rather than evidence. By considering this author's account of social and political history, a different conclusion would be likely to emerge. Different evidence would be seen as relevant. For example, Ferreira covers in an "Author's Note" an overview of the White settler invasion and mistreatment of indigenous Africans, but then presents the first democratic South Africa (after the 1994 election) as so horrible that "human life came to be regarded as cheap" (xi). This is a glaringly biased interpretation, but one that is completely in line with White anti-democratic forces in South Africa.

Such an untenable viewpoint is apt to arise when one uses European norms as the only basis of analysis. In *Zulu Dog,* nearly every detail in the post-Apartheid world comes across as an alien intrusion into South Africa's supposedly viable and attractive White society. White prejudice is criticized by the author, but he describes indigenous cultural details in ways so damming that those White biases appear valid. In his account, indigenous belief systems and the government's neglect of post-1994 violence are conditions that would encourage Black–White animosity. The implied solution (and the one offered to the Black African protagonists) is a return to paternalistic White control and Black peonage. (In Chapter 7 we look closely at this scenario.)

An Antidote for Institutional Racism

The Children's Africana Book Award (CABA), including the "Honor Book" awards, are given each year to authors and illustrators of children's books about Africa. CABA was established in 1991 by the Outreach Council of the African Studies Association, a non-profit corporation devoted to bringing together persons with scholarly or professional interests in Africa. The credibility of the prize is largely anchored in the African Studies Association's reputation as one of the largest and most active learned societies of its kind in the world. (It was founded in 1957.) Adding further to the prize's influence is its association

tion with two online services: Africa Access Review (a database created for children's books and edited by Brenda Randolph),[6] and Michigan State University's H-Net Services (H-Afrteach@h-net.msu.edu), which also carries Africa Access reviews. (Beverly Naidoo's *Out of Bounds* [2001, 2003] is a CABA winner and is covered in Chapter 12.)

Of special importance is the publication of CABA book reviews in the journal *Sandofa*, which is edited by Meena Khorana from its base at Morgan State University. By involving reviewers who make African Studies a particular field of interest, CABA reviews often end up going against the grain, as in the case of *Over a Thousand Hills I Walk With You* (2006). This novel about the Rwandan genocide in 1997 has received the Batchelder Award and has been given starred reviews for being "beautifully crafted" (*School Library Journal*), "compelling" (*Booklist*), and "remarkable and inspiring" (*Publishers Weekly*). But it skews the long history of a workable Hutu–Tutsi balance of power and its decline into repeated conflicts when the relationship was manipulated by neo-colonial Western governments and commercial investors. The value of this work, especially its ties to the life of an actual genocide child-survivor, is largely undone by author Hanna Jansen's use of this child (who became her adopted daughter) as a way to show Rwanda as a place of extreme "tribalism" and "naked hatred" (Randolph, 80–81). The vital role of personal, individual responsibility for anyone's premeditated death is not minimized by the novelist or the CABA critics. But the author places side by side the beheading of the child protagonist's uncle (considered a Tutsi leader) and the murder's alleged rationale: Tutsi "snobbishness and illicit wealth" (Jansen, 127). This is a glaring distortion of Hutu–Tutsi history and co-existence. And the book's concluding "Timeline of Rwandan History" is not very helpful, since it excludes historical material that would call into question Jansen's interpretation of events.[7]

* * *

Prizes, according to James English, are a rich opportunity "to test and affirm the notion of art as a separate and superior domain," as something "nontemporal, noneconomic" (52). However, perceiving art as "separate" and basing prizes on that premise only underscores an array of contradictions. Colonialism, for example, is deeply implicated in the prize business. English writes:

> [C]ultural prizes—long intertwined with the apparatus of colonial indoctrination, and widely deployed to that end in schools and colleges—became (without altogether surrendering this earlier function) part of the struggle to formulate . . . a coherent indigenous national culture. (265)

In children's literature, prizes have contradicted respect for indigenous African cultures, as the examples cited from the Batchelder, Phoenix, Bergh, and online awards suggest. Brenda Randolph alluded to this problem in an interview in *NEA Today*: "Africa remains the most poorly taught region of the world in U.S. schools. Much of what is taught about Africa is based on old Western icons. But Africa is about people, not animals and huts" ("Teaching Africa ... "). Regrettably, in books listed on "best book" lists we are subject to the biases of organizations sponsoring those lists. We are allowed to know Africans primarily as people mired hopelessly in tragedies of their own making. Given an error of such magnitude, it is not surprising that the realities of Africa seldom find their way into "best books"—realities that would help children find their way beyond an imposed institutional racism.

Works Cited

American Library Association - Association for Library Service to Children. 2007. "ALSC Mildred L. Batchelder Award: Terms and Criteria." http://www.ala.org/ala/alsc/awardsscholarships/literaryawds/batchelderaward/batchelderterms/batchelderaward.cfm

Apple, Michael. 1995. "The Politics of a National Curriculum." In *Transforming Schools*, eds. Peter W. Cookson, Jr. and Barbara Schneider, 345–370. New York: Garland.

Bess, Clayton. 1984, 2004. *Story for a Black Night*. Boston: Houghton Mifflin. New edition by Graphia Books.

Burroughs, Edgar Rice. 1912. *Tarzan of the Apes*. New York: Grosset and Dunlap.

Carmichael, Stokely and Charles V. Hamilton. 1967. *Black Power: The Politics of Liberation in America*. New York: Random House.

English, James F. 2005. *The Economy of Prestige: Prizes, Awards, and the Circulation of Cultural Value*. Cambridge, MA: Harvard UP.

Feagin, Joe R. and Hernán Vera. 1995. *White Racism: The Basics*. New York: Routledge.

Ferreira, Anton. 2002. *Zulu Dog*. New York: Farrar, Straus and Giroux.

Jansen, Hanna. 2006. *Over a Thousand Hills I Walk With You*. Translated from the German by Elizabeth D. Crawford. Minneapolis, MN: Carolrhoda Books.

Kelly, R. Gordon. 1974. *Mother Was a Lady: Self and Society in Selected American Children's Periodicals, 1865–1890*. Westport, CT: Greenwood Press.

Kessler, Cristina. 2004. *Our Secret, Siri Aang*. New York: Philomel.

Kidd, Kenneth. 2007. "Prizing Children's Literature: The Case of Newbery Gold." *Children's Literature* 35: 166–190.

KidsPOD: Protecting Our Diversity. http://kidspod.com/synopsisZuluDog.shtml

Morrison, Toni. 1992, 1993. *Playing in the Dark: Whiteness and the Literary Imagination*. Cambridge, MA: Harvard UP; New York: Vintage Books.

Naidoo, Beverley. 2001, 2003. *Out of Bounds: Seven Stories of Conflict and Hope*. London: Puffin Books; New York: HarperCollins.

Okonkwa, Chidi. 1999. *Decolonization Agnostics in Postcolonial Fiction*. Houndmills, UK: Macmillan.

Parents' Choice: Reviewing Children's Media. http://www.parents-choice.org/aboutawards.cfm

Quintana, Anton. 1982, 1999. *The Baboon King*. In the Netherlands: *Dehavianenkonig* (1982). Translated from the Dutch by John Nieuwenhuizen. New York: Walker.

Randolph, Brenda. 2007. "Picture Books Sweep the 2007 Children's Africana Book Awards." *Sankofa: A Journal of African Children's and Young Adult Literature* 6: 74–84.

Sharra, Steve. 2001. "*The Baboon King*: Institutionalizing Anti-African Bias in Children's Literature." *Children's Literature Association Quarterly* 26: 2 (Summer): 96–99.

Small, Stephen. 1994. *Racialized Barriers: The Black Experience in the United States and England in the 1980s*. London: Routledge.

Stolz, Joëlle. 1999, 2006. *The Shadows of Ghadames*. In France: *Les Ombres de Ghadamès*. (1999). Translated from the French by Catherine Temerson. New York: Random House.

"Teaching Africa in U.S. Schools." 2007. *NEA Today*. http://findarticles.com/p/articles/mi_qa3617/is_200101ai_n8949397

Wheeler, Sara. 1967. "The Mildred L. Batchelder Award." *Top of the News (TOP)* 23: 2 (January): 180–181.

Part II
Neo-Imperialist Stories, 1994–2008

Chapter Four
Eurocentric Feminism in *The Shadows of Ghadames* and *Our Secret, Siri Aang*

> I am not making a culturalist argument about ethnocentrism .... [M]y argument holds for any discourse that sets up its own authorial subjects as ... the yardstick by which to encode and represent cultural Others. It is in this move that power is exercised in discourse.
> —Chandra Mohanty (64)

> To meaningfully explain the phenomenon called African feminism, it is not to Western feminism but rather to the African environment that one must refer.
> —Obioma Nnaemeka (9)

To "Third World" women, imperialism has many guises, including the way Western feminist scholarship dominates the distribution of ideas. American and European feminists are active not only in circulating their own culture-bound presuppositions about womanhood but also in utilizing children's literature as a means for doing so. In particular African populations, as in Joëlle Stolz's *The Shadows of Ghadames* and Cristina Kessler's *Our Secret, Siri Aang*, are being used as a channel for images of oppressed girls and women.

I: Muslims and Feminism in *The Shadows of Ghadames*

Bilkisu, a Muslim co-wife, has a characterization that cannot be judged simply by how she's presented by the author as bold and gregarious, as racing like a tomboy on the rooftop with Malika (the other co-wife's daughter). This is truly an unusual behavior for a Muslim woman under the veil in the 1800s. But it is in line with Stolz's Western-inspired agenda. Her portrait includes traits reminiscent of the conventionally rebellious Western woman. She functions, in short, as propaganda for global feminism. The women of Ghadames are confined, for the most part, to the rooftops of the town and live submissive, secluded lives—lives of deprivation. This condition is not only the fault of Islamic males (at least as they exist in Western media). The media generally paints virtually all males of color in the underdeveloped world with this same brush. By revisiting this stereotype, Stolz knows she needs to create an ally to bring about needed change in the city of Ghadames, and Bilkisu is the chosen one, alongside Malika as her undisputed disciple-daughter.

Stotz's story could be easily misunderstood as a simple novel for children. It reads that way. And it is not surprising to read commentaries about the book that are misleading. The *Kirkus Reviews* admires the weaving together of sights, sounds, and rhythms of life in Ghadames, as well as the novel's cast of distinct characters, but emphasizing the rhythms of Ghadames is making a long stretch. Depictions of characters in their own space is handled haphazardly, and Stolz's observations of people of strict religious/cultural traditions—this is at best inconsistent. Even reading between the lines yields little about the texture of the Mahmud family's daily life, since important aspects of Berber history are overlooked. Or rather, we see only the parts related to Islamic restrictions on women.

Stolz shows a male-dominated Muslim society in Libya in the late 1800s and the way two wives and their children are either compliant or resistant. To drive home the point that Berber laws are cruel and irrational, this French journalist creates three protagonists: two mothers and the eleven-year-old Malika, who live as "shadows" under the shade of Muslim men. She organizes her cast around contrasting pairs that help her underscore this theme. The wives come from different geographical regions, speak different languages, have different skin colors, have ease or difficulty in conceiving children, and are either strict or relaxed vis-à-vis Muslim laws. The children are a boy and girl, dark and light in color, educated and uneducated, and either free or severely restricted in their movements. Women do not only conceal themselves behind veils; they are not allowed to speak to men, remain in the same room with men, pass men in the street without retreating to a recess in the wall, or engage in occupations outside the home unless they belong to the servant class. Most striking is their confinement on the roofs—a rule that applies also to female children. Malika has a strict, fundamentalist mother, Meriem, and a co-mother, Bilkisu, who really "mothers" Malika in the important things: for example, disobedience to Muslim laws if logic and compassion require it.

Readers follow the fate of these characters but see little of the husband and father in the Mahmud family. He's traveling in Tripoli and we're not told how he might have reacted toward the wounded stranger that the women bring into the house to save from a veritable lynch mob. Bilkisu is the charitable wife, even though her care of the stranger, Abdelkarin, means that she could be "disallowed" forever. That is, she could be returned in disgrace to her parent's house for having disobeyed tradition and having dishonored her husband. Meriem is, at first, ready to let the man die rather than break Islamic-based rules. Yet we see that Meriem is not malicious, but rather a person well-trained in the region's belief system. And she tries to pass on this learning to Malika: men and women, she tells her daughter, are like the "sun and moon"; they "meet only at the beginning and end of the night" (10). Thus the fugitive (now hidden in a pantry on the roof) must be kept secret until he can be whisked away during an annual women's festival. During one day each year, the women become revelers (dancing, luring a jinn, undressing, etc.); in a word, they come out from under their "husband's shadow" (25). Except for trips to the baths while men pray at the mosque, Meriem has not set foot outside the house since her marriage—that is, for fourteen years!

This storyline, while underscoring the restrictive life of women, makes repeated references to the young protagonist's impending marriage. This eleven-year-old wants to read and write like her brother, Jasim, but there is a strict ban on education for girls. She wants to resist the tattooing of her whole body to ward off supernatural attacks. She wants to be spared confrontations with a less-than-friendly senior wife (as in Bilkisu's case). She dreads the constant threat of informers on the rooftops (women who either see or imagine the violation of a taboo). She grieves over the prospect of denying an education to her own daughters. She knows her values and problem-solving talents must be suppressed as she accedes to being a "shadow." As Stolz portrays it, Malika's life expectations are almost entirely negative. To what extent is this doleful picture painted by an ill-informed Westerner?

Chandra Mohanty sees this stereotype of the "Third World" woman as ensuing from two invalid suppositions. First, there is an *uncritical* way of defining "universality." And second, there is an assumption that women have "identical interests" irrespective of ethnic and class differences (65). Most of the sharp contrasts in the novel presuppose just one normative referent—namely, Stolz and *her* culture.

This is apparent as the author editorializes about the Mahmud family and other Muslims. She tells readers that "this habit of taking several wives suits most men too well for them to see its drawbacks" (58). Polygamy, she says, "engenders a lot of sufferings and sometimes dreadful rivalries," and that, in turn, "endangers the fortune and unity of families" (58). Moreover, "women shouldn't know the same things as men, for men and women belong to two different worlds ..." (71).

Characters

Characterization is about building subtle layers of revealing information. To find the meaning in *The Shadows of Ghadames,* it is necessary to walk with the characters, to watch how they are maneuvered from one developmental stage to another. It is to see them reach the point where they can be recognized in their wholeness. Malika has an amiable personality and such a passionate devotion to her father that she feels "a superstitious fear of letting my father leave on a trip without saying goodbye to him" (3). She believes his safety depends on this duty. She pleads for the chance to see the departure of the caravan at the city gates, but her mother, Meriem, orders her to get dressed and look after her hair. "More than anyone else in Ghadames, Meriem insists on a strict adherence to traditional practices" (5). She "has the features of a queen": "straight forehead," "delicate mouth," and bluish facial tattoos that "have magical significance" (5). Her husband, we're told, idolized her as "a perfect woman in a perfect city" (57). Bilkisu (second wife) is a completely different person. She doesn't share Meriem's superstitions and is as eager as Malika to "break up the monotony of our reclusive existence" (10). We see how tall and lithe Bilkusi is, and how she attracts Mahmud's attention with her frequent laughter, but there is a virtual silence about her Hausa heritage and her homeland in northern Nigeria. We never connect her region with her character. Some Islamic observances in Nigeria would have differed from those in Libya, and would have helped explain her free-spirited thinking. They would have helped explain the self-confidence that Meriem queries her about: "Where did you learn these things?" (27). Instead of allowing some context for Bilkusi (other than the label "wife from the journey"), she is allowed only this over-generalized statement about taking risks for the sake of another: "Instinct tells me that this is how we must act or else we're lost" (27).

As for Jasim, Bilkusi's son, he joins the cast of unsympathetic males as he taunts Malika: "'You're just a girl! I am the one who gets to go with our father. . . . Your place is with the women'" (6–7). Jasim knows full well his life-long privileges as a Muslim male, yet he has learned a strict code of honor. After losing a bet, he willingly gives his sister his writing board and stylus. As noted above, Malmud (who is the center of this family's universe) is barely sketched in. What kind of Arabized Berber is he? Which of his wives does he prefer most? His attributes are simply inferred since his primary role is in representing the tradition-bound society. His departing words to Malika are unequivocal: "We live in an ancient city. Don't ever forget that" (6). Perhaps in a feminist novel, a man's extensive, tradition-bestowed power is enough to render clearer definitions unnecessary.

Abdelkarim, the fugitive the women will rescue, is characterized as a rude, impertinent fundamentalist even as the Malmud women are saving his life. He bends traditions himself by adopting a variation on the town elder's version of Islam. But still he yells at his rescuers: "'What are you doing? Tak[ing] off my gandourah! Who are you to dare touch me?'" (44). (There is blood on this garment from his head wound and the women have offered to wash it.) He tells Bilkisu, "'Women should never act on their own initiative without consulting a man who has authority over them. All too often they are guided by the devil'" (46). Abdelkarim will be changed by his contact with the Malmud household, but throughout much of the novel he represents a personality type that is both immature and churlish. He symbolizes the fanaticism of a true believer. Nonetheless, Malika eventually wins him over to the point where he will begin giving her reading lessons.[1] He even admits that "the Koran is for everyone. It is the word of God" (71).

Plotline and Relationships

Plot development is not a major feature in Stolz's novel, but it enables the author to contrive relationships serving the feminist theme. Relations between Bilkisu and her own son are minimized by the author, and the same applies to Mahmud's connections with his son. However, Malika and Bilkisu are shown with a stronger bond than the one Malika has with her own mother. And that unshakable trust between Malika and Bilkisu enables readers to become acquainted with the child's innermost secrets—to feel her stresses and bewilderments as she shares them with her mentor. On Meriem's part, Maliku is the child she feared she might never have, and thus her vigilant attempt to keep Malika on her side. Arguably, it is a mother's love and possessiveness vis-à-vis her daughter that allows Meriem to make the one cultural violation she is willing to make—namely, the disobedience involved in the fugitive's rescue. That rescue is the plot's one dramatic moment, and the details that follow are largely shaped by the Malika–Meriem–Bilkisu triangle. Actually, a disciple-daughter or a disciple-son connection is not uncommon in polygamous homes. The young and junior wives sometimes bond with the children of senior wives. They play an important social role as mentor, friend, and confidant. In Malika's case, Bilkisu is such a friend, a person that is easier to trust than her own birth-mother.

It is not surprising that at the sound of chasing feet, the strong-willed Bilkisu tiptoes downstairs alongside a shocked Malika. "'I am going out to look . . . I have to know what happened'" (23). So off goes the surrogate mother to pick up the battered Abdelkarin. At this point the plot calls forth new relationships. Abdelkarin is impatient and full of youthful conceit. He doesn't really seem to realize his predicament. He is Koranic bookwise but doesn't realize that when you are on a long journey and being carried on someone else's back, you don't say "the distance is long and I am tired."

Aïshatou, a traditional healer, comes into the story to assist the wounded man, but she is introduced by Stolz in stale colonialist terms. She is like the "witch doctor" to White perception, the voodoo queen: " . . . suddenly there is a shadow at the doorstep. It is Aïshatou, the healer. She is even taller than I remember and as broad as a tower. Her skin is so dark that it looks bluish around the temples" (30). Stolz ridicules this overweight "doctor" in her "ample dress" (32), and even as Aïshatou calms the patient ("'We will get you safely out of this house and out of this city'"), she is disrespected. Abdelkarin only complains: "I don't want to leave this city . . . I've been given an important mission that must be successfully completed" (73). Now readers are faced with a character that has to be understood beyond what the author tells them. What is the mission? For what purpose? Why was the Aissaouia Brotherhood so desperate to get rid of him when he is, after all, a true-born orphan of their ancient city? Is Abdelkarin a traitor? Bilkisu, Malika, and Meriem do not question him. But he did let them know that like other Muslim men of very strict faith he does not tolerate women who break the Koranic laws, whatever the circumstances. In the end, however, Malika's intellectual astuteness, directness, and spontaneous expressions of feeling impress Abdelkarin. When they part (after Abdelkarin has been dressed in women's veils and smuggled into the women's festival), he tells Malika: "I learned several things while I was hidden on your rooftop. For example that the world of women is not as stupid as I thought" (102). As for Malika, her mind was still fixed on the idea that she was "just a girl" until her new friend explains: "Girls deserve to be taught just as much as boys. It's because they aren't taught anything that they wallow in all that foolish nonsense, all that magic stuff and coffee dregs" (79). Abdelkarin and Malika are both caught in a transitional place between past and present, conservative extremism and revolutionary impatience. He admits that this ancient city is not ready for his assigned mission. And Malika has been given a rare opportunity: the chance to show Abdelkarin that the women of Mahmud's house cared about him.

History and Accountability

Malika's story is imaginary, but Ghadames is no fantasy; it is a city near the Algerian and Tunisian borders in southern Libya. Stolz has chosen Africa for this make-believe tale, and therein rests a clear responsibility. When writers choose the "underdeveloped Third World" as their subject, it is incumbent upon them to know something of history. "Global village" and "global economy" have become catchwords, and critics often generalize about authors "of world fame" and stories "read all over the world." But the terrain that Western book people are laying claim to is often under the cloud of centuries of white supremacist domination.

The Shadows of Ghadames is a historical novel and implies the need for some accountability in the handling of setting. Malika's family members are Berbers of the Ghadames tribe, one of twenty-nine ethnic groups identified by George Peter Murdock (112–114). This tribe established its caravan center in western Libya and managed to withstand foreign invasions until shattered by Arab conquests and Bedouin immigrations. Many Berber communities became Arabized in language and to some extent racially mixed.

Stolz has decided to make the Madmud family a polygamous one, even though that family arrangement is highly unusual in the region selected for the novel's setting. According to Murdock, there is "a strong preference for monogamy among nearly all Berber peoples . . . " Moreover, "in most of these cases, it is confined to a few wealthy men or results . . . from the operation of preferential levirate" (117). Mahmud is, perhaps, an Arabized Berber who has adopted the Arab culture of polygamy. But since this custom is particularly repellent to Westerners, it can be used effectively as propaganda. Stolz uses it to stress Muslim women's problems and to make polygamy integral to her Berbers-are-backward theme.

Bilkisu was no doubt raised in a polygamous Nigerian family and understands the intrigues that are sometimes found in polygamous homes. Her upbringing would have prepared her to deal with them. But not only do readers receive no clues about Bilkusi's homeland; they also know Bilkusi as the kind of "liberated" woman who finds opportunities to unsparingly speak her mind. The contentious fugitive, for instance, sees that he has met his match when Bilkisu reminds him of his initial residence in a woman's womb. He had best bridle his complaining mouth! In isolation, this scene appears uncharacteristic, since Bilkisu is now living in a fundamentalist Muslim milieu. In Kano, Nigeria, non-aristocratic Muslim women did not live in seclusion in the late nineteenth century; this conservative lifestyle was not common across class lines in Nigeria until the 1920s (Adamu, 233–234). A nineteenth-century Bilkisu would have been well advised to avoid exhibiting Nigeria's less restrictive customs. All told, this Nigeria woman's portrait is less than historically convincing when she is painted as intemperate in conversation and rambunctious in her activities with her co-wife's daughter.

Meriem's circumstances are totally dissimilar. She is Mahmud's cousin, and her well-to-do family marries her into this wealthy, solidly conservative merchant's family. She is an easy target for depiction by a Western feminist, since she will adopt traditional beliefs without question. A secluded life is all she has ever known. Yet in analyzing women's gender-related lives in Africa, an approach centered exclusively on inequality and subordination is inappropriate, since Islamic-based restrictions are not necessarily "reproduced in all other aspects of their lives" (Adamu, 239). African feminist scholars have reported on the numerous complex means by which African women have subverted both domination and dependency. But how many strategies and complexities are child readers allowed to see?

African feminism relates to cultural and philosophical specificity. Motherhood plays a large role in the Stolz novel, but in the view of Obioma Nnaemeka, "African feminism's valorization of motherhood . . . should not be pitted against the demotion of motherhood/maternal politics by radical feminism in the West" (9). The African environment, according to Nnaemeka, should guide the place and importance of motherhood if Western writers wish to explain it. Similarly, the African worldview helps guide African feminists' use of words such as "balance," "connectedness," "reciprocity," and "compromise." Western feminists use such terms in relation to a different historical experience.

* * *

As missionaries tramped across Africa selling Bibles and crosses as Christian symbols, so Stolz and other European and Euro-American children's writers parade before Western readers and lure them into believing that people of color are backward—even so primitive they are victims of their own uncivilized ways. In Stolz's case, *The Shadows of the Ghadames* could have been a remarkable piece of storytelling, different from so many other books. She needed only to be sincere with characterizations and more honest with socio-historical facts. Saving the life of one devout Muslim (Abdelkarin) from an angry mob of other devout Muslims has philosophical as well as dramatic potential. Additionally, African feminism could have been powerfully rendered in the relationships within a Nigerian–Berber co-wife family. But the age-old "Darkest Africa" myths got in the way and made even feminist ideals stumble off course.

II: Maligning the Maasai in *Our Secret, Siri Aang*

Cristina Kessler in her author's note tells her readers: "I first came in contact with the Maasai in 1975, as a Peace Corps Volunteer in Kenya. They dazzled me with their elegance, style and pride" (211). A very unusual commendation coming from a White writer. As a whole, *Our Secret, Siri Aang* is based on the unexpected transformation of the Maasai people and their culture. The girl-child protagonist, Namelok, is a twelve-year-old Maasai whose traditional name means in English "sweetest one" and who serves as the author's main vehicle for informing readers and advocating change in Namelok's community.

Most African governments, because of their dependence on foreign aid and Western monetary policies, allow their traditional culture to be replaced by invading foreign cultures. And in the case of *Our Secret, Siri Aang*, the author lets her readers know that she wrote the book "to document another culture before it totally changes from nomadic to sedentary" (212). Ironically, however, Kessler depicts a present-day Maasai community as if it is hopelessly frozen within an antiquated socio-political system. Her twenty-first-century Africans see little of their immediate, contemporary world. Instead, whatever the author could find out about highly conservative historical periods in Kenya, she felt justified in attaching to contemporary Maasai groups. This will be a noticeable feature in the pages that follow.

The main plotlines are strung together to highlight polygamy, initiation (i.e., "female genital mutilation"), conservation, and the rights of women. In contrast, the author uses the conventional stereotypes from Euro-American novels to portray male characters. For the most part they are lazy, chauvinistic, self-righteous, and unproductive.

Namelok is the product of a polygamous family. Her father, Reteti ("helpful one"), has four wives. The author does not explain in detail the profession of Reteti; however, as Reteti belongs to one of the many pastoral groups in Africa, the reader can deduce that Reteti is a cattleman.

At the outset, the story establishes a meeting between Namelok and a mother rhinoceros whom she has come upon in the bush while the mother is giving birth. Excited by what she has witnessed, Namelok names the baby Siri Aang (Our Secret), collects the wood she had been in the process of collecting, and starts back to the Enkang (the circular enclosure where family and livestock live). Significantly, "Our Secret" is not just a name conjured up by Namelok. It is the author's metaphor for her protagonist. At first, the reader is informed by Namelok that "this is a secret; one I will share with no one. Not even with father" (9). With this mysterious show of privacy, the reader comes to understand that Namelok's father is her confidant, but he becomes less so after Namelok's life-changing experience in the bush. She has become a wild animal lover, protector, and conservationist. She has sworn to protect both mother and Siri Aang. She murmurs affectionately, "I love how comfortable you are with my presence" (32).

Protecting wild animals in the African bush is not an obsession among Africans, but has become the preoccupation of White people in these very recent years. In many novels, autobiographies, and travelogues in the past, we find the "Great White Hunters"—adventurers paid to shoot down lions and other animals. In short, Whites from many European countries went on safari to Kenyan parks to hunt for animal trophies.[2] In evading the long historical record of this practice, Kessler is providing entertainment for an audience that she is not adequately informing—an audience being fed on the colonialist belief that Africans do not attempt to hold their own in the face of White interests.[3] Moreover, as the author looks on from a vantage point outside the culture, she doesn't notice the way the Euro-American's affection for animals, be they domestic or wild, is different from that of the African. African hunters do keep hunting dogs, but they protect and care for them in ways different from the ways of Westerners. What is so transparent to Africans is the hypocrisy of Western occupiers who abused the forests and wildlife of Africa for years and years. None of their destructive practices had anything to do with African interests, but suddenly Africa is the culprit.

As foreign interventions continue in the story (now in the form of poachers near Reteti's compound), the elders complain but still break the conservation laws themselves by embarking on a lion hunt. The youths treat their parents' ancestral traditions with wholesale opposition. And traditional values are replaced by foreign values without proper selection, choice, and taste.

Traditions and Youthful Anxieties

Both girls and boys are depicted in *Our Secret, Siri Aang* as personally threatened by long-standing Maasai traditions. The slightest support for social change is treated by Maasai leaders as a traitorous act, and Namelok is dealing with this through three well-kept secrets, all connected to Maasai rituals.

The first secret was the naming ceremony of Siri Aang. Raising her right hand and then pulling back her first finger, she said to the baby rhino, "You were born before my eyes." Pulling back on her second finger she said, "You will always be my family," and "grabbing her third finger to hold with the first two, she finished, 'And I will never tell anyone about you'" (41). To complete the naming, Namelok announced to the bush and to the parent, "'Emuny Narok'" ("Black Rhino"). "'This baby shall be called Siri Aang, which means 'Our Secret.'" To the baby she said four times: "'May that name dwell in you.'"

The second secret was necessary on the morning when Namelok was shocked to find blood on her thighs. No one else must know, especially her mother because it would change her life forever. However, on the third month of Namelok's period, her mother discovered her secret as Namelok bent over the twilight fire. "'Namelok-ai, your time has come. There is blood on the back of your *kikoy*! Soon you will be a woman'" (48). The shock on Namelok's face convinced her mother that it was her first time. As tradition dictates, the mother was overjoyed. "It was what every Maasai mother waited for, and every Maasai girl looked forward to" (48). In no time the news had reached the first wife, Namana, who then passed it to the other wives. Namunyak was a proud and happy mother. "'My sweetest one' she called her daughter. 'Why the frown? You should be happy, for soon you will be initiated and marry the man your father chooses'" (48).

Her third secret came after an event at the neighborhood store run by a greedy, shifty, cheating shopkeeper. Namelok had come to purchase something and the shopkeeper had short-changed her. The local teacher, who was present and had seen what had transpired, asked Namelok to open her hand so he could check the change she'd been given. True to character, the thieving merchant had cheated her out of ten shillings. "'Come to school,'" says the teacher. "'You'll learn to count and add and subtract, to read and write ... Just think of the money you could save your family'" (45). Namelok did not go to school and did not think it possible, knowing as she did that her father would not even discuss the subject. But at a later encounter, Joseph (the teacher) writes Namelok's name on a piece of paper and lets her keep it. She is surprised, but at the same time realizes that she wants to go to school. With the paper carefully tucked in her *kikoy* and rubbing against her skin, she walks away, patting this new treasure. Then she stopped and said aloud, "'Now I have three secrets to keep'" (47).

Surprisingly, Western children's novelists continuously harp on the trivialities and backward life that they themselves create for the African characters in their novels. Adult characters are powerless, lacking in motivation, and uninspired in what they do in their rundown communities. But many Western writers also approach their task with a specific political campaign to wage, and in *Our Secret, Siri Aang* the battle is about clitoridectomy (female circumcision).

Genital Cutting: Male and Female

It is a sensitive subject. Namelok, a girl of twelve, would not (in an actual African community) have confronted her mother in public about *emuratare* (initiation) and marriage. That would not have been a common practice even in urban areas. And for Namelok to later express regret to her father is also unconvincing: "'aaa, I knew later that I should not have spoken in public, for this is a matter for a mother and daughter to discuss'" (204). Clearly Kessler has nothing to replace the traditional rites she is so blithely trying to destroy, so she tries to follow a middle course: "I decided that I will follow tradition when I get back [to the kraal]." And she explains to her father, [This is] for my mother, for my family, but I will not force my future daughters to do this" (204).

Kessler introduces the anti-circumcision message by way of a radio broadcast, letting readers hear the broadcaster arguing against female circumcision and noting that surgery is conducted without the benefit of anesthetics (93). Angry shoppers turn off the shopkeeper's radio and lash out at the broadcaster: "'[She] cannot be one of us with such foolish thoughts.... Who is this crazy woman, challenging our ways?'" (93). But both the shoppers and the broadcaster offer no opinions about male circumcision, a related initiation ritual. Nor is anything said about the logic of anesthetics for both sexes.[4] According to Corrine Kratz, "Where both [male and female circumcision] are practiced, they can only be understood fully in relation to each other" (618). Being part of a spiritually oriented *rite of passage*, as Kratz explains, it is not surprising that a single word refers to both male and female operations in many African languages. Moreover, "this correspondence is often central to the way their practitioners understand them" (618). A Nigerian anthropologist, E. Babatunde, explains the religious aspect of the rite in these terms:

> The logic of the practice is couched in the anthro-pological term of prestation, a gift that you give under pain of sanction for which you receive a gift in return. The logic of clitoridectomy is that by taking a tiny bit of the sacred instrument of fertility as an offering the god of fertility will bless you with more children. (qtd. in Steady, 108)

From this perspective, one way to change female initiation customs is to reduce the high value placed on bearing many children. In countries where health care delivery has been substantially improved, the public pressure that promotes much child-bearing has receded (Steady, 108).

Throughout Africa, meanings attached to female circumcision encompass identity formation, morality, bodily aesthetics, definitions of adulthood, and ideologies of fertility, to name but a few examples (Kratz, 617). In her novel, Kessler insists that without circumcision, "a Maasai girl would never be considered a woman," would "never be able to marry a Maasai man," and would "never bear legitimate children" (62). These generalizations sidestep the complex, ritually important meanings of circumcision, and also shed no light on the political issues that accompanied both colonial and anti-colonial campaigns in relation to initiations.

Kessler's anti-circumcision program echoes the colonialist programs designed to abolish genital cutting in women. In the early twentieth century, European missionaries and colonial administrators targeted various local customs (including clitoridectomy) as being in violation of Christian behavior, but their efforts to ban them only added further momentum to the anti-colonial movements already under way. Specifically, African responses to the proposed ban spurred the people's creation of more independent schools and churches (Kratz, 618).

Education and Tradition

Another variation on the "primitive" theme occurs by way of Namelok's brother, Saitoti, and his education. Saitoti's father tells him, "You are a warrior, circumcised and trained together with your age-mates in the skills of battle, cattle raiding and lion hunting. . . . In time you will [join the] Elders that lead our community. Make your mother and me proud" (26–27). According to this set of "traditions," Maasai communities seem oblivious to Kenyan law. They claim their independent right to wage war, steal cattle, and violate environmental protection laws. But how does this agenda connect with modern Kenya? Who is it that Saitoti is being ordered to engage in battle? Whose herds will he rob? Why will he shame his parents unless he defies the government-appointed conservation officers? We're told that "Maasai are the protectors of animals" (5, 53, 85). But when a lion threatens a cow, the villagers secretly plan a lion hunt rather than involve the nearby game reserve rangers. Justifying his traditions, Father claims that the government wants to "stop our *ilmurani* [boys from ten to eighteen years] from warriorhood days" (66). It appears as if young men will be blithely decimating the lion population whenever Elders give the command (67). Father seems positively clueless about any connection with Kenyan citizenship. "'All these changes,' he complains. 'I hate them!'" (67). The author's argument centers on the notion that Africans lack viable societies. Also, they are destructively "tribalistic" and have not noticed how Maasai intertribal wars (prevalent in the late 1800s) have been largely eliminated. They have not accepted any connection with a postcolonial nation. Only Namelok is characterized as flexible, as "redeemable" in this modern age.

Namelok's longing for education revolves around her self-esteem and the local teacher's assurance that she will be able to outwit a cunning shopkeeper. But these plot twists have little to do with Maasai connections with education.

Maasai girls generally receive formal schooling through the fourth grade, thus gaining the reading, writing, and math skills required for commercial endeavors. Historically, the business ventures of women have been important to the nation's economic stability. As for boys in a nomadic society, their participation in a pastoral economy has been the reason underlying their minimal schooling. Finn Kjaerby explains:

> In contrast to agricultural societies, where the labour power of school-aged children is more marginal and temporary, . . . children in pastoral societies are heavily and continuously engaged in herding, day in and day out, and this explains the reluctance of pastoralists to send their children to school. . . . [T]his reluctance is not due to conservatism or ignorance. . . . (qtd. in Rigby, 170)

To help in resolving this problem, some East African pastoral communities have transferred the herding job to young initiated men ("junior warriors"), as well as to elders, "so that young boys (*ilaiyok*) can go to school . . . ." (qtd. in Rigby, 170).

Folklore

Folklore has been introduced as another tool to reinforce the author's theme about Maasai inflexibility. The novel contains a creation myth which, in Kessler's hands, becomes a means for indicting the Maasai as perpetrators of wars and thefts. According to this myth, the female God, Enkai, created cattle in response to a Maasai request, and designated the Maasai as perpetual owners of all cattle (Kessler, 81–85). Namelok's father explains that in his younger days, "cattle raids were a Maasai right rather than a breaking of someone else's laws . . . .[A Maasai household] was expected to increase the herds through cattle raids . . . ." (75). Here the author is extending the uses of creation myths far beyond their cultural meaning. Typically, such tales throughout the world have involved a God-given gift, as well as conditions as to how the gift will be managed. Mismanagement brings on punishment (e.g., banishment from Eden). The Creator's first acts are symbolically important as art and as a means for clarifying collective values. But as in Kessler's case, they can be put to a variety of uses.

Declining Father–Child Relations

How well does Retiti understand his daughter? She had caught him committing a crime that his daughter abhorred: poaching on the game reserve. On Retiti's part, he wanted to know what his daughter was running from when she confessed her anxieties about the upcoming *emuratare* and marriage. To him, it looked like cowardice: "'I cannot believe that a child of mine, male or female, is a coward'" (205). Any reader will understand full well that this girl is no coward. But what is she? A Maasai traditional girl or a caricature devised by a Western writer?

Retiti sits in front of the fire his daughter has made at their make-shift camp in the bush. He ponders the circumstances that have forced him to commit the unforgivable. He has been a party to the killing of the mother rhino and has consequently left the baby rhino without a mother to protect it.

His anger and shame could not be understood at first by his daughter. He had overheard the *Ilmurani* talking among themselves about men who promised to pay money to those who led them to a rhino. Retiti had thought that if he had money he could buy some land so "no one could plant on it or ban them from grazing there" (188). He knew where he could go with his family to resume the true, free Maasai life. Then by coincidence he sees his son posing for a tourist, which is against Maasai traditions, and he feels forced to accept the poachers' offer: a fee of seventy-five thousand shillings. "'Don't you see, my sweetest one? I wanted the money to set my family free. . . . I had a son posing for pictures and a daughter who wanted to delay her *emuratare* and go to school. Both things are so distant from a true Maasai's life or mind. These are the things that drove me to a terrible and shameful act'" (192).

Deep in the bush, father and daughter were agreed that "changes are coming" and Namelok posed this question to her father: "'Isn't it better to be part of the change happening than just to be a victim of it all?'" (209).

Maasai Society: Functional and Diversified

The confusion about contemporary Kenyan reality on the one hand, and colonialist assumptions on the other hand, leads to many of the misrepresentations in *Our Secret, Siri Aang*. Kessler repeatedly mentions how a Maasai "respects all animals of the wild" (5), but then plunges ahead with a pitch about Africans threatening the environment. She mentions ineffectual game reserve workers, but takes no real account of government initiatives on behalf of conservation. She makes no attempt to understand the range of current choices vis-à-vis land use, technology, and education. Lawless cattle-raiding presupposes a homogeneous nomadic culture, yet for many decades choices have been available that have included a change from semi-nomadic to sedentary living. Especially during and after the 1960s, Maasai families increased their residency on collectively organized ranches (Hedland, 2–3). Namelok's father *may* have wandered from one kraal to another, always believing in a traditionally defined status quo as a solution for his family. But he was not necessarily stuck in the trap Kessler devises for him. It was not inevitable that he would so close his mind that he would reduce the opportunities needed by his offspring. Today's Maasai children see the way their communities build dams to preserve water, operate electrically motored pumps, utilize government-built watering stations and clinics, immunize their herds, and so on. Today's Maasai sometimes construct cement houses, thus reducing the time earlier populations spent on repairing mud/thatch dwellings and repelling insects and snakes. As noted above, they reorganize herding practices to accommodate their children's school attendance. Women who have helped bring about such improvements have nonetheless wished for the sisterhood that nomadic living enhanced. Even though the distance between houses on collective ranches is not great, women have noted in contemporary studies the way ranch life has reduced the camaraderie they enjoyed in carrying out chores and bringing up children (*Our Life: A View of Maasai Women*, 1995).

Put simply, the Maasai pastoral system has become "integrated into the market economy and increasingly subjected to the political and administrative control of the state apparatus" (Talle, 4). And although biased research studies have failed to show the role of Maasai women in political matters, their influence has been substantial. Anthropologists have made the mistake of separating two "spheres": the "private" (read: domestic and female) and the "public" (social and male). Yet "the Maasai themselves do not draw any clear distinction" (Talle, 9). As shown in detail by Aud Talle, decision-making within households is political in nature, with brides, wives, and mothers playing a strong role as councilors and as mediators "between men and the larger world" (9).

Western feminists, despite little understanding of African culture, make pronouncements extolling women's rights and condemning polygamy, female initiation, conservation as practiced in Africa, and other such well-publicized subjects. *Our Secret, Siri Aang* is loaded with commentary on all of these subjects. Yet at times Kessler does not sound like a feminist, Western or otherwise. Despite the novelist's interest in feminine justice (e.g., her interest in promoting independence for Namelok), she does not express much awareness of Maasai women in the current century, and she inexplicably resorts to negative animal metaphors to belittle women. She writes about weaver birds that "flitted about their nests, scolding one another with incessant chattering notes, just like the women emerging from the hut" (11). Here women are generalized as persons with nervous, gossiping personalities. Namelok scrambled "like a dung beetle in the path of an anteater" (58), and was seen by her father as being "as jumpy as a wildebeest surrounded by hyenas" (54). Nanana (father's first wife) "planted [her eyes] on her husband's face like a tick stuck on a cow's hide" (76). Is this the imagery Kessler came away with after nineteen years of knowing and studying Maasai groups?

* * *

As Joëlle Stolz spreads her Western-style feminism by capitalizing on the West's conflicts with Muslims, so Kessler portrays Maasai communities as too torpid, self-inhibiting, and politically isolated to be agents of their own best interests. She seems unaware that Africans in the midst of rapid changes may be simultaneously victims and participants in those transformations. That is, planners may have failed to consult enough common citizens—people that have been forced into the role of voiceless, marginalized people. They may have been reluctant to admit that economies will remain colonialist economies unless the vast majority of the people become actively involved.

As for fiction writers, they will play a more positive role if they can reject distortions of African realities, take up the study of African history, and abandon the "dying races" motif that children's literature has been steeped in for eons.

Works Cited

Adamu, Fatima L. 1998. "Gender Myth About Secluded Women in Hausa Society of Northern Nigeria" in *Gender Perceptions and Development in Africa*, ed. Mary E. Modupe Kolawole, 231–241. Lagos, Nigeria: Arrabon Academic.

Hedland, Hans G. B. 1971. *The Impact of Group Ranches on a Pastoral Society* (Staff Paper No. 100). Nairobi, Kenya: University of Nairobi, Institute for Development Studies. .

Kessler, Cristina. 2004. *Our Secret, Siri Aang*. New York: Philomel.

Kratz, Corrine. 2005. "Female Circumcision in Africa." In *Africana: The Encyclopedia of the African and African American Experience*, 2nd ed., eds. Kwame Anthony Appiah and Henry Louis Gates, Jr., 616–620. Oxford, UK: Oxford University Press.

MacKenzie, John M. 1986. *Imperialism and Popular Culture*. Manchester, UK: Manchester, UP.

Mohanty, Chandra. 1984, 1988. "Under Western Eyes: Feminist Scholarship and Colonial Discourses." In the UK: *Boundary 2* , 12: 1; 13: 1 (Spring/Fall, 1984): 333–358; in the US: *Feminist Review*, 30 (1988): 61–88.

Murdock, George Peter. 1959. *Africa: Its Peoples and Their Culture and History*. New York: McGraw-Hill.

Nnaemeka, Obioma, ed. 1998. "Introduction: Reading the Rainbow." In *Sisterhood: Feminisms and Power From Africa to the Diaspora*, ed. Obioma Nnaemeka, 1–35. Trenton, NJ: Africa World Press.

Our Life: A View of Maasai Women. 1995. Nairobi, Kenya: National Museums of Kenya, Centre of Biodiversity.

Rigby, Peter. 1985. *Persistent Pastoralists: Nomadic Societies in Transition*. London: Zed Books.

Sada, Ibrahim N., Fatima L. Adamu, and Ali Ahmad. 2006. *Promoting Women's Rights Through Sharia in Northern Nigeria*. Centre for Islamic Studies, Ahmadu Bello University, Zaria, Nigeria. http://www.dfid.gov.uk/pubs/files/promoting-woman-sharia.pdf

Steady, Filomina Chioma. 2006. *Women and Collective Action in Africa: Development, Democratization, and Empowerment with Special Focus on Sierra Leone*. New York: Palgrave Macmillan.

Stolz, Joëlle. 1999, 2006. *The Shadows of Ghadames (Les Ombres de Ghadamès)*. Translated by Catherine Temerson. Yearling (Random House, Inc), 2006. (Originally published by Bayard Editions Jeunesse, 1999).

Talle, Aud. 1988. *Women at a Loss: Changes in Maasai Pastoralism and Their Effects on Gender Relations*. Stockholm: University of Stockholm.

Chapter Five
White Supremacy in Isabel Allende's *Forest of the Pygmies*

> In terms of their own history, [peoples of Africa] are very obviously developed peoples. They can be seen as "underdeveloped" only in terms of the quite different histories of other peoples, whose own development has emerged and taken shape in quite different circumstances.
>
> —Basil Davidson (233)

> Imperialism knows no law beyond its own interests.
>
> —Kwame Nkrumah (xiv)

Isabel Allende is an international bestselling author. In the world of literature, she is deemed "the most widely read woman writer in Spanish in the last half of the twentieth-century" (Zapata, 17). Her much anticipated entry into the young adult book empire began with a trilogy in 2002: *City of the Beasts* (an adventure story set in the Amazon river basin), *Kingdom of the Golden Dragon* (2004), which takes the reader to the Himalayan mountains, and *Forest of the Pygmies* (2005), which plunks her protagonists into the midst of a tropical rain forest in "Darkest Africa." The main characters are multinational, intergenerational and, in one instance, biracial. Yet this question soon surfaces vis-à-vis *Forest of the Pygmies:* is it written to engage the diverse adolescent populations in today's "global village"? Or contrariwise, is it steeped in ridicule and mockery, not only of "Pygmies" and Bantus, but of Africa in general—African cultures, languages, phenotypes?

Like many Euro-American novelists, historians, cartoonists, and "scientists," Allende shrewdly reminds Caucasian readers about their superiority, about the indisputable greatness of Western wayfarers, colonizers, missionaries, and journalists. The book's cover begins this process with a diabolical image on the jacket (a painting of a malevolent face mask), and following this illustration is the inscription "Journey into the heart of darkest Africa."[1] For adolescent minds of whatever nationality (including Africans and those of African descent), the impression will be complex and disturbing. Africa is, after all, utilized primarily as a backdrop for Allende's explicit themes about environmental protection and the independence of women, yet taken as a whole, the narrative corresponds with the mask's insidious message: namely, that when contrasting European and American nations with African nations, the latter necessarily requires the "saving" intercession of the former. The notion of such a "White Man's Burden" has for centuries functioned as a rationalization for the appropriation of another's lands, liberty, and wealth.

White supremacist depictions of Africa are ironic in Isabel Allende's case since her adult fiction is widely commended for its solidly based social commitment. Commenting on this Chilean novelist, Celia Correas Zapata contends that "all of Isabel's works [with one exception] exhibit an undeniable social commitment" (204). In *Forest of the Pygmies*, Allende turns this important feature on its head. That is, the novel fails as social commitment since it rests upon little acquaintance with the African socio-political world.

Storyline and Characterization

Characters from the two earlier novels in the trilogy have regrouped in Kenya to record the first elephant-led safari in Africa. Kate Cold is an American journalist on special assignment for the magazine called "International Geographic." Her grandson (Alexander) accompanies her, along with Nadia Santos, the Canadian–Brazilian teenager from the first novel. Barobá, Nadia's pet monkey, is a constant presence in all three books, helping Allende string together repeated messages about treating animals humanely. Alexander and Nadia are the God-sent saviors of the "Pygmies." Alongside Barobá, they have all it takes in bravery, ability, self-sacrifice, resourcefulness, and extra-sensory perception to cope with helpless "Pygmies," servile Bantus, and a sadistic village leader. They had learned from Brazilian indigenes to shape-shift (as in the first novel), and this knack saves their lives more than once in *Forest of the Pygmies*.

Grandmother Kate serves the women's liberation theme by way of her self-conscious nonconformity. She is Hollywood's fearless heroine; she glories in disheveled clothes, gruff manners, and no-nonsense relationships (her grandson's unpardonable sin is in referring to her as "grandmother"). Adding further to the independent woman theme, Allende creates "Angie," an African woman with her own air transport business. But then she undercuts the characterization by making gratuitous references to her supposedly inordinate size. She is "voluminous" in appearance (125), equipped with "considerable girth" (34), embodying a "bulk... too substantial to conceal" (124), an "ample bosom" (89), an "ample knee" (249), a form summed up as "considerable flesh" (85). Angie moves on and off stage like a minstrel buffoon, splitting eardrums with her "Comanche yells" (54, 59, 259).

To shift the safari adventure to a rescue-the-missionaries tale, Allende needs the help of Brother Fernando, a Catholic missionary from Spain. From the outset his white supremacist orientation is clear. When Kate learns that a "reign of terror" is financed through contraband, she complains, "'Don't the authorities do anything about it?'" (97). The Brother enlightens her: "'Just where do you think you are, lady? Apparently you don't know how things are done in this part of the world....'" (97–98). Missionaries are the antidote for "this part of the world"; they face danger while the Africans bolt. They "were the only ones who persevered" (55). When ordered out of the village by the dictator, "they didn't leave. They tried to help our tribe" (182). They "would have healed the children's sores [had they survived assassination]" (116). In Rwanda, we're told, "only missionaries stayed and tried to help" (182). Allende devises repeated opportunities for displaying the Brother's role as "serving Christ" (e.g., his dangerous mission on behalf of the missing clergymen, his bravery in facing an attacking boar, his role as referee between the battling village tyrant and "Pygmy" leader). Saintly Western religionists serve as a means for signaling a gap between "civilization" and a benighted "part of the world."

In contrast to the religious paragons of the West, Allende introduces a "priestess," Ma Bangese. "Everything about this woman (this "mountain of flesh") associates her spirituality with horror and excess. She is surrounded with figures that are "wet with the blood of sacrificed animals" (13). When Alexander meets her in an African market place, she grabs him with "two powerful hands" ("hands that had immobilized him"), yanks him into her "hut," and forces him "to sit before her" (12, 13). With "bulging eyes," "deep roar," and "smoke that brought tears to the young people's eyes" (smoke from puffing black leaves), she is presented as hugely unappealing in contrast to the idealized Catholic "Brother." As for her "hut," this term is usually a reference to a residence; a "hut" will not be found in a marketplace, no matter what kind of business transaction is under way. And word usage is also a problem when Allende moves voodoo from its actual geographical locations (Brazil, Haiti, and other Caribbean islands) to Africa. There are no voodoo priests or priestesses in Africa, as there are also no "witch doctors." The novelist seems more in touch with dime novels and sensational imperialist travelogues than with credible sources.

Forest of the Pygmies is ridden with the imagery characteristic of imperialist literature from the past three centuries. This literature (whether by explorers, "scientists," philosophers, or missionaries) is replete with contempt for the Black population. In his early nineteenth-century lectures, Hegel instructed his students that "we must lay aside all thought of reverence and morality—all that we call feeling—if we would rightly comprehend [the Negro]; . . . [the] accounts of Missionaries completely confirm this . . . " (93). Africa, he noted, "is no historical part of the World; it has no . . . development. . . . What we properly understand by Africa, is the Unhistorical, undeveloped Spirit . . . ." (99). In *Sunday Reading for the Young* (1877), Africans are referred to as being "but one degree removed from the level of brute creation—the sole trace of civilization about them is that they cook their food, and that, it may be assumed, in the crudest manner" (qtd. in Pieterse, 35). The work of the nineteenth-century anatomist, Robert Knox, includes a description of the "Hottentots": "[They are] of a dirty yellow colour. . . . The face is set on like a baboon's. . . . " (qtd. in Pieterse, 42–43). In the twentieth century, the myth of mental and physical inferiority persisted: "[N]o change or treatment and environment will . . . make the black man's mind and spirit, any more than a black man's body, that of a white man" (qtd. in Rich, 90).[2]

In Allende's book, both the Bantu and "Pygmy" groups are delineated in inaccurate and derogatory ways. Although a "Pygmy" leader plays a positive role in defeating a malicious dictator, "[t]here was nothing beautiful about [the leader's] out-of-proportion limbs and torso, or his flat-nosed face and shortened forehead . . . " (267). "Pygmy" feet are positioned to run "like ducks"; their speech ranges from "jabbering" (109) to "chattering like magpies" (241). The actual group that Allende features in the story, the Aka people in the Central African Republic, is never referred to except by a derogatory label. According to Stanley Frankland, "The analytical concept "pygmy" . . . generally has been discarded as a term of classification because of its derogatory overtones of dwarfism" (62).

To the novelist's credit, she does offer some information from anthropological studies, as when she describes husbands and wives as "equally sharing the care of the children," or communities without hierarchies or gender discrimination, or a society free from violence among its members (Allende, 179). However, this cultural detail is seldom woven into the texture of the narrative. What dramatically unfolds are scenes recounted in stock Eurocentric clichés: "[T]hey weren't interested in civilization" (179); their dances were "degrading" (132); they were "a pandemonium of people twisting and jumping around" (132); they represented "a collective dementia" (132). As for their religion, it was a constant promoter of fear and self-flagellation.

In a similar way, Bantus are demeaned: they are either the dictator's sycophantic servants, or henchmen who beat up "Pygmies" and stumble with drunkenness. As with "Pygmies," their religious system boils down to a life of constant terror (e.g., "[T]he night is peopled with demons and the day with ghosts" [277]). And in a proverbial blame-the-victim argument, we learn that "to liberate the slaves [of the dictator]" the novel's young protagonists "had to shatter the indifference of the Bantus; because they hadn't opposed tyranny, they were accomplices to it" (236). Indeed, the plotline puts both Aka and Bantu communities in complete submission vis-à-vis enslavement, rape, impoverishment, child abuse, lack of education, lack of medicine, and death in a crocodile-infested pool! How does the regional president (the dictator) activate all this brutality and misrule? Allende makes him three persons in one: a "witch doctor" concealed behind a ceremonial mask, a military commandant concealed behind dark glasses and battle gear, and the regional ruler who is viewed by the citizenry as divinely chosen. As commandant, he threatens and entices Bantus to police the "Pygmy" slaves, who must supply enough ivory tusks to amply enrich the regime. Everything works brilliantly because the faint at heart won't go near the place: "[O]utsiders couldn't live that far from civilization. They got sick; they went mad" (182).

It is important to be conscious of anti-African commentators (whether past or present), while also understanding that these reporters have not been encountering in Africa a "vacant land"—a "blank slate." A real place, culture, history, and political economy were in full view.

Realities of Aka Life

"Pygmy" groups—for example, the Aka, Mbuti, and Twa—are specialists in forestry. A rain forest requires a unique type of exploitation if its seasonal products are to be collected, but contemporary researchers have debunked the idea that forest harvesters "live in forests the year round" (Blench, 45–46). Studies indicate that "the forest does not yield enough carbohydrates . . . for people to live there independently [that is, independent of farmers who supply such products as yams]" (Hewlett, *Intimate Fathers*, 14). Therefore, over at least the past hundred years, the Aka have routinely harvested edible plants on the forest's periphery. Additionally, they have established dwelling places near the Bantu village farms, becoming part of a seasonal labor force (Hewlett, "Cultural. . . ," 225). Farm products, plus Bantu metalworks and extensive commercial channels, have contributed to a viable economic life throughout the Aka regions. At the same time, benefits for the Bantus included meats, gathered foods, and medicinal plants collected by Aka families. In ancient times, they benefited from the services of Aka guides through densely forested areas (Bahuchet and Guillaume, 193). In a word, the short-statured people were by no means "confined and isolated in their forest cocoon" (Bahuchet and Guillaume, 191). In Allende's novel, the Aka groups are incorrectly positioned in near-total isolation.

In the nineteenth century and beyond, colonial rulers had an inhibiting impact on both Bantu and Aka societies. French colonial administrators, for example, gave Europeans monopoly control over products such as ivory, rubber, and the much-coveted skins of duikers. When Bantus were forced to become ivory collectors, they relied upon specialized Aka hunting skills. This specific Bantu–Aka partnership continued until elephant herds became much reduced in number (by about 1910). According to Serge Bahuchet and Henri Guillaume, Bantu labor was also used in harvesting rubber, a compulsory occupation imposed by the French and one reinforced by the colonial government's tax levies—payments being payable only in rubber (199–120). Direct colonial domination is seen in the way Aka settlements were regrouped near rivers and roads, making them accessible to colonial administrators and readily available as involuntary laborers (204). In *Forest of the Pygmies*, Allende claims that "Pygmies" valued independence to the point where they "had not been subjugated even by European colonizers, but in recent times many of them had been enslaved by the Bantus" (127). An independent lifestyle *was* a much-valued aspect of Aka life, but since 1974, their communities have become integrated into Bantu society. Their living arrangements have evolved in ways that produce flexibility vis-à-vis the Bantu, while still maintaining customs such as strong communal solidarity. Allende's insistence upon a static, blindly immobile "Pygmy" population simply fails to correspond to the historical record.[3]

By perceiving the Aka as a strictly primordial people, the novelist has been tempted to treat domestic traditions, religious beliefs, and hunting methods as basically frozen in time, as unaltered by the forces of space, time, and human agency. This is perhaps a convenient means for manipulating dramatic tension, but by excluding African realities, the writer is disserving both African and non-African readers.

White Supremacy and Flawed "Magical Realism"

Magical realism was, potentially, an ideal creative approach for Allende's young adult novels. *Forest of the Pygmies* is crammed with witches, warlocks, totems, hallucinatory journeys, shape-shifts, conversations with the dead, predictions of the future, and a capacity to make the human body invisible. Book reviewers have noticed in *Forest of the Pygmies* important aspects of magical realism, qualities that distinguish most of Allende's adult fiction.[4] But a magical realist novel is not simply an example of the conventional literary fantasy. It is a blend of supernatural happenings and strong social realist content. This combination of natural and supernatural worlds brings forward the insights of socio-political observation alongside poetic, other-worldly conceptions. But clearly the "realistic" side must be genuine. In the present case, Africa is primarily glimpsed through popular culture and a white supremacist lens. Praising Allende's first adult novel, *The House of the Spirits* (1985), Kavita Panjabi emphasizes the importance of the novelist's social criticism: "[The novel's strength] lies not in fantasy, but in [the protagonist's] confrontation of the economic and sexual organization of her social system" (11). The lack of such confrontation in Allende's "African" novel produces distortion and underdevelopment, as well as a questionable use of spirituality.

A case in point includes the way Africans are all but hypnotized by a punitive, spirit-based belief system, while the visiting teenagers, Nadia and Alex, have lofty "trance" experiences. "Pygmies," for instance, believe it is fatal to pass through the "lands of the ancestors" since trespassers disturb spirits that take revenge on the living (111–112). Moreover, the theft of an important amulet—the very "soul of their people"—has left the population soulless (113). Without the soul-imbued object, all sacred meaning has been removed from their primary occupation (hunting elephants and other beasts) (172). In contrast, Nadia and Alex have trances in which the spirits shed a "great light on everything." Reality is viewed from "a richer, more luminous perspective" and fear (even the fear of death) is "left behind" (235). Incredibly, the youngsters are privileged to a "silent dialogue with the ghosts" and thereby learn how foolish are the "Pygmy" beliefs:

> Alex and Nadia learned that the spirits do not cause illness, misfortune, or death, as they had heard; suffering is caused by the wickedness and ignorance of the living. Neither do they destroy people who violate or intrude into their domains, because they have no domains and it is not possible to offend them. Sacrifices, gifts, and prayers do not reach them; their only usefulness is to mollify the mourners making the offerings. (208)

In this imagined utopia (where "earthly souls, along with all things in the universe, are particles of a single spirit . . . "), the local inhabitants are inexplicably stricken with self-imposed terror (210–211).

Turning to feminist connections, we see a tie-in with magical realism, as when Allende is called a "magical feminist." This term has been coined to refer to Allende's "blend of politics, spirituality, and magic" (Benjamin and Engelfried, 185). Yet in *Forest of the Pygmies* the feminist content is less than consistent.

Nana-Asante (the deposed queen of the Bantus) exhibits extraordinary courage, and upon her return to power is asked how she will improve relations between Bantus and "Pygmies." "I will begin," she says, "with the women. . . . They have more goodness within them" (288). Here is a male–female hierarchy that is rejected by many feminists, knowing as they do that hierarchies typically breed injustice. But in spite of the "more goodness" notion about women, the novelist does offer credible contrasts among varying female personalities. Angie, for example, does not surprise us with her obsessions about lipstick and snazzy clothes, while Kate Cold scorns any costume other than ill-fitting shirts and shorts. Still, one suspects that Kate's wardrobe is virtually a *costume*, a way to disguise her preoccupation with becoming an old, enfeebled person.

Finally, there is the "terrorized harem" of forced-marriage wives (120). After the tyrannical ruler dies in his man-made crocodile pool, the wives are liberated as "happy widows" and, in gratitude, bestow their jewelry on Angie (290). Angie is already weighed down with jewels, but she loves these gifts until Brother Fernando confiscates them. "Brother Fernando demolished [Angie] with one of his apocalyptic glances and held out his hands" (291). It seems women are still babes with trinkets and a father figure to keep them in line. Angie submits to humiliation at the hands of Brother Fernando, and Kate's sixty-plus years inhibit a positive self-concept. By putting Brother Fernando in charge of Angie's possessions and by making ageism (not age per se) a pronounced problem for Kate, Allende contradicts some of the feminist strands put forward in her story.

The spiritual rituals of the Aka may have initially attracted Allende to the Central African Republic as a setting, but whatever the lure of fantasy, magical realists do not typically shy away from significant policy matters such as gender politics and grinding poverty. Phil McCluskey notes: "[I]n a Latin American context, magic realism is often seen as the fictional manifestation of immediate reality" (qtd. in Schroeder, 23). Reyhan Harmanci, critic for the *San Francisco Chronicle* and usually an Allende fan, recognized the "reality" shortcomings in *Forest of the Pygmies*. Harmanci comments: "Allende eschews her usually charming mix of magic and realism and just piles on the magic" (E–3).

On one level, Allende does know the "immediate reality" of life in exile, abuses of power, and similar political catastrophes. Her father's first cousin, Chilean President Salvador Allende, was assassinated to make way for the late General Augusto Pinochet. The extermination, as well as the "disappearance," of thousands of people occurred under Pinochet's administration. In "Writing as an Act of Hope" (1989), Isabel grieves over the Chile of the 1980s: "We are living in the worst economic, political, and social crisis since the conquest of America by the Spaniards. . . . Social inequality is greater every day, and to avoid an outburst of public rancor, repression also rises day by day" (qtd. in Zinsser, 47–48). This history must still produce haunting effects on Chileans, yet there is no evidence that it has made a difference in Allende's Africa-based story. All told, the white supremacy myth, as well as the intentional selection of specific African subjects, makes it imperative that this content be given serious consideration. But this imperative has remained among the author's unrealized responsibilities.

White Supremacy and Artistic License

Social responsibility in the arts entails a mix of aesthetic and public policy concerns. It depends upon a well-conceived social *and* art-driven philosophy. Frequently, however, this philosophy has been seen as an undue restraint on the creative imagination. Children, we are told, can endure practically any image or idea. So how is social responsibility to be defined and made

practical? How should we rate authors who bring a negative connotation to skin colors, nose shapes, and other immutable traits? In *Forest of the Pygmies*, not only is the "Pygmy" population inherently unattractive; it is so backward that survival depends upon guidance from a newcomer in Africa: an American teenager. In an interview, Allende has expressed her attitude toward the moral dimensions of literary technique: "Beware of authors," she says, "who pound their 'moral messages' into you" ("Interview With Isabel Allende"). However, are not her white supremacist scenes in *Forest of the Pygmies* as obvious in their message-sending as her feminist and environmentalist scenes? She has not been evasive in advertising feminism and wildlife conservation, but in her treatment of Africa, she has managed to extend the life span of white supremacy.

Haki Madhubuti, an African American poet and publisher, speaks urgently in an interview about accepting the "mission to accurately deal with the world" (240). Yet in children's literature the material "is often downright treacherous . . . ." (245). Proposing a remedy, Madhubuti cautions that "you cannot stand on the outside and just observe and think that you've going to get the truth or the answer. . . . You have to become culturally immersed in that people, in their mores, their science, religion, music, technology, art, their language" (246). Such a program charts a pluralistic course for creative writers. Moreover, the necessity of dealing "accurately with the world" is the business of all educational professionals. The case is made by Mawuena Kossi Logan: "All efforts to deal with prejudice and equal opportunity are labor lost when cultural bias has already been established in the child at a time when he or she cannot judge the accuracy of white supremacist materials." Logan continues, "It is not by accident that although culture changes continually, the image of Blacks did not essentially change until Black writers began to be admitted to the children's book field in the 1960s" (184–185). It is now a half century later, but images of Africans in Western children's literature remain essentially the same as when "Darkest Africa" became a disparaging nineteenth-century cliché.

In recent decades historians such as Logan, Patrick Brantlinger, and Jan Nederveen Pieterse have paid particular attention to imperialist narratives: "An adolescent quality pervades imperialist literature. . . . Africa was a setting where British boys could become men, and British men . . . could behave like boys with impunity" (Brantlinger, 190). "[B]ecause imperialism," writes Brantlinger, "always entailed violence and exploitation, and therefore could never bear much scrutiny, propagandists found it easier to leave it to boys to 'play up, and play the game'" (190).

In producing white supremacist propaganda, authors still turn frequently to Africa as their chosen setting. And even when otherwise capable of creating art, as in Allende's case,[5] writers squander their skill with uninformed and xenophobic depictions. Put bluntly, the calls for artistic freedom remain unaccompanied by an equal concern about how much the disproportionately powerful can get away with.

Works Cited

Allende, Isabel. 2002. *City of the Beasts*. Translated from the Spanish by Margaret Sayers Peden. New York: HarperCollins.
———. 2004. *Kingdom of the Golden Dragon*. Translated from the Spanish by Margaret Sayers Peden. New York: HarperCollins.
———. 2005. *Forest of the Pygmies*. Translated from the Spanish by Margaret Sayers Peden. New York: HarperCollins.
Bahuchet, Serge and Henri Guillaume. 1982. "Aka-Farmer Relations in the Northwest Congo Basin." Translated by Sheila M. Van Wyck. In *Politics and History in Band Societies*, eds. Eleanor Leacock and Richard Lee, 189–211. Cambridge, UK: Cambridge UP.
Benjamin, Jennifer and Sally Engelfried. 2004. "Magical Feminist." In *Conversations With Isabel Allende*, rev. ed., ed. John Rodden, 185–199. Austin: University of Texas Press.
Blench, Roger. 1999. "Are the African Pygmies an Ethnographic Fiction?" In *Central African Hunter-Gatherers in a Multidisciplinary Perspective: Challenging Elusiveness*, eds. Karen Biesbrouck, Stegan Elders, and Gerda Rossel, 41–60. Leiden, Netherlands: Universiteit Leiden, Research School for Asian, African, and Amerindian Studies (CNWS).
Brantlinger, Patrick. 1988. *Rule of Darkness: British Literature and Imperialism, 1830–1914*. Ithaca, NY: Cornell UP.
Curtin, Philip D. *The Image of Africa: British Ideas and Action, 1780–1850*. Madison: University of Wisconsin Press, 1964.
Davidson, Basil. "Africa Recolonized?" In *Amistad 2*, eds. John A. Williams and Charles F. Harris, 229–260. New York: Vintage Books.
Frankland, Stanley. 1999. "Turnbull's Syndrome: Romantic Fascination in the Rain Forest." In *Central African Hunter-Gatherers in a Multidisciplinary Perspective: Challenging Ellusiveness*. eds. Karen Biesbrouck, Stegan Elders, and Gerda Rossel, 61–73. Leiden, Netherlands: Universiteit Leiden, Research School for Asian, African, and Amerindian Studies (CNWS).
Harmanci, Reyhan. 2005. Rev. of *Forest of the Pygmies* Isabel Allende. *San Francisco Chronicle* (May 29): E–3.
Hegel, Georg Wilhelm Friedrich. 1956. *The Philosophy of History*. With prefaces by Charles Hegel and Translator J. Sibree, and a New Introduction by C. J. Friedrich. New York: Dover. (Original posthumous manuscript published 1840)
Hewlett, Barry. 1991. *Intimate Fathers: The Nature and Context of Aka Pygmy Paternal Infant Care*. Ann Arbor: University of Michigan Press.
———. 1996. "Cultural Diversity Among African Pygmies." In *Cultural Diversity Among Twentieth-Century Foragers*, ed. Susan Kent, 215–244. Cambridge, UK: Cambridge UP.
"An Interview With Isabel Allende." (n.d.). http://readinggroups.co.uk/Authors/interview.aspx?id=610&aid=136
Kirkus Reviews. 2005. Review of *Forest of the Pygmies* by Isabel Allende. April 15, 2005: 467.
Logan, Mawuena Kossi. 1999. *Narrating Africa: George Henty and the Fiction of Empire*. New York: Garland.
Madhubuti, Haki. 1985. "An Interview with Haki Madhubuti (Don L. Lee): Poet, Publisher, Critic, Educator." In *The Black American in Books for Children*, 2nd ed., eds. Donnarae MacCann and Gloria Woodard, 239–252. Metuchen, NJ: Scarecrow Press.
Nkrumah, Kwame. 1973. *Toward Colonial Freedom: Africa in the Struggle Against World Imperialism*. London: Panaf Books. (Originally published 1962)
Panjabi, Kavita. 1991. "'The House of the Spirits,' Tránsito Soto: From Periphery to Power." In *Critical Approaches to Isabel Allende's Novels*, eds. Sonia Riquelme Rojas and Edna Aguirre Rehbein, 11–20. New York: Peter Lan.
Pieterse, Jan Nederveen. 1992. *White on Black: Images of Africa and Blacks in Western Popular Culture*. New Haven, CT: Yale UP.
Rich, Paul. 1993. "Race, Science, and the Legitimization of White Supremacy in South Africa, 1902–1940." In *Colonialism and Nationalism in Africa: A Four-Volume Anthology of Scholarly Articles*, vol. 2, eds. Gregory Maddox and Timothy K. Welliver, 81–102. New York: Garland.
Rohrlick. Paula. 2005. Review of *Forest of the Pygmies* by Isabel Allende. *Kliatt* (May).
Schroeder, Shannin. *Rediscovering Magical Realism in the Americas*. Westport, CT: Praeger, 2004.
Zachary, Nancy. 2005. Review of *Forest of the Pygmies* by Isabel Allende. *VOYA* 28: 2 (June): 141.
Zapata. Celia Correas. 2002. *Isabel Allende: Life and Spirits*. Translated from the Spanish by Margaret Sayers Peden. Houston, TX: Arte Publico Press, 2002.
Zinsser, William, ed. *Paths of Resistance: The Art and Craft of the Political Novel*. Boston: Houghton Mifflin, 1989.

Chapter Six
Anti-African Themes in "Liberal" Young Adult Novels

Feminism (Western feminism) is part and parcel of Western cultural imperialism.
—Obioma Nnaemeka (83–84)

One of the prime impulses in the European conquest of large parts of the globe had been the exploitation of wild animal products.... Hunting was at the same time a mark of the fitness of the dominant race, ... an emblem of imperial rule.
—John MacKenzie (145, 170)

An anti-African mindset seems to be dominating contemporary children's literature, as it dominated Western literature in earlier eras. In Cristina Kessler's *No Condition Is Permanent* (2000), the traditions of the West African nation, Sierra Leone, are twisted out of all recognition. Eric Campbell's *Papa Tembo* (U.K. edition, 1997; U.S. edition, 1998) maligns East African peoples. What we see in these novels is a demonstration of how writers who view themselves as progressive and liberal in their advancement of ideas such as feminism and environmental preservation can blithely engage all of the familiar stereotypes in the Western imagemaker's toolkit. We also see how they can depart from their intended themes and contrive biased notions about cultures foreign to them.

These two novels display the patterns that recur in scores of contemporary fictional works with African settings:

- Africans are ridiculed for their lack of "high" (Western) technologies.
- Africans are disparaged for medical practices that differ from Western health practices.

- African officialdom is presented as largely corrupt and unable to grasp Western business practices and ethics.
- Africans are accused of using natural resources in ways that are ecologically unsound, while they are simultaneously shown as being primitive peoples naturally suited to inhabit wild, undeveloped landscapes.
- African skin tones are obsessively emphasized (e.g., in Kessler's book "[the skin] glistened like fresh hot tar" [23], or "shone like black, wet marble" [44], or "black carbon paper" [53], or "wet ebony" [75], or "resembled a jet black Siamese cat" [132]).
- African spirituality is shown to be inferior to Western spirituality.
- African community and family traditions are maligned as Western customs are extolled.

We found that the Kessler and Campbell novels maintained these unfortunate literary traditions in their consistent reiteration of Eurocentric assumptions.

Mis-stated Feminism in *No Condition is Permanent*

Cristina Kessler was a Peace Corps volunteer in Sierra Leone from 1981 to 1983, and she states that her characters in *No Condition Is Permanent* are related to her journal entries from that period. The central adult character is seen returning to Sierra Leone after an absence of about fifteen years. The return visit is for the purpose of stamping out the female initiation rite entailing circumcision (i.e., clitoridectomy, or as some opponents label it, "female genital mutilation").[1] This mother and anthropologist does not realize that the rite is scheduled for the same time as her return visit, but once she discovers this, she fears for her free-spirited, fourteen-year-old daughter, Jodie, who has accompanied her. Jodie has become best friends with a young woman who will participate in the rite. The mother's alarm seems justified since her stubborn offspring will not be dissuaded from interfering in the ceremony, and consequently, mother and daughter are run out of the village. But after two years, a letter arrives that vindicates the "do-gooders": that is, girls in the village promise to rebel against circumcision for the sake of their future daughters. Also, the older women have found a way to forgive the impetuous American teenager.

In arguing against clitoridectomy, Kessler largely employs the tactics listed above: "comic relief" stemming from African encounters with technology; dramatic tension derived from images of unhealthy conditions; social commentary about families oppressed by male tyranny; a moral indictment of spirituality; and a portrayal of dancing as either comic in its exaggeration or depraved in its orgiastic excesses. As for the environment, it is not shown as lacking in proper protection (unlike the Campbell novel), but it seems quite dysfunctional. The people apparently subsist with only a rice crop and a dried fish business—neither of which prevents their extreme poverty.

At first, the setting unfolds comically. The American fourteen-year-old, Jodie, is a wise-cracking, smart-ass narrator and is not to be taken as a fully reliable reporter. However, the authorial voice is ever present, and from that perspective, everything in Africa is unsafe. There appears to be as many reptiles as people inhabiting the houses and make-shift privies. Every family has lost a relative to lethal snake bites (121). Travel is unsafe since the airport has few lights and many potholes, and cars and buses have engines "that sounded like a blender full of loose screws" (23). A top speed of thirteen miles per hour is not unusual (44). Open sewers and rotting meats in the marketplaces created "a stink strong enough to scorch paint" (1), while the people in the bus produced "a killer stink," a smell that "singed my nose hairs and burned the roof of my mouth," as the narrator, Jodie, remembers it (46).

Such descriptions set a mood of general anxiety, while the characterizations degrade specific aspects of Sierra Leonean society. With respect to family life, Khadi (Jodie's Sierra Leonean friend) offers a depressing proverb: "A bad man is better than an empty house" (134). Sierra Leonean men are quite despicable as a class, although Kessler rarely allows them to appear "on stage." They are treated as responsible for the multiple wife system, and for the threatening circumcision that allegedly kills some girls and causes multiple injuries in others (105–106). Moreover, the men are responsible for denying girls any formal education (89), and they reserve the right to abstain from all "women's work"—forms of labor *they* define as beneath their dignity (136).[2] Such an appearance of domination conceals completely the role of age-old West African tradition. In the West African belief system, the woman is a symbol of two forms of fertility: the womb and the soil. The woman converts these elements into life-sustaining features that support survival: child-bearing, crop cultivation, and the drawing of water to cook with. These tasks differentiate her from the men, but this is a matter of difference, not status or level (Brathwaite, 3–4). "Cooperation between two sexes," writes Ghanian lawyer Akua Akyea Brathwaite, is quite different from the Western-style rivalry that involves "a [female] class striving to gain social equality with a class of men" (3).

In the general area of spirituality, Sierra Leoneans are condemned in Kessler's story for their "juju" or "black magic" (3). This subject opens the novel, and Kessler's description of a "witch-like" woman includes "eyes... like snake eyes," decorations and an amulet made from snake skin, and a "face older than time" (2). She speaks in "muffled grunts" and "stalked toward [Jodie]," causing a "long shiver [to] run down [her] back" (2). Kessler notes in an Afterword that her own journal entries from 1981 to 1983 supplied her with this character. But using a biased, Western lens, she interprets this woman's religious beliefs in fearsome terms: "I didn't know [says Jodie] if she had been throwing good energy or bad energy my way. It was important to know in a world of juju—black magic and witches. The only thing I did know was that my market stroll was no longer fun" (2–3).

No Condition Is Permanent is a conventional change-of-heart novel, with Jodie learning to curb her chauvinism and self-righteousness, but the focus is on what Khadi learns. Readers are led to consider how Khadi discovers the evils of circumcision, the evils of juju, the evils of male domination, the evils of educational deprivation, and so on. Readers are told that these Africans are a friendly and music-loving people; however, Jodie's mother explains that a "secret society [the Sande Society that educates girls for womanhood] and juju can make sweet people do strange things" (111). Additionally Kessler treats even the musical scenes with derision. When the women are cleaning fish on the beach, one woman begins "shaking her big bottom from side to side":

> The women laughed with glee as she started wrenching her pelvis back and forth in a frenzied way. One started clapping and the others joined, driving the beat faster and faster and the dancer's hips too. Her head lolled back and she smiled toward the sky, shaking everything she had with total wild abandon. (69)

Jodie's mother counsels her daughter about how admirable it is when "people just make their own fun" even while watching "[their kids] die from malaria" (70–71). But we now learn that Mother has ulterior motives. She tells Jodie, "That's why I've worked so hard for their respect these first weeks. . . . Maybe now I can get to it [the circumcision that I want to talk about]" (68). Here is a classic case of the way Western feminists can label "Third World" women as "traditional," and then portray them as "politically immature women who need to be versed and schooled" (Amos, 7).

Mother wants to get to the point and talk about killer infections. Mother does not want to admit that clitoridectomy can be arranged in a clinic, that medical assistance (entailing the use of novocaine, penicillin, and tranquilizers) is a safeguard against after-effects (Brathwaite, 11–12). Moreover, mother does not want to talk about the broader meaning and importance of Sande rituals. K. L. Little describes them in wholly positive terms:

> A general and important feature resulting from both Poro [the male society] and Sande schools is the sense of comradeship imparted. Initiates obtain a feeling of participating in a national institution. The common bonds of the society unite men with men, and women with women, as fellow members over a very wide area, and to an extent which transcends all barriers of family, clan, tribe, and religion. It is this corporate sense arising largely out of the memory of experiences shared at an impressionable age which is mainly responsible for the extra cultural significance of Poro and Sande. It is something, quite apart from a person's social status

and position, upon which he or she can draw at any time for mental and moral reassurance. (202)

To have made reference to this reality would have increased the work's intellectual integrity. And to have avoided sweeping indictments would have increased credibility. The circumcision process, for example, is condemned for producing "a helluva lot of pain and high rates of terrible infections. It can also mean sterility, as well as making sure that the women never have any pleasure during sex" (105). How does this Peace Corps returnee know about the "pleasure" factor? Was she sleeping around with Bukama men? Was she listening to their complaints about local women? This returnee has been unsuccessful in securing information about the commencement of the Sande initiations, so is it likely that the local women would have told her about their sex lives? And if sterility is such a problem, why is Africa treated as a primary culprit vis-à-vis population explosion?

In structuring her story around two culturally diverse young women—one in a tank top and one topless—it seems that Kessler is urging a pluralistic viewpoint. However, instead of showing parallel growing experiences in the lives of these two adolescents, Kessler is quite one-sided in calling for change. The Americans have everything right, and all that needs changing in *their* sphere is the immaturity of a headstrong girl from California. In short, Jodie is just a typical developing child, like all children. Sierra Leone, however, is *not* just a nation like other nations, having its own distinctive history. It is presented as essentially unacceptable, as permanently backward.

"Backwardness" is overemphasized throughout the novel. It would seem that the notes and diaries of early adventurers and missionaries are still the primary resource for storytellers. Those journals were replete with the falsities and half-truths that found their way into works by Conrad, Haggard, Henty, and a host of other writers who could see Africans only as Stone Age types or bearers of all the cardinal sins. Kessler picks up on these stereotypes while eliding the actual cultural practices in a rural Sierra Leonean community. We have no glimpse, for example, of the customary protocol that would precede a new friendship between adolescents. We do not see Khadi's parents, the visit they would make to the Californians, or the way Khadi would help connect her parents or other relatives with the newcomers. We do not see the way the adults would issue an invitation to Val and Jodie or the way this visit would include the breaking of bread before Khadi and Jodie would have had a chance to cement their friendship. And even though Val, Jodie's mother, had been in this community fifteen years prior to the action in the narrative, the child of Val has been unknown, so the teenagers would not have gotten together spontaneously without parental involvement or oversight from someone in the extended African family. In short, the popular proverb "It takes a village to raise a child" is not simply a catch phrase. With everyone caring for everyone else, parental participation is ever present in children's lives, in their problems, altercations, household duties, and calls for guidance.

The novelist tries to zero in on Khadi's village through the use of the Krio language, but on many occasions she mistakes "pidgin" English for Krio. Where Krio is spoken (in Sierra Leone and Gambia), people would not try to ask someone to "back off" by saying "yu no able fo join Sande. Ah de say like so yesterday. Na lef it, du ya, ah beg" (102). Instead they would definitely warn the person, but without being insulting: "Yu nah 'traenja, nor put han pan whetin' yu nor sabie. Yu understan? Whosie dehn nor call yu nor go dae, ehn nor pwel business for yuself." It is possible that both publisher and novelist tried to work out a simplified dialect they thought young readers could handle. But there can be no excuse for the misrepresentation of the Sande society, for falsely labeling Sande a "secret society," and for painting such a jaundiced picture of this institution in educational, religious, cultural, and hygienic terms. Kessler's mis-statements should have been enough to suggest a "Not Recommended" rating for the book, but instead the *Bulletin of the Center for Children's Books* calls the book "Recommended" (Stevenson, 212). Both the novelist and the reviewer seem to agree about what a so-called Third World woman is like. According to Indian scholar Chandra Mohanty, such a woman is widely perceived in the West as leading "an essentially truncated life based on her feminine gender (read: sexually constrained) and being 'third world' (read: ignorant, poor, uneducated, tradition-bound, religious, domesticated, family-oriented, victimized, etc.)" (65). It is hard to read *No Condition Is Permanent* without seeing this subtext shaping every scene. And on the other hand, the Western women (Jodie and her mother) are represented in the way Western feminists typically represent themselves: "educated, modern, as having control over their own bodies and sexualities, and the 'freedom' to make their own decisions" (Mohanty, 65). Similar kinds of polarization, says Mohanty, can be found throughout European and Euro-American discourse, as when "Third World" peoples are engaged in "the lesser production of 'raw materials' in contrast to the 'real' productive activity of the first world" (65).

Recognizing these "First World–Third World" binaries is important, since they are typically used to privilege one group over another. All told, Kessler fits Valerie Amos and Pratibha Parmar's description of Eurocentric feminists: "Because they are not acquainted with traditions outside of their own cultures and histories . . . [their theoretical foundation] denies as valid any modes of struggle and organization which have their origins in non-European philosophical traditions" (8).

Conservation and the Case of *Papa Tembo*

The depletion of the planet is largely a Western affair. Americans alone consume hundreds of times the resources consumed by Africans, according to historian Thomas Spear (18). But novels for children are telling a different story. They are blending together popular conventions from Western literature, while simultaneously highlighting the prospects of endangered species. This is the combination in Eric Campbell's *Papa Tembo,* a mixture that is also replete with anti-African images. Why, then, is this novel so appealing to Western book critics? In reviews in four leading journals the novel was described as "vividly written," conscientious," "touching," "thought-provoking" (Foldy, 132), having "adventure aplenty" (Bush, 10), written with "great authority, . . . [and] a gift for storytelling and a reporter's eye for arresting detail" (Cart, 1990). Moreover, Campbell is successful "at investing his characters with symbolic weight and at introducing haunting, magical elements" (Cart, 1990), while writing "masterfully" and packing "a suspenseful novel" with "vivid descriptions and a gripping story line" (Lent, 273). Not a single review makes mention of the African people. Although Campbell utilizes them in carrying out his conservationist program, they have no place in the commentaries about this story.

Campbell builds his novel around three familiar literary conventions or types. He employs the devices of Romanticism, making the young hero an almost Christ-like figure in her mystical ties with the wild. Campbell connects with the back-to-nature movement of the nineteenth and early twentieth centuries. ("Papa" elephant is reminiscent of characters in early animal "biographies.") And the stock characterization of the Great White Hunter proves useful: the ex–game warden is among the many hunters in literature who have been emblematic of imperial invincibility. At the same time, African characterizations in Campbell's novel also have historical roots. The indigenous peoples are stereotyped as stupid, filthy, degenerate, and cruel, as is exemplified by one British military explorer's observation in 1908: "[The Nigerians] have no physique, no intelligence, their habits are of the dirtiest description, and nothing gives them so much pleasure as the sacrifice of human blood" (qtd. in Hudson, 16–17).

The setting of this story is East Africa, where the African ivory trade has been most extensive, and this is where a young English girl has her fantastic bonding with elephants. She simply "walked right up to the stricken beast," a young elephant whose foot is trapped and injured in a snare. She "plunged her fingers into the crimson gash . . . located the wire buried deep in his flesh," removed the wire, and remained long enough for the chief elephant bull, Papa Tembo, to show his appreciation (113). Her scientist-father has been watching the whole encounter, and his career in the sciences is important to the overall story line.

Alison, the novel's young savior-of-elephants, has the advantage of a scientific upbringing and an intuitive capacity to communicate with animals. Her supernatural ability is treated as a cosmic phenomenon, even one that the elephants recognize. Much of the novel focuses on the bond between the two groups of innocents: children and beasts. Alison and Papa Tembo, writes

Campbell, "were locked in a strange silent communion" (206–207). "Whatever strange forces were at work between Alison and the great mysterious animal, they [Alison's father and brother] were not to know or understand" (203). Throughout the story, Alison uses a "sixth sense" to discover where the animals are and what may be happening to them. She serves as a symbol for the West's professed right to rule, embodying as she does that ethos in both spiritual and physical terms. Campbell stresses the beauty of both child and animal innocence as he shows Papa Tembo acknowledging the solidarity between himself and Alison. After the bull elephant has snapped the snare's wire, and after Alison has untangled the wire from the young elephant's bleeding leg, Papa Tembo expresses his gratitude:

> [A]lison looked up at the elephant's great head towering above her. For a second their eyes met, and in that brief, tiny meeting all her fears were stilled. The eyes held no threat, no anger, no danger . . . .
>
> Slowly the elephant reached out his trunk toward her and, with infinite gentleness, touched her hair. So delicate was the touch that Alison barely felt it . . . .
>
> She reached up her trembling hand and touched her hair. It was slightly damp where the velvet wetness of the trunk had passed over it . . . .
>
> His touch, and the smell of him had, in that brief moment, entered her heart. (116–117)

The Romantic tradition has been essentially reproduced in this glorified child–beast connection. And we need to note the handling of the whole elephant herd, the way each member has a name and an important family position. (Victoria is the Mama whose calf, Daffodil, has just been saved, while pregnant Aunt Cleopatra observes the scene.) Animals have become "people" in this story, while some of the people (especially the indigenous Africans) have become "animals."

In the early twentieth century, British popular journals carried stories with similar anthropomorphic treatments of animals. Peter Broks has studied these stories and other cultural symbols from the back-to-nature movement in *Pearson's Magazine* from 1890 to 1914. He tells of "The Story of Rip, a Weasel," "The Autobiography of a Partridge," "The Biography of a Bat," "Jack the Otter," and scores of other "biographies" or, depending on the style of the writing, "autobiographies" (155, 161, 163). The style here is particularly important. The intimate, anthropomorphic style signaled "a transition from a cryptic to a sentimental anthropomorphism" (156). There was a new demand for "empathy together with the constant emphasis on man as the enemy." In effect, writes Broks, "[there was] a call for a new relationship with nature" (156). This call in children's fiction meant more "mawkishness" and "soggy idealism" (156). It meant "the urge to view the animal world in human terms" (David Allen, qtd. in Broks, 156). Campbell seems to have caught this urge.

Alison says of the elephants: "Funny, isn't it? They're so strange. And yet so much like us" (60).

In contrast to the conservationism of Alison and her family (her father is conducting a study that is in its fourteenth year), the novelist depicts Africans as a consistent threat to the environment. Alison's father, John Blake, explains African land abuse to his children. "Half the point of this study is that this area is becoming overgrazed by Masai cattle. You've seen the Masai herds. Sometimes one herd is one hundred animals now. . . . [We] may have to help these elephants move" (56). The Maasai community is again set up as the environmental villain when we learn that in Papa Tembo's youth, a Maasai cattle herder "needlessly, petulantly threw a spear at him. It embedded itself in his flank" (45). Papa Tembo had a long agonizing struggle with the ensuing infection. This description of "needless" injury associates the Maasai with the novel's primary antagonist, Lauren van der Wel, who felt "the sheer pleasure of the killing, the joy of the slaughter" (41) and who is mentally deranged—"a psycho," as Mike Taylor, the safari leader, noted (188). When Taylor seeks help in locating van der Wel, the Maasai headman calls elephants "vermin" (88), and this descriptive term is used again in the novel's concluding lines: "The elephant is a vermin. He destroys crops and frightens villagers. The only answer is to utilize him or kill him" (n.p.). These words are attributed to Peter Musavaya (an actual ranger in Zimbabwe) and date from 1996. Campbell juxtaposes this statement with idealistic ones from W. V. Hudson in 1892: "[When elephants] perish, something of gladness goes out from nature, and the sunshine loses something of its brightness" (n.p.). It is unlikely that readers will miss the message of White altruism versus Black culpability.

In actuality, the Maasai followed a self-protective policy, eliminating animals only when they threatened their stock or their gardens (MacKenzie, *Empire of Nature,* 164). The idea that Africans abused their homeland is refuted in the record of various cultural groups and their hunting practices. MacKenzie reports, for example, that the Acholi people "had a longstanding tradition of organized tribal hunting which ensured that too many animals were not killed and that no area was hunted over too frequently" (*Empire . . .* , 275). The Western conservationist agendas (which included "game reserves") were *externally* derived and tended to impact negatively on indigenous peoples. These reserves were constructed in ways that ignored "the long-evolved relationship between people and nature . . . [tending] to profoundly threaten traditional mechanisms of subsistence and thereby to threaten and alienate whole cultures from their environmental contexts" (Grove, 42). Such an alienating type of conservation conveniently justified the seizure of the most economically advantageous lands for European settlement (e.g., the hilly regions where the climate was allegedly healthier [MacKenzie, *Imperialism . . .* , 10]). Additionally, the colonial authorities often disallowed Africans the right to hunt, even during the most severe famines (MacKenzie, *Empire . . .* , 163–164).

The hunter as an emblem of Western power appears in *Papa Tembo* in episodes featuring the same cast that Campbell used in *The Place of Lions* (1991): Taylor (one-time game warden who now runs a safari business) and his American customer, Hyram Johnson. In the earlier story, this pair (along with the driver, Benny) chase Somalian poachers, and now they are trying to restrain the demented White man, van der Wel, who has tried to kill Papa Tembo, but has been so badly injured by the elephant that he spends the rest of his life seeking vengeance.

Taylor is a rash, sardonic leader who managed a game reserve until the Tanzanians supposedly abandoned all environmentalist principles. As in the earlier novel, Taylor sees nothing wrong with his own vigilante-style policing operations. According to this narrative, Africans are incapable of conceiving or administering just laws. Virtually all the African characters, except Benny the servant, are either cheats or the servile employees of the mad man. They are depicted as outside the modern world of order, environmental understanding, and basic morality. Taylor's self-appointed "police" initiatives are not unlike the imperialist usurpation of indigenous authority over land and government. The history of British colonial rule includes accounts of punitive expeditions that were organized by the British military against various African communities (MacKenzie, *Empire* . . . , 159).

All the plot developments and characterizations point to the rightness of imperial rule in this novel. The scientific team and the safari leader are on hand when van der Wel traps the elephant herd in a location where he can burn the animals alive. Alison tackles van der Wel as he is preparing to shoot Papa Tembo; Papa Tembo kills van der Wel; Taylor frees the herd and it escapes from the deadly inferno. In an epilogue, we learn about Papa Tembo's death and about the apparent extrasensory perception that enables both Alison and the elephant herd to know precisely when it occurs.

Africans are seen only as a hindrance in this drama, except for Benny and his humorous encounters with Western technology. Benny, as well as African taxi drivers, provide so-called comic relief as they "whisked away [airport passengers] in loud crashings of tortured gearboxes and great clouds of black smoke from ruined engines" (17). Benny treats Taylor's Land Rover with similar abandon, as when the machine "tilted almost vertically down a slope and slid, into a gully bottom," throwing the passengers "violently backward and forward" (75). Benny also has a new cassette player (a purchase made from Hyram Johnson's fifty-dollar gift), and the music is forever "blasting from the car stereo" while Taylor threatens to "shoot it" (46, 10).

Africans, it seems, reject conservation, the care of cars, and also good government. Bribery and the confiscation of travelers' belongings are subjects introduced in the first two dozen pages. Before traveling from the United States to Tanzania, Hyram Johnson mails Taylor two hundred dollars in order to "bribe whoever needs bribing [to] get all the 'petroli' you can" (12). Inside the airport, Hyram observes a "negotiation" about a missing visa:

Hyram recognized "this for what it was—a well-rehearsed charade in which the actors were all aware of their respective roles. When the required posturings were over, money would change hands and the man would be allowed in" (15). Hyram places twenty dollars inside his health certificate as a means of passing through customs (16). The airport officials complete their work with the passengers and then "gloat over the flight's confiscated goods" (17). Garages do not function at all except within a dishonest system, as Taylor explains to Hyram: a "closed" sign on a garage is deceptive, since "every petrol pump in the country has 'closed' on it. It doesn't mean it *is* closed. This is Africa" (71). In this scene, Benny closes a deal by using a hundred-dollar bribe with the "sleep-numbed man" who operates the garage—a necessary donation before the man will open the pump at all (74).

Campbell offers no explanation for the pervasive criminality, except through his explicit association of "primitives" with law-breakers. He makes a point of showing Africans as being far removed from modern times, as simply unable to grasp anything beyond their own self-serving rules. In this novel legal principles seem entirely outside an African's line of vision, and what law enforcement the government does provide is presented as intolerable. A jail, for example, is "a stinking pit with rats and cockroaches crawling all over your head" (187). Is this because the people are "ancient," as the author repeatedly states, or because they are "phantoms" (83)? When Hyram first sees the Maasai herders returning home with their cattle, he is looking through a pair of binoculars: "Viewed through a magical lens, reality, time and distance are suspended. Here, through glass, a scene of biblical antiquity was taking place" (82). Moreover, nighttime is not just darkness in Africa: "Night, African night, returns a man, even a man of the twentieth century, to what he was at the dawn of time" (120). Similarly, mountains do not give up their "hold on time" (78). "In all the millennia, life has not come to her slopes" (78). "To go to Ol Doinyo Lengai is to take a journey not just in distance, but in time" (77).[3]

But why is Campbell's interest in time linked with assertions about criminality? His thesis that Africa is static is juxtaposed with claims about lawlessness:

> [Hyram] became acutely aware of the strangeness of where he was....
> Their features [the Maasai's], transformed by shifting light, suddenly seemed more savage, more primevally alien than before. For a split second he felt a jolt of fear as the knowledge took root that they were in a very different world. A world that had changed little in thousands of years. A world of magic and ancient savagery where life meant little. (90–91)

Here we have "magic" (spirituality) associated with cheapness of life, and as the plot develops, Campbell presents African spirituality as a series of vile customs. In the "Ritual of the Night" (a means of gaining reassurance about the safety of a hunting expedition), the "witch doctor" brings a very rotten elephant heart for the men to eat, and the author makes much of maggots crawling over hands and mouths. Whenever Africans are present, there is also reference to an offensive "stench," whether the Maasai are preparing food (80), or being in the sun with rancid oil on their skin (162), or preparing a ritualistic ceremony (125–126).

And so it goes. Household customs, religious beliefs, government transactions, and protection of lands and stock are all presented in a negative light. Imperialism seems justified. Children are encouraged to feel a great aversion toward Africans. But there is never a dull moment, and potentially this makes the reading experience quite insidious. White children may love identifying with Alison, the elephant savior; they will smile at the humanized animal portraits ("Cleopatra . . . has huge eyelashes that she flutters and all the bulls adore her" [24]); they will laugh at Benny's reckless driving and at the sarcastic banter between Mike Taylor and Hyram Johnson; they will tremble at the whip lashes of the demented van der Wel and the disgusting amulets of the "witch doctor." On the other hand, for children of Africa, children of African descent, or other children sensitized to prejudice, there will more likely be an angry, anxious, and confused response, for regardless of the book's excitement and heart-tugging sentiment, there is hardly a moment that does not abuse African character, distort cultural practices, and falsify history.

In 1998, Kenyan novelist Ngũgĩ wa Thiong'o noted in an interview that "the child's capacity for wonder is clear, and we need to also make the world more understandable to children." He spoke of how the child reader cannot always detect propaganda: "Narratives tend to be strong enough to carry the child along without the child recognizing what is actually happening. Children may not question how the bad guys are defined—how the successful colonizer is allied with the 'good' and those opposing colonization are associated with the 'bad'" (Ngũgĩ). In *Decolonizing the Mind* (1986), Ngũgĩ compares the cannon and the canon (including school curricula). It is the latter, he says, that makes a conquest permanent. "The cannon forces the body and the school fascinates the soul" (9).

We can, to some extent, agree that reading has not been common to the African. But Western education was not made available, even after Europeans had been in contact with Africans for more than a thousand years. Moreover, traditional African education was persistently thwarted when, even after World War II, Africans were severely punished for speaking their own languages, for mastering the art of drumming, for mask dancing, or for performing other cultural acts. Drums were deemed sacrilegious; old men and women were labeled warlocks, juju men, and witches; "secret" societies were banned by colonial governments as potentially dangerous.

In referring to the language of literature, African American librarian Augusta Baker stated in 1963: "[I]f we lack the skill to speak *precisely*, our thought will remain confused and ill-defined" (emphasis added, 75). In any particular society, feminism and environmentalism may be understood and articulated "precisely" because the society as a whole is understood. But in an unfamiliar society, that necessary precision may well be lacking. Progressive ideas are transportable, but they will always exist within a distinct social context.

It is no small matter when children are subjected to anti-African propaganda. It is common knowledge that wars fought over land have caused unnecessary aggression, but it is less often admitted that pen-on-paper calamities are another unnecessary disaster. Like mass-produced armaments, pen-on-paper destructiveness is well-thought through and well-planned. It is sometimes well disguised as a literature for the young. Kessler and Campbell have both lived in Africa, but they incorporate in their novels a long-standing white supremacist perspective. They downgrade Africa in ways that essentially serve Western interests, and they rob children of authentic impressions of a continent and its inhabitants. Their novels hardly warrant the term "entertainment." On the contrary, children miss out on the complex and enriching worldviews they have every right to enjoy.

Works Cited

Amos, Valerie and Pratibha Parmar. 1984. "Challenging Imperial Feminism." *Feminist Review* 17: 3–19.
Baker, Augusta. 1963. "What Makes a Book a Good Book." *The Instructor* 73: 47–48. Rpt. in *Readings About Children's Literature*, ed. Evelyn R. Robinson. New York: McKay, 1966: 74–77.
Brathwaite, Akua Akyea. 1995. "Practices Affecting the Reproductive Rights of West African Women." Unpublished manuscript, University of Iowa.
Broks, Peter. 1990. "Science, the Press and Empire: 'Pearson's' Publications, 1890–1914." *Imperialism and the Natural World*, ed. John M. MacKenzie, 141–163. Manchester, UK: Manchester UP.
Bush, Elizabeth. 1998. Review of Eric Campbell's *Papa Tembo*. *Bulletin of the Center for Children's Books* 52: 10.
Campbell, Eric. 1998. *Papa Tembo*. New York: Harcourt.
Cart, Michael. 1991. *The Place of Lions*. New York: Harcourt.
———. 1998. Review of Eric Campbell's *Papa Tembo*. *Booklist* 94: 1990.
Foldy, Kate. 1998. Review of Eric Campbell's *Papa Tembo*. *School Library Journal* 44: 10: 132.
Grove, Richard H. 1990. "Colonial Conservation, Ecological Hegemony and Popular Resistance: Towards a Global Synthesis." *Imperialism and the Natural World*, ed. John M. MacKenzie, 15–50. Manchester, UK: Manchester UP.
Hudson, Brian. 1977. "The New Geography and the New Imperialism: 1870–1918." *Antipode: A Radical Journal of Geography* 9: 2: 12–19.
Kessler, Cristina. 2000. *No Condition Is Permanent*. New York: Philomel.
Lent, Laura L. 1998. Review of Eric Campbell's *Papa Tembo*. *VOYA* 21: 273.
Lightfoot-Klein, Hanny. 1989. *Prisoners of Ritual: An Odyssey Into Female Genital Circumcision in Africa*. New York: Harrington.
Little, K. L. 1949. "The Role of the Secret Society in Cultural Specialization." *American Anthropologist* 51: 199–212.
Logan, Mawuena Kossi. 2001. "Labor Party Reforms Versus Imperial Literary Practices." *The Lion and the Unicorn* 25: 391–411.
MacKenzie, John M. 1988. *The Empire of Nature: Hunting, Conservation and British Imperialism*. Manchester, UK: Manchester UP.
———., ed. 1990. *Imperialism and the Natural World*. Manchester, UK: Manchester UP.

Mohanty, Chandra. 1988. "Under Western Eyes: Feminist Scholarship and Colonial Discourses." *Feminist Review* 30 (August): 61–88.
Ngũgĩ wa Thiong'o. 1986. *Decolonizing the Mind: The Politics of Language in African Literature.* London: Currey.
——. 1998. Personal interview with Donnarae MacCann. University of Iowa, May 1.
Nnaemeka, Obioma. 1995. "Feminism, Rebellious Women, and Cultural Boundaries: Rereading Flora Nwapa and Her Compatriots." *Research in African Literatures* 26: 2: 80–113.
Spear, Thomas. 1990. "The Environment: White Man's Burden." *Christian Science Monitor* (November 30): 18.
Stevenson, Deborah. 2000. Review of Cristina Kessler's *No Condition Is Permanent*. *Bulletin of the Center for Children's Books* 53: 212–213.

Chapter Seven
Crime and Crime Syndicates in *Many Stones* and *Zulu Dog*

[T]he term *"swaart gevaar,"* Afrikaans for "black hordes," [was] used by the apartheid regime when rallying the country's whites against their self-presumed God-given right to rule. Americans present themselves to Africans as all-knowing, when, in fact, their perspectives are influenced by the often distorted views of Africa in textbooks and the media.

—Charlayne Hunter-Gault (111, 34)

With good reason the *New York Times Book Review* used "Truth and Reconciliation" as its headline for a review of Carolyn Coman's *Many Stones* (2000). Hazel Rochman, like other reviewers of this book, commends the author's comparison of a fractured family with the opposing sides in a warring South Africa, and the possibility of reconciling them. Coman once commented in an interview in *TeenReads Newsletter:* "I don't pick troubling material because I want to make a political statement." But whatever her motivation, *Many Stones* is a thoroughly political novel.

Urban crime is presented as a major issue, and as in Anton Ferreira's *Zulu Dog* (2002), the authors actually mean *Black* urban crime. Both novelists pull plots from the Western press, Coman spinning her story around the murder of a young Fulbright scholar, Amy Biehl, and Ferreira drawing upon the car-jacking that crime syndicates turned into a chronic condition during the transition to post-Apartheid government. Given the way crime is depicted, readers may form the impression that the 1994 one-person/one-vote election (the *first* democratic election in South Africa) was really a regressive event. A backward step since unlike acts of violence in earlier decades, robbery and homicide are no longer spurred by the political ideals of Apartheid and anti-Apartheid forces. Instead murders are treated as representing pure malice. Sadistic behavior by indigenous Africans enters into the plotlines in both narratives, but the realities of post-1994 law enforcement and the programs designed to meet South Africa's new legal challenges—these are nowhere in sight.

As Coman focuses on urban Black crime, she offers the South African Truth and Reconciliation Commission (TRC) as a force that will potentially alleviate race-based tensions. In *Zulu Dog*, Ferreira displays the harm inflicted on a Black family by crime syndicates, while he also voices accusations about Mandela's so-called chaotic government. One White farmer changes his mind, but only when a Black child's dog rescues his daughter. Throughout the novel, the "failed state" theme is connected with Black rule exclusively, even when the author puts glaringly racist White farmers on display as a way to distance himself from overtly racist language.

I. *Many Stones*

Author Carolyn Coman is conscientious in depicting a family tragedy and its psychological effects. Teenaged Berry and her parents are Americans trying to cope with Berry's sister's murder at the hands of South African criminals. South Africa was selected by Coman as the backdrop for a long-standing quarrel between Berry and her father, a disagreement connected with his divorce and with sibling rivalry rather than the murder. Was the decision to move this family quarrel to South Africa inspired primarily by the news report about Amy Biehl's death? Or did the novelist start with ideas she wanted to share about South Africa's Truth and Reconciliation Commission, the Soweto township, Nelson Mandela, the Robben Island prison, the gap between rich and poor, and similar politically important issues?

Berry expresses an intense dissatisfaction with her father. Since one of her many grievances is her father's know-it-all attitude, Coman convincingly uses him as the conveyor of knowledge about urban South Africa. From the comfortable surroundings of a swanky hotel suite, father discusses with Berry an upcoming tour of Soweto—a place of collapsing outhouses, babies hospitalized with AIDS, and one shack where a woman with six children invites tourists inside to voice their shocked response. Berry compares the outhouses to latrines she used at summer camp and the woman's miniscule shack to her childhood playhouse. Father has warned Berry that "crime is out of control here [in Johannesburg]" and the point becomes clear as father and daughter visit an upscale restaurant in the otherwise deserted city. Coman uses the imperturbable Black waiter (a man who has suffered enormously from Apartheid torture and murder) to reinforce what she is trying to suggest to readers about the wisdom of the TRC's pacification mission.

Racism and "Reverse Racism"

A vacation in the wine-producing countryside opens the way for Berry and her father to observe what Berry calls "a real live racist" (151). She is the owner of their bed-and-breakfast hotel, a woman who endlessly bad-mouths the Black labor force. The workers, she says, "will be falling down in the streets in a few hours" since "they *cannot* hold their liquor" (125, emphasis in original). They are incapable of work, and when it comes to governing the country, "*they don't even want to, really they don't*" (127, emphasis in original). Coman is successful in bringing a racist mentality into the open, but only on one level. On another plane, Berry never meets an indigenous African without reacting in a racialized and/or historically implausible manner. The author seems unaware of the racist connotations. Non-White physical appearances are to Berry odd: the priest at the school commemorating her deceased sister is "a man whose blackness *shines*"; the Black driver working for the hotel has black hands with "pink palms"; the driver taking Berry and her father to the upscale restaurant is "hyper-alert, like a smart dog or cat, darting around, herding us toward the restaurant" (103, 40, 58). In terms of emotion, Phillip (the waiter at the restaurant) appears dismissive of unspeakable crimes. He describes how one of his brothers was shot and thrown into a pit, and the other one tortured to the point when he can no longer walk or speak. "'It is very sad,' Phillip says . . . , '*but!*' and his smile returns, flashes: 'We have a new country now . . .'" (62). Berry is thinking of her murdered sister and is not ready to change the subject, but Phillip and her father, "they have moved on . . . they are both going on, together, they are up there in their good-news plane . . ." (46). "Moving on" is a theme in this novel, even when placed in an implausible context. (This will be discussed below in relation to the TRC.) But there is another kind of racism introduced at the bed-and-breakfast inn: "reverse racism."

Suzanne, "the real live racist," scolds one of her African workers like a child, and Berry finds this embarrassing and objectionable. She rolls her eyes at the woman because "I want her to know I hate Suzanne, too. . . . I'm sorry she has to stay and be yelled at like a little kid. . . . [But] there isn't a chance she'll look at me and we'll connect. I am one of *them* to her, the same way she is one of *them* to Suzanne" (132). In other words, Blacks hate Whites, as Whites hate Blacks. The playing field is level.

This illustrates "reverse racism." It is another way for Coman to engage in what historian Terry Bell calls an apartheid strategy: "equating the violence of resistance with the violence of repression" (238). "Reverse racism," says Joe Feagin, is actually an "oxymoron" since it circumvents the central issue, namely, the systemic racism still oppressing people of color. Beliefs and impressions may be similar in different groups, but racism is more than an attitude. It can only be measured through an analysis of lived experience—historical and contemporary. As Feagin explains, "white racism is a legacy of imperialism, whereas the black version is a reaction to the experience of racism" (qtd. in Cashmore, 373). This is an important qualitative distinction. "Reverse racism" involves an unsupportable view of history, but Coman brings it up again when she has Berry "wonder[ing] what it would be like to kiss a black man. . . . I wonder if he would ever wonder that about me. Or if he only hates us" (40).

The TRC: Atrocities Reduced to Common Sinfulness

"Reconciliation" is the issue confronting the American family, and Coman utilizes the TRC for conveying her version of unconditional forgiveness. Berry's visit to Robben Island unveils the novelist's position. The tour guide had been imprisoned for twenty years on the island, but assures the tourists that he is not bitter: "'It is time to get on with other things, with reconciliation.'" "Maybe," says Berry, "his history gave him the chance to get bigger, and he took it" (114). Justice is not presented as part of the equation. In this story, becoming a "bigger" person revolves around the TRC's religion-based path to a better future. A regard for law is largely set aside (a process that would include tangible evidence, legal argument, cross-examination, and a jury of one's peers). Coman illustrates the TRC in her ultimate father–daughter truce, but how will this idea be implemented in relation to crimes against humanity? What legal remedies exist for those who were mysteriously eliminated by government decree and placed in unmarked graves? What legal consequences exist for the perpetrators? What position does officialdom take in relation to injustices of such unprecedented magnitude?

One of the novel's basic flaws is the way Apartheid is placed on a par with the challenges of an aggrieved American teenager whose father favored her sister. The strategy of devising two reconciliation models—one that is personal and American and the other national and South African—looks neatly symmetrical, but the question of *scale* can be ignored only at the cost of trivializing an immense human rights failure. The two Americans have no great distance to travel in achieving peace with each other, and we don't learn much about Laura, the sister, except with reference to her liberalism (e.g., "God, Laura loved him [Mandela]!") (106). But in the end Berry feels reconciled with her father when he unabashedly weeps at Laura's memorial service. In Berry's eyes, her father has always had an excessively managerial personality, but now he cannot manage his tears. Berry's symbol of growth is in thanking the students and priest at the school where Laura had been a volunteer: ". . . thank you very much—for letting us be part of everything with you" (158).

The author's strategy throughout is to flatten out histories that clamor for differentiation. When a vulture circles Robben prison, father leaps at the chance to make everything equal: every nation, he says, has things to be ashamed of (107–108). When Berry hears the guide tell about prisoners' letters being censored, she says to herself that this kind of censorship "*was* torture" (111). When men are seen hanging around bars, Berry comments: "They have nothing to do and it shows all over them, like having nothing to do has become who they are" (101). Berry is admittedly a young unreliable narrator, but in this scene the author uses her to steer the subject from crimes against a people to what appears to be a scarred Black personality.

According to Rashida Manjoo (an Advocate of the High Court of South Africa), "the most important principle of the TRC was recognition of the *humanity of the other* without racial, religious or economic distinctions" (15, emphasis in the original). This description generalizes a principle that the TRC (under Bishop Desmond Tutu's leadership) placed within a religious framework. That is, amnesty for members of the Apartheid regime was handled within the universal perspective of human weaknesses and sinful behavior in their broadest sense. "It was based," writes Terry Bell, "on the concept of confession and absolution. The systemic nature of apartheid was clearly not an issue. Apartheid was to be regarded rather as a sin, with its roots in frail human nature" (239). In Coman's novel, the young protagonist asks her father, "So is it working *here*, in South Africa? The truth and reconciliation thing?" Her father replies, "Jury's still out" (71).

Yet the novelist stands in for this "jury" and is clearly not troubled with doubt. "Remorse was not required by the commission. They asked for full disclosure and acknowledgment—that's what they consider the key to moving forward" (Coman, 72). At the actual TRC hearings, Bishop Desmond Tutu "operated as a religious figure, . . . garbing himself in a purple cassock and reverently lighting the candles as if he were officiating at a sacred service." In addition, he called on religious organizations to "provide liturgies for corporate confessions and absolution" (Graybill, 27).

These performances were part of a complex political drama and a method of legitimizing opinion instead of law in the dismantling of Apartheid. South African president F. W. de Klerk knew Nelson Mandela, the leader of the African National Congress (ANC), as someone with a long history of opposition to the National Party—someone whose twenty-seven-year prison experience had not altered his anti-Apartheid outlook. Justice minister Dullah Omar had made the case for Mandela and other prisoners by stressing that the struggle for liberation was rooted in the principle of human rights. On the other hand, he said, the quest of the Apartheid state to sustain itself through repression was "'an affront to humanity itself'" (Bell, 241). Backed by his military establishment, de Klerk rejected such an analysis and, in practice, won the day. Amnesty included "indemnity from both civil and criminal prosecution, in exchange for full disclosure of unlawful acts committed in the pursuit

suit of a political objective . . . ." (Manjoo, 13). What readers of *Many Stones* will probably never realize is that the "disclosure of unlawful acts" did not occur as anticipated, and that Coman's sanguine fiction conforms only to "the 'fairytale' transition . . . widely disseminated across the world" (Bell, 286).

Crime and Systemic Racism

In *Many Stones*, which aspects of urban crime are laid before young readers and which aspects are concealed? We are told repeatedly that thieves first robbed Laura (a volunteer aid worker) and then smashed open her head with a rock. Their murderous action had nothing to do with Apartheid or resistance to it; it was not only brutal, it was gratuitous. Coman is sending messages by way of this plotline, yet she seems uninterested in the actual crime scene in the years of Mandela's government. She took no notice of the unique obstacles that the post-Apartheid government encountered as it tried to bring a measure of equality to civil society. One such problem was the need to integrate the police forces from the "Homeland" areas within the overall police department (an integration that began in 1994). Numerous Homeland police officers were illiterate. Moreover, they had not been denied employment in the police force despite possession of a criminal record. These personnel problems hampered law enforcement, as did also the power vacuum that occurred as the newly elected Black government was replacing the Apartheid regime. But despite the difficult task of reconstituting the law and order infrastructure, studies have shown that the crime problem was to some degree localized or contained (e.g., most of the murders occurred among people who knew each other, and among those homicides, most occurred in areas with large unemployment, easy access to firearms, income inequality, and a high level of poverty in general) (Hunter-Gault, 59). Carolyn Coman has failed her readers by failing to research this complex subject. All told, the assault on Laura is believable, but not a common feature in urban street violence, and new programs were having some success in addressing chronic, underlying causes.

Allister Sparks has emphasized the way an acceleration of crime was already under way in the 1980s. First, profits from drugs were on the increase as the use of narcotics increased; second, European fortune hunters, as well as some from the Middle East, were smuggling gold, diamonds, ivory, drugs, and other prized objects into South Africa from across the northern border. (Northern nations such as Angola, Zambia, and what was then called Zaire had ineffectual police forces and governments that failed to stem the traffic.) South African gangs used motor vehicles as bartering items in the north, and hence car-jacking reached astronomical levels. All of this lucrative business eventually attracted international smuggling networks (Sparks, 226–227; Terreblanche, 42). Moreover, the Apartheid government neglected its recruitment of regular detectives and focused most of its attention on developing counter-revolutionary police (e.g., the "Special Branch"). Some of these anti-ANC specialists felt abandoned in the face of the TRC and turned to the *committal* of criminal acts (Sparks, 229). Additionally, the very legitimacy of the police force was reduced as the result of glaring race discrimination. In 1996, for example, seventy-five percent of police stations were located in White areas; poor Black neighborhoods were still poorly protected, even as they endured the brunt of criminal activity.

One problem with the TRC is the way it backed away from considering systemic racism, and doing so after initially gaining support for the Commission by promising to deal with it. Racism permeated the Apartheid government whether in educational planning, law enforcement, job and housing regulation, marriage laws, and any number of other types of control. By definition, "systemic racism is a characteristic of societies in which most major aspects of life are shaped by . . . core racist realities" (Feagin and Houts, 416). In South Africa the "core" was unjust enrichment for Whites and unjust impoverishment for Blacks. Given these privileges and deprivations, both of which were passed along over generations, it is not surprising that vested group interests became entrenched.

Thus we find urban crime being systemic in nature. It was accelerated when young people were systematically blocked from employment, education, or any other road to a viable future. At the outset, Apartheid's main architect, Hendrik Verwoerd, made discrimination an important tenet for his regime: different races, he said, would have different syllabuses at school, since none would be educated "to have expectations in life which circumstances in South Africa do not allow to be fulfilled" (qtd. in Sparks, 221).

While the background for urban crime is too complicated to discuss at length in its relationship to novel-writing, yet the social responsibility of novelists includes acquaintance with that background, once they introduce the subject. An understanding of South African justice and injustice is not served when authors ignore the realities, and when they are rewarded by the Western educational establishment for doing so.[1]

To Coman's credit, she does bring to *Many Stones* a quality that she greatly values. In her *TeenReads* interview she states: "I come to love my characters and deeply appreciate how hard life is for them sometimes" (www.Teenreads. . .) That affection is easy to recognize and feel in her novel. But why bring Berry (and the readers) to a region that the writer will describe in a largely superficial, ill-informed, and racialized manner? With that approach, the work becomes a contradiction—an experience imbued with appreciation for White characters and what they represent, and indifference toward Black characters and what they are symbolizing.

II. *Zulu Dog*

Violent intimidation and well-organized crime syndicates are center stage as Anton Ferreira introduces a young Zulu and his three-legged dog. Vusi

Ngugu's father has a taxi business that he can either shut down, or refuse to terminate and be murdered as a consequence. He has no other options. The new, democratically elected government will not help him, for there is little law enforcement for the Black population. Mr. Ngugu is a modest but aspiring businessman who, at the end of the novel, is left with no economic opportunity except employment by a White landowner. Both self-determination and self-respect are undermined as he is forced to trade his independence for White protection from Mafia-type Black entrepreneurs. Ferreira accurately links crime and poverty; however, his criminal world is entirely Black-instigated and Black-directed. Sampie Terreblanche, a leading Afrikaner academic, makes a similar linkage, but without the "blame-the-victim" connotation. He writes, "a mutually reinforcing dynamic exists today between crime and violence on the one hand and the process of pauperization on the other" (406).

Post-Apartheid Crime and Corruption

Besides depicting the violence on the roads, the novelist shows an array of lawless conditions in the post-apartheid society: for example, drug traffickers operate freely, the police are easy to bribe, legal redress is practically non-existent, the coffers of government exist mainly for the personal benefit of politicians, and White farmers are plagued by Black poachers. All this is presented to readers, while Ferreira also inserts a few belligerent White voices: anger about "black idiots running the country now" and disgust about "what a mess they've made since 1994" (93, 94). In brief, the author seems bent on impressing children with his version of Black criminality, while also unfolding a story about how a poverty-stricken Black child (Vusi) and a well-off White child (Elizabeth) become great friends. Among the White and Black adults any friendship seems unlikely until Vusi's dog saves Elizabeth. That changes Elizabeth's family, but the book's basic economic power relationships and authority remain intact. Elizabeth's father (a man who often cursed the "bloody kaffirs") is glad that a dog intercepts the attacking leopard, but we see no other motivation as he offers a job to the ex–taxi entrepreneur.

The novelist indirectly criticizes blatant prejudice on the one hand, while simultaneously expressing a deep disillusionment about the post-Apartheid regime. With respect to law and order, the South Africa of *Zulu Dog* is a hopeless case.

Even Vusi's school is a place where Black officialdom exercises its corrupt intensions:

> Not much government spending has reached Msinga, [the teacher] thinks. The educational budget is all spent in the cities, where the children of the government officials go to school. The people in the countryside have to make do with what's left over, if anything (70).

What's left over is a two-room hovel with rat holes in the walls and leaks in the roof (66, 68).

Black children under Apartheid were specifically and purposefully deprived of equal schooling, but now we are to believe that the Black majority will again deprive these children. This is an untenable assumption since it grossly overlooks the quality and scale of Apartheid's use of education for social engineering. The National Party had systematically politicized education as a way to "produce not only certain kinds of people, but produce them in certain quantities and of certain qualities" (Samuel, 270). And this was for the purpose of maximizing White wealth and, in the process, maximizing Black impoverishment. In the Apartheid system, "every single aspect from pre-school to university level is marked by an inequitable balance biased in favour of whites" (271).

Amazingly, Elizabeth's father rails against Mandela because under his leadership "the standard of schooling is appalling" (94). And while Mr. Montgomery will soften his protests after his daughter's rescue, the numerous charges against the new government are never contradicted.

Child readers are allowed to know nothing about the way schools for Blacks were designed under Apartheid as a weapon against each new generation—as a means to carefully shape the young into an exploitable labor force.

Indigenous Culture as the Enemy

Cultural causes for inept Black rule are implied when the author introduces "granny," a spirit medium. Granny supposedly represents the "African mind" by concocting medicinal remedies from decaying animal parts, talking with ancestors, fearing dwarfs, and making spiritualism a tool for "healing and hexing" whomever she chooses. The African hero of this story, Vusi, avoids his grandmother because her "hut" is a ghoulish mess of clinking bones, dried animal skins, empty eye sockets, and numerous monkey skulls. Yet in speaking to his friend, Vusi defends his granny with the comment that "she is very clever . . . she can cast many, many spells" (147). Elizabeth is appalled. "She used my hair to cast a spell on me? . . . My father was right—you are superstitious, you do believe in magic" (148). Given what Ferreira shows us about granny, it is not hard for a Western reader to agree with Elizabeth and her prejudiced father. Moreover, the boy's family shares most of granny's beliefs, so the author's strong indictment of African spirituality (as he interprets it) extends beyond one elderly woman.

Racism, as it functions in this story, is less about race per se and more about culture. It is reflected in what Ellis Cashmore terms "cultural racism." Biological differences are not at issue, but other characteristics are portrayed as so extreme that those characteristics appear to be as immutable as genetic differences. The holders of these attributes are treated as parasites, as a thoroughly undesirable population (Cashmore, 96–97).² In his "Author's Note," Ferreira describes such a population as resulting from the end of the Apartheid regime, one that *would* be reasonably viewed as parasitic:

> [T]he country was awash in weapons, which now ended up in the hands of criminals. Human life came to be regarded as cheap, expendable. The poverty of most blacks provided abundant incentives for robbery. The police ... were held in contempt. (xi)

As Vusi's family is planning to flee from their rural homestead in Kwa-Zulu-Natal, the children are "aghast," and become the mouthpiece for the author's views of urban life: "They have heard ... nightmare tales ... about all the shacks jammed up against one another ... [about] thugs and gangsters everywhere" (164).

The senior book editor for Parents' Choice, Kemie Nix, appears to believe every word about a post-Apartheid South Africa as a dysfunctional state. She calls Ferreira an author who "realistically present[s] problems of South Africa." He does, in fact, deliver what the Western newspaper headlines present, but the problems, as portrayed in the novel, have been isolated from their South African context. Dorothy N. Bowen for the *School Library Journal* agrees that Ferreira is a reliable commentator: "[He] presents an authentic picture of the chasm between the haves and the have-nots" (224). On the contrary, he gives readers a blame-the-victim picture of haves and have-nots. Only Cheryl-Ann Michael from the University of the Western Cape brings up the problem of "have-nots" and its relation to land rights. She points out that "the idea of the sharing of land and profits, a solution that has had some success in post-apartheid South Africa, is not approached in this novel."³ Rather the novel "veers dangerously towards the suggestion that white patronage provides an adequate answer [to the poverty issue]" (see Michael's online review). At every turn, we see this novel suggesting that Whites must take charge if they are to rescue law-abiding Blacks from an incompetent Black government.

For Vusi's family, classic colonialism has been resurrected. The Ngugus have returned to the White-owned land that, prior to conquest and occupation by Europeans, was African land. For a young audience, the well-meaning Montgomery paternalism may obscure the way friendly relations are actually *unfriendly* with respect to how costs and benefits are distributed within the population. Economics can only be touched on in a novel, but the way the author seems nostalgic for Apartheid, and the many ways he debases the Black population—all this adds up to mis-education for the reader.

* * *

In *Many Stones*, for Berry's father to warn that "crime is out of control here" and for African street vendors to wear signs stating "I don't do crime" (in other words, *I'm* not part of a crime wave)—this hardly offers children an unbiased set of images. Instead, this only adds to the "Africans-are-dangerous" propaganda that the American media seem to relish.

In *Zulu Dog*, the claims about "chaos-under-Black-rule" have been made while ignoring the necessary context. Admittedly, a violent struggle did occur between these African parties—the African National Congress and the Inkatha Freedom Party (IFP)—but much needs to be understood about this conflict. The stakes need to be understood. The overt forms of struggle only ended with a compromise at the last minute that induced the IFP to join in the election and keep South African unified. However, during the outbreaks of fighting, white supremacist Apartheid groups, as well as the South African police, were giving assistance to IFP fighters; thus the final conflict resolution rested on a much more fragile base than appearances indicated. In short, the "law and order" problem for the new government had roots going all the way back to the 1820s. The IFP wanted an independent post-Apartheid state that would include all the territory ruled by Shaka, the renowned leader of the Zulus, in the early nineteenth century. The IFP joined the unified South Africa plan only after three million acres of land were transferred to the Zulu monarch, thus keeping this land outside the control of the new government (Thompson, 253). In the end, wherever colonial control has usurped indigenous sovereignty, land ownership remains a central human rights issue.

Crime in South Africa was, therefore, not about vicious "thugs," or about a government that couldn't restrain the crime syndicates arriving from all directions. Yet such a false history is exactly what young readers are being fed.

Works Cited

"Author Profile: Carolyn Coman." 2000. TeenReads: http://teenreads.com/authors/au-coman-carolyn.asp

Bell, Terry, with Dumisa Buhle Ntsebeza. 2001, 2003. *Unfinished Business: South Africa, Apartheid & Truth*. Observatory 7935, South Africa: RedWorks; New York: Verso.

Bowen, Dorothy N. 2002. Review of Anton Ferreira's *Zulu Dog*. School Library Journal 48 (September): 224.

Cashmore, Ellis. 2005. "Cultural Racism." In *Encyclopedia of Race and Ethnic Studies*, ed. Ellis Cashmore, 96–98. London: Routledge.

———. 2005. "Reverse Racism/Discrimination." In *Encyclopedia of Race and Ethnic Studies*, ed. Ellis Cashmore, 373. London: Routledge.

Coman, Carolyn. 2002. *Many Stones*. New York: Puffin Books. (First published in the United States by Front Street in 2000)

Feagin, Joe and Leslie A. Houts. 2005. "Systemic Racism." In *Encyclopedia of Race and Ethnic Studies*, ed. Ellis Cashmore, 416–418. London: Routledge.

Ferreira, Anton. 2002. *Zulu Dog*. New York: Farrar, Straus and Giroux.

Graybill, Lyn S. 2002. *Truth & Reconciliation in South Africa: Miracle or Model?* Boulder, CO: Lynne Rienner.

Hunter-Gault, Charlayne. 2006. *New News Out of Africa: Uncovering Africa's Renaissance*. Oxford, UK: Oxford UP.

Manjoo, Rashida. 2003. *Peace and Reconciliation in South Africa: What Lessons?* Colombo, Sri Lanka: Muslim Women's Research and Action Forum.

Michael, Cheryl-Ann. 2003. Review of Anton Ferreira's *Zulu Dog*. H-AfrTeach, H-Net Reviews (June). http://www.h-net.msu.edu/reviews/showrev.cgi"path=6550157636329

Nix, Kemie. 2002. Review of Anton Ferreira's *Zulu Dog*. Parents' Choice. http://www.parents-choice.org/produce.cfm?product_id=9221&award=xx&from=Dog%20

Rockman, Hazel. 2000. Review of Carolyn Coman's *Many Stones*. New York Times Book Review. November 19: 64.

Samuel, John. 1992. "Education in South Africa: Strategic Issues for the Future." In *Power and Profit: Politics, Labour, and Business in South Africa* (The Innes Labour Brief), eds. Duncan Innes, Matthew Kentridge, and Helene Perold, 270–277. Cape Town: Oxford UP.

Sparks, Allister. 2003. *Beyond the Miracle: Inside the New South Africa*. London: Profile Books.

TeenReads. 2003. Interview with Carolyn Coman (Jan. 14, 2000). http://teenreads.com/authors/au-coman-carolyn.asp

Terreblanche, Sampie. 2002. *A History of Inequality in South Africa, 1652–2002*. Pietermaritzburg, South Africa: University of Natal Press and KMM Review Publishing.

Thompson, Leonard. 1995. *A History of South Africa*, rev. ed. New Haven, CT: Yale UP.

Chapter Eight
"Doomed Races" in Elana Bregin's "Ella's Dunes"

> The [Bushman] has become a mere human fossil.... [T]here is nothing left for him but to disappear.
> —Jan Smuts (qtd. in Dubow, 51)

> One of the fundamental characteristics of 19th century European imperialism was its systematic destruction of communities outside the "mother country."
> —Irving Louis Horowitz (18)

Imperialism and its outcome—the destruction of targeted communities—has gained support from entrenched pseudo-scientific ideas. One such belief places so-called lower races on the path to extinction. In Elana Bregin's "Ella's Dunes" (2004), the targeted group is a San community in South Africa which has taken up residence in a game park designed to entertain White South African tourists. Bregin's adoption of the "doomed races" theory becomes explicit when the father of the teenaged narrator, Annette, explains to his daughter why the game park is necessary to the survival of San communities: "'They're ... the last survivors'" (19). If left on their own, they face "'Starvation! Complete poverty! Drinking themselves to death'" (28). The reference to alcoholism brings together the extinction theme with a variety of stereotypes that permeate the narrative, for example, "Bushmen" as warlike, animal-like, static, mysterious, and furnished with "wild forests of hair" (27). A third strand in this short story (the lead story in *Memories of Sun: Stories of Africa and America*, 2004) is the Africans-on-exhibit theme.

Africans were actually placed in museums, fairs, theme parks, and zoos in the nineteenth and twentieth centuries and were a huge hit with the public. (Zoos in Germany and in the United States in 2005 and 2007 have perpetuated this racist tradition.)

The voyeurism of fairs and zoos will receive a closer look on a later page, but we begin with an overview of the plotline and characterizations, the San land problem, and the "doomed races" theory.

"Best Friends" in a White Supremacist Plot

Friendship between two adolescent girls (Annette and Ella), and a re-united father and daughter drive the plotlines in "Ella's Dunes." These lines intersect when Annette complains that her father's game park treats members of the San community like inmates in a zoo. Her father (the park's tourist guide) explains that his "zoo" is a necessity. That is, either Ella's group is put on display in "San Rock: Bushmen Craft and Culture Farm," or else, like others in the "dying" San populace, they will "stand on a highway in the middle of nowhere, hoping that the occasional speeding car will stop and buy from them" (28–29). And with their meager earnings, they will then "drink themselves to death" (28). With this explanation, we are to believe that Annette has been set straight about Black South Africans vis-à-vis exhibitions, since for the first time in her life she respects her dad: "'I could hear in his voice how much he cared about them . . .'" (29). Readers will supposedly be as impressed as is Annette by the idea of bringing the San off the highway and placing them on display.

Following Annette's parents' divorce, Annette had rarely seen her father, and as the two are becoming re-acquainted, Dad is useful to the author in the role of teacher. He serves as Bregin's stand-in as he lectures his daughter about the San in relation to their "place." "'Their place,'" he says, "'is the Kalahari.'" Yet "'even if they had the land, they wouldn't be able to survive on it without some way of earning their keep. This is not the old days anymore. Everyone has to pay their way in this mercenary world. The Bushmen are no exception'" (29). It appears that in some mysterious way the Bushmen have lost their land, but this is of no consequence since they apparently don't know what to do with land in any case. Besides poverty, "'there's nothing else for them there. They have no land, no money, no way of earning a living.'" In contrast, at the "Culture Farm," they "'have full bellies at night [and] their children can go to school'" (28). Bregin seems basically in tune with the beliefs of the twice-elected Afrikaner prime minister, Jan Smuts, who insisted that the Bushman had become "a desert animal . . . as much as the rest of our desert animals and plants." And though still living, was "verging on extinction" (qtd. in Dubow, 51).

Another part of the author's history lesson centers on specific "Culture Farm" exhibits. When tourists arrive, the San perform a quick change act:

> Clothes were stripped off, the cups and pots and other traces of civilization hurriedly swept up and hidden in the *skerms* ["huts"]. Before my eyes, the group transformed themselves into the Stone Age people of the history books. The men wore nothing now but loincloths of animal skin, the women, skirts of animal hide. (25)

Fourteen-year-old Ella was "sullen and unsmiling" as she "sat bare-chested like all the women, my crystal pendant oddly out of place between her breasts" (26).

Whatever is placed in a San "tourist village" exists primarily in relation to what will appeal to tourists, and Bregin seems to have this same audience in mind when she is telling readers that "cups and pots" constitute for the twenty-first-century San "traces of civilization." What is Bregin's purpose in misrepresenting the San perspective in a story that is itself a twenty-first-century production? Steven Robins notes that in everyday San experience, the dichotomy of "modern" and "traditional" does not exist. Instead,

> The hybridized conditions of everyday life in the Kalahari include "local" knowledge, practices and identities as well as San access to "exogenous" cyber-technologies, fax machines, cellular phones and international indigenous peoples' conferences and conventions in Europe and North America. (369–370)[1]

Annette is impressed by the short stature of the Bushmen as they stand among the tourists, and in these scenes we are told that she can adopt the San perspective. She "looked through his eyes and my heart sank for the Bushmen. It struck me suddenly what little people they were. So misplaced here, with their cracked desert faces, their animal skins and wild forests of hair" (27). This description represents neither an actual San identity nor the San self-concept, but only a set of insinuations linked to the "doomed race" myth. And the author's characterization of Ella has similar implications. She remains throughout at as stereotypical creature of nature, seen with her brother as bobbing "through . . . the bushes, [as] trott[ing] barefoot through the hot and thorn-strewn dust, moving in effortless rhythm, as graceful as antelope" (17). So fragile and unearthly is Ella's existence that survival does seem unlikely. She is:

> full of magic. Her little brother stood beside her, small and shy. They seemed so light, as if their bones were made of air, as if they could blow away like birds into the sky at any minute. I was afraid to breathe too hard, in case I made them vanish. (18)

In one of his fatherly lectures, Annette's dad has told her that the "Culture Farm" is home to "Cape Kalahari Bushmen.... Among the few left who still have knowledge of the old ways ... and losing that knowledge fast. Without land of their own to live on, they can't survive" (19). He seemingly pleads the case for the San when he tells Annette, "'They should be given the land back.'" But then adds, "'There's politics involved'" (29) Why is land not a resource for the San, whether or not they engage in hunting, gathering, herding, or farming? Has this claim something to do with eugenics and its treatment of intelligence as something inherited and disproportionately allotted to certain groups? Eugenicists believed that political power could be used to block the increase of "unfit" persons and enhance the growth of "fit" populations. And this idea, writes Nancy Stepan, could be "easily grafted on to existing race ideas in science" (114).[2]

Since Ella's parents have, for some unexplained reason, remained in the Kalahari after sending their daughter to the "Culture Farm," what are we to think about their prospects for survival? What do contemporary studies indicate about the Kalahari? For one thing, there has been a diminished supply of wild plants due to a persistent drought, and also a less abundant supply of game in the large ranch areas where San communities are situated. However, the San are "some of the most active indigenous peoples in Africa in terms of ... sustainable community-based development" (Hitchcock, 1). Their mixed economies include herding their own livestock and working as herders for White ranchers as well as for Black pastoralist groups. Moreover, they "participate extensively in the regional and world economy" (Hitchcock, 1). Bregin's notions about no land "to live on" suggest a degree of hopelessness that is unsubstantiated in the research about San communities. They divert attention from the San struggles on behalf of human rights and land rights.

Annette decides to spend her time at the San campsite, and as the story winds down, we hear more about what she calls a "strange bond" with Ella (30). For example, Ella dresses Annette in a topless animal skin outfit similar to her own. "'I let her strip me, felt the strange, cool texture of the skin skirt against my own skin, fought the urge to cross my arms across my breasts'" (34). Annette admits that she is shy in this non-Western attire, but "Ella's eyes held a challenge that I couldn't defy.... 'Now you look more Bushman.' She nodded approvingly, rubbing dust into my skin to dull its whiteness" (34). Putting dirt on pale skins as a way to suggest dark skins is a racist idea, but one that recurs in works by White authors who are reaching for a multicultural effect. As for the dressing–undressing scene as a whole, it smacks of exhibitionism. Annette notes the way "other Bushmen laughed in delight to see me so transformed," and she joins their "stomping, hopping kind of dance" around the fire (34).

Annette's father has already explained to his daughter that one advantage of the "Culture Farm" is having the opportunity to send children to school. But Ella's school experience is utterly untenable. When Dad says she is "fine" in her present school, Annette promptly debunks that claim. Ella lets herself be driven to school each day by Annette's father, but she secretly avoids entering the building. How could she continually face the gibes about being "a stupid Bushman," or endure her classmates' cultural misunderstanding of her topless performance for tourists (33)? How could she continually endure teachers who "shout at her because she's got no English and she can't do the work" (33)? Annette has reported that her father "cared about them [the San]," but where is his response to Ella's unbearable learning environment?

Bregin's stream of misinformation needs to be seen against the backdrop of the land problem, the evolution of the "doomed races" concept, and the history of European and American exhibitions.

Land Claims

Typically anthropologists have grouped the San among forager societies. Foraging, however, was a survival strategy forced on this group by those denying them access to the resources they had depended on prior to seventeenth-century Dutch colonization (Holmann, 8). As for the European settlers, this was a strategy for forcing the San into the role of farm laborers, and later into the role of trackers during military conflicts in bush country. Few employment opportunities existed in the towns due to inordinate race prejudice. These economic limitations were contributing factors in the San population decline.

Bregin's portrait blames the victim and rarely touches upon contemporary San realities. San political organizations such as the FPK (First People of the Kalahari) have been involved in landholding claims, school organizing, the development of farm cooperatives, and other pro-active initiatives. The FPK has articulated the following ongoing agenda:

> Striving for political recognition, for secure access to natural and financial resources, for increased human rights awareness, ... for self-sustainability through development projects, and for a common identity and pride in their culture. (Holmann, 13)

This plan does not represent a mere wish-fulfilling gesture. In today's South Africa, the San is the only group granted the label "indigenous group," and it is the only one authorized to submit land claims (Holmann, 6). San communities, notes Robert K. Hitchcock, "are making progress in their efforts to obtain rights to land and to compensation for resources lost in the past" (5). Under the Restitution of Land Rights Act of 1994, the /Khomani group received 25,000 hectares of land outside the Kalahari Gemsbok Park, as well as rights over the tourism in the park. Local people, writes Hitchcock, are playing a decision-making role.

Nonetheless the San still battle policies that inhibit self-sufficiency and self-determination. They are still victims of cultural property thefts and other forms of commercial appropriation.[3] The pseudo-scientific mind-set of earlier epochs does not change easily, and two centuries of "dying race" theories have left the San particularly vulnerable to race prejudice, harassment of their children, and inequitable government practices. While "Ella's Dunes" is explicit about extinction for the San, this position is not at odds with "scientific" findings of anthropologists, geologists, historians, and other academics. Their theories abound vis-à-vis "doomed races."[4]

Africans as "Fossils"

In view of both scholarly and popular opinion, it is not surprising that Prime Minister Smuts referred to the short-statured people of the South African Cape as "mere human fossils" (qtd. in Dubow, 51).[5] And if elaborate discourses on this subject were not enough, the learned prophet-scientists also *recommended* that "lower races" be helped along in their disappearance. By 1949, this phenomenon had received a new name—genocide: "the structural and systematic destruction of innocent people by a state bureaucratic apparatus" (Horowitz, 17). Groups who were initially targeted for this destruction were those residing in the spots most coveted by Europe, places where European nations were cranking up their expansionist programs. They were places rich in land, in mineral resources, and in exploitable laborers.

In South Africa, the dying race hypothesis served a number of purposes of immediate relevance. For example, its emphasis on racial differences was useful following the Anglo–Boer War (1899–1902), when extreme Afrikaner–British divisions needed immediate repair. Racial segregation was an immediate issue when expanding Black servant populations induced "black peril" anxieties and demands for heightened social control in cities. Darwinian rhetoric was increasingly heard, as when the *Transvaal Leader* editorialized in 1904:

> We can say with scientific certainty that the process of evolution must be so prolonged as to deprive any speculations based on it of present political interest. . . . The very formation of the negro skull is so antagonistic to the theory [of ethnological equality with Caucasians], recalling as it does the Neanderthal head, which is admittedly a member of the European race which existed many thousands of years before the dawn of history. (qtd. in Rich, 85)

In the previous year, the South African Association for the Advancement of Science had been founded, and its various units developed theories about segregation, African educability, and the African's "peculiar characteristics" (Rich, 91–92). In studies of children, White children's differences were "usually interpreted in terms of environmental differences, while those between Whites and Blacks were perceived in terms of heredity" (Rich, 95).

The "dying race" doctrine was not being seriously challenged as long as its misguided biological support remained intact. However, eugenics and other race-related "scientific" arguments became largely discredited after they had been put to use by Nazi Germany in the 1930s. When the Apartheid ideology gained momentum following the South African National Party's 1948 victory, its ideas centered more on cultural differences among "peoples" than on questionable measurement methods.

Simplifying an Apartheid philosophy for the sake of child audiences, Elana Bregin introduces the social control of Blacks by way of a cultural center/game park. In this way the future of the indigenous population appears quite benign, even as this populace is portrayed as facing inevitable doom. Bregin's story echoes pronouncements about decline from early twentieth-century academics such as George Chatteron Hill:

> Nothing can be more unscientific, nothing shows a deeper ignorance of the elementary laws of social evolution, than the absurd agitations . . . against the elimination of inferior races. . . . By reason of its genius for expansion, [the "British race"] must necessarily eliminate the inferior races which stand in its way. Every superior race . . . was obliged to do it. (qtd. in Cashmore, 110)

"Ella's Dunes" is clearly a historical throwback, and at the same time lends support to a popular, ongoing form of entertainment: the creation of exhibitions featuring living, breathing Africans.

Zoos, World Fairs, and Other Spectacles

The "San Rock: Bushman Craft and Culture Farm" has on its company vehicle a logo featuring a crouching "Bushman" with a drawn bow. Annette asks her father: "'Aren't they San people?' He grimaced. 'Ya, that's the popular term now. But they prefer the old name. They say that San is what others call them'" (19). Of course Dad favors the use of the "old name" since the San community is valuable to him when its connection with ancient times can pull in more customers. But irrespective of its commercial relevance, the use of the term "Bushman" is comparable to the use of "Hottentot" for the Khoikhoi—both words being Dutch inventions. ("Bushman" is based on the Dutch word "Bosjesmans.") By the 1990s the use of "Bushman" in

San communities had been generally discontinued, and it was largely discontinued in academic circles in the 1970s (Lee, 9). In the West, given the racist and sexist connotations of "Bushman," contemporary book publications usually have "Bushman" in their index but refer the reader to "San." "Ella's Dunes" promotes the old terminology.

In any case, "Hottentots," "Bushmen," and "Pygmies," could be gaped at in Paris, Amsterdam, London, Hamburg, St. Louis, and other cities in enormously elaborate zoos and World Fairs. These spectacles consisted of events deemed popular with Westerners such as mock battles and ritualistic dancing (sometimes alluding to cannibalism). A Black child was allowed to walk about uncaged at the Antwerp zoo and was a major attraction. But also in Antwerp, three out of sixteen Congolese entertainers died in the midst of their zoo experience and four more became seriously ill (Pieterse, 95). In the Bronx Zoo in 1906, a young Congolese was placed in an exhibit called the "Monkey House," and the *New York Times* offered enthusiastic support. The *Times* applauded the "joint man-and-monkey exhibition" and the zoo director's comment about seeing "no difference between a wild beast and the little Black man" (Miller and Ejikeme).

According to historian Jan Nederveen Pieterse, such "zoological" displays served Western audiences in the way exoticism generally attracted people. He writes: "The Other is not merely to be exploited but also to be enjoyed, enjoyment being a finer form of exploitation" (95). After machine guns became a means for decimating populations in Africa and elsewhere, the African spear or assegai became largely a decorative object to Western eyes. As for imperialism, it became associated with an increasingly politicized "natural history" (96).

In Bregin's story, the author's presentation of Ella illustrates the voyeurism connected with colonial and neo-colonial exhibits. Ella must display her body as a showbiz attraction and then sit in a White-populated classroom where students saw that display as pure degradation. As unthinkable as this is, Bregin's story pre-dates by just one year the mock African village built in the Augsburg zoo in 2005. *Die Tageszeitung,* a German newspaper, opposed the protest against the exhibit despite the show's racist connotations (Attikpoé, 69). In another example, the Woodland Park Zoo in Seattle opened an exhibit in 2007 called "Maasai Journey: An African Adventure." In a protest by two history professors, zoo-goers were asked to imagine a zoo in Africa "where visitors are encouraged to 'Meet an American and learn how their lives intersect with the large mammals of the Rocky Mountains'" (Miller and Ejikeme, 9). Zoo officials were only mildly impressed by the analogy. In their first press release they had emphasized the fearsomeness and primitivism of Maasai warriors; now as a debate began to surface, they switched the actor-warrior title to "educator." As Char Miller and Anene Ejikeme point out, the exhibit embodies the "quintessential Western fantasy about darkest Africa." And the Maasai in particular are used to symbolize an imagined gap between

African and Western-style civilization. One can only wonder whether zoo-keepers, storytellers, and newspaper editors consider imperialist exhibitions as the best place to learn about Africa.

Afrikaner Literature and the Apartheid State

In the wake of centuries of negative stereotyping, the incorporation of the so-called Other into one's own sense of self is not easy. Yet identity is a mental construct, and in the case of Beverley Naidoo's fiction (to take one example), we can glimpse the way direct engagement in the anti-Apartheid resistance movement has had some effect. It has enabled her to reverse the perceptions and popular myths embraced by many of her South African compatriots.[6] In contrast, it is not hard to see the "separateness" agenda of the Afrikaner state in Bregin's "Ella's Dunes." The San community is treated as a lost cause, as incapable of action that constructively impacts the future of San children. We are told that the San are landless, and this deprivation is truly part of their history. But if the writer decides to introduce the subject, on what grounds can the legislative program driving that land loss be deliberately concealed? Will readers not come away with a distorted image of San history? Admittedly, in a tale about youthful relationships, political details are handled selectively. But landlessness is a political matter and has a bearing on the political rights of young and old. Silence on this matter can only trivialize the status of the San as an autonomous, self-defined people.

The way Black characters are portrayed in White-authored fiction is one piece in the Western imperialist mosaic. It can signal the way a White myth-structure is embraced as a cultural norm or, contrariwise, is recognized as a powerful and destructive imposition. Bregin's story is not something responsible educators can offer children, but it does invite questions. To what extent have "Dark Africa" myths been seriously confronted? To what extent have power relationships been understood? To what extent is the Other imagined as a stereotype or a threat?

Works Cited

Attikpoé, Kodjo. 2006. "African Images in Current German Fiction for Children and Young Adults: A Denial of African Culture." *Sankofa: A Journal of African Children's and Young Adult Literature* 5: 62–70.

Bregin, Elana. 2004. "Ella's Dunes." In *Memories of Sun: Stories of Africa and America*, ed. Jane Kurtz, 13–37. New York: Greenwillow Books.

Cashmore, Ellis. 2005. "Doomed Races Doctrine." In *Encyclopedia of Race and Ethnic Studies*, ed. Ellis Cashmore, 108–112. New York: Routledge.

Dubow, Saul. 1995. *Scientific Racism in Modern South Africa*. Cambridge, UK: Cambridge University Press.

Hitchcock, Robert K. 2002. "Human Rights, Development, and the San of Southern Africa." In *What Place for Hunter-Gatherers in Millennium Three?* eds. Thomas N. Headland and Doris E. Blood, 1–8. Dallas, TX: SIL International and International Museum of Cultures.

Holmann, Thekla. 2003. "San and the State: An Introduction." In *San and the State: Contesting Land, Development, Identity and Representation*, ed. Thekla Holmann, 1–35. Köln, Germany: Rüdiger Köppe Verlag.

Horowitz, Irving Louis. 1982. *Taking Lives: Genocide and State Power*, 3rd ed. New Brunswick, NJ: Transaction Books.

Lee, Robert. 1993. *The Dobe Ju/'hoansi*. Fort Worth, TX: Harcourt Brace.

Miller, Char and Anene Ejikeme. 2007. "A Zoo Replays Old Stereotypes of Africa." *Christian Science Monitor* (September 7): 9.

Pieterse, Jan Nederveen. 1992. *White on Black: Images of Africa and Blacks in Western Popular Culture*. New Haven, CT: Yale University Press.

Rich, Paul. 1993. "Race, Science, and the Legitimization of White Supremacy in South Africa, 1902–1940." In *The Colonial Epoch in Africa*, vol. 2, ed. Gregory Maddox, 81–102. New York: Garland.

Robins, Steven. 2003. "NGOs, 'Bushmen' and Double Vision: The /khomani San Land Claim and the Cultural Politics of 'Community' and 'Development' in the Kalahari." In *San and the State: Contesting Land, Development, Identity and Representation*, ed. Thekla Holmann, 365–400. Köln, Germany: Rüdiger Kölppe Verlag.

Stepan, Nancy. 1982. *The Idea of Race in Science: Great Britain, 1800–1960*. London: Macmillan, in association with St. Antony's College, Oxford.

Chapter Nine
Disease and the "Darkest Africa" Myth: Novels About AIDS and Smallpox

> Because social structures limit the choices people make, stopping AIDS requires eliminating the barriers that deprive women of control over their sexual interactions, and deprive poor people of control over their lives. . . . Changes on the interpersonal level are insufficient.
> —Brooke Grundfest Schoepf (25)

> The devalorization of life has as its corollary the the media penchant for associating the Third World with violent, unnecessary, random death, or with disease. . . . whereby "the dead or dying body has become in itself the visual sign of human reality in the Third World."
> —Ella Shohat and Robert Stam (24)

Novelists proclaiming a genuine desire to wage war against disease have sometimes turned their pen against Africa. Such is the case in Allan Stratton's *Chanda's Secrets* (2004) and Deborah Ellis' *The Heaven Shop* (2004), both about AIDS, and Clayton Bess' *Story for a Black Night* (1982, 2004), a novel about smallpox. All these novelists go to some lengths to treat dying bodies as the "Third World's" reality and to claim a pre-industrial mind-set at work in twenty-first-century urban and rural districts. It would appear that no conceivable plotlines are imaginable to Western authors unless they first develop a fearsome "Dark Africa" context.

I. *Chanda's Secrets*

Stratton has taken numerous negative reports about Africa, plus age-old popular stereotypes, and scrunched them together to create *Chanda's Secrets*.

Readers will see the multiple sufferings of AIDS, but more than that, they will see Africa in general as horrifying. A novel about AIDS is potentially informative, but it can also be used as a dumping ground for cultural racism. Racism does not necessarily connect with the idea of "race" per se, but it "may have functional equivalents, culture being one of them" (Cashmore, 96). Since the 1960s, the idea (or theory) of a genetic basis for differences has not been as prevalent as differences anchored in a cultural context. Diverse classes, social behaviors, and educational disparities become functional equivalents of "race" when they generate serious ill-treatment: attacks, aversion, abhorrence, banishment, or hate crime.

Western newspaper and TV reports have little to say about Africa unless there is news about starvation, civil wars, or scandals within governments. The mythology about "Darkest Africa" is frequently discernable in these reports. Harilaos Stecopoulos has pulled together a series of anxieties that he associates with this myth. He sees U.S. fears about Iraq, fears about nuclear attack, and fears about AIDS as related phenomena, all attached to the "Dark Africa" fantasy. He writes:

> In the Niger affair, the United States sought to use the darkness long ascribed to Africa as a means of rendering [Saddam] Hussein even more frightening than he already appeared. After all, who . . . would doubt the possibility of such a fearful transaction on a continent that had been represented as particularly demonic in recent mass-market journalism? . . . The tragedies of Ebola and HIV/AIDS epidemics segue seamlessly into the horror of nuclear proliferation and radiation poisoning. . . . [T]ales of the heart of darkness help dramatize the need to combat evil in the world. (223)

Stratton's emphasis on African dysfunctions and ethical weaknesses are spread throughout his narrative. From the moment Chanda's father dies (he suffocates in a mine with failing rescue equipment) to the death of her mother from AIDS, African communities are plagued with interpersonal violence, negligence, or both. Prior to working for the mining company, Chanda's mother and father were disowned by her father's cattle-owning family because the couple had ignored the family's marital plans for them and eloped. The mining company no longer provides a house for Chanda's widowed mother so she finds work as a domestic. But the new employer will throw mother and daughter in the street unless the mother becomes his mistress. Only when he starts molesting sixteen-year-old Chanda does the mother flee to another region, marry an elderly barber, is again widowed, and inherits the barber's house. She marries a construction worker, but when their baby dies from AIDS, he becomes a habitual drunk. His own lengthy suffering from AIDS is graphically described, and upon his death Chanda's mother begins to gradually weaken with the AIDS infection.

Throughout the novel children suffer constantly as the result of misplacements among relatives, separation of siblings, and prostitution as a means to earn money to hold parentless families together. Chanda's best friend becomes HIV-positive after a gang rape and a knife attack that disfigures her face. There is no viable health care (a nurse helps by merely handing Chanda some rubber gloves when she seeks assistance for her stepfather). The schools are staffed by teachers who are often so ill that even kindergartners have little supervision, a condition that almost costs Chanda's five-year-old sister her life in a junkyard with an uncovered well. A fraudulent HIV drug inventor rips off customers because they are illiterate and cannot read the labels on his phony concoctions. A coffin maker rips off clients with fraudulent credentials as a mortician. Religionists offer cold comfort, and a prying neighbor spreads gossip and fear as she denies AIDS and covers up her son's death. Chanda's stepfather steals her mother's hard-earned money and uses it to support a prostitute and hasten his own decline into alcoholism.

Chanda and her mother are two momentary survivors of all this humanly created suffering. Stratton presents graphic descriptions of the AIDS symptoms, but concentrates on characterizations of supposedly backward, superstitious people. For the author they serve as a stark contrast to Chanda, the author's intelligent, industrious, compassionate hero. The condition Brooke Schoepf notes as a cause of the spread of AIDS—namely, the way poor people have no control over their lives—seldom enters into this novel. Instead, people are their own worst enemy.

Characterizations

Auntie Tafa, the next-door neighbor, is continuously present as an obnoxious snob. She is the neighborhood's proverbial busy-body and serves the novelist as his source for "comic relief." Since Chanda is the narrator, we see Tafa's foolishness from Chanda's perspective and feel how Tafa must grate upon the nerves of a sixteen-year-old. But this woman's stream of advice to Chanda's mother, and her mother's gracious response, is the way mother becomes characterized as an exceptional human being, someone Chanda wants to emulate. Saving this excellent woman from AIDS is not treated overtly in the novel until the last pages, but this goal hovers over the story and skillfully increases dramatic tension.

Bringing in Mrs. Gulubane, a "spirit doctor," is Tafa's idea and serves one of Stratton's major interests. He seems to relish creating a throwback to nineteenth-century imperialist descriptions of "witch doctors."[1] The following lines are reminiscent of earlier Western fiction about spirituality and ritualized worship:

> [Mrs. Gulubane] pulls a length of rope from her basket, folds it in two, and beings to whip herself. Strange noises rattle up her throat. Spittle flies

from her lips. Her eyes roll into her head. "HI-E-YA!" She throws back her arms, stiffens, and slumps forward in a heap.... Mrs. Gulubane's face contorts into the face of an old man. Her voice changes, too. It's low and guttural. She swallows air and belches words. "An evil wind is blowing from the north." (115, 116)

Chanda explains to her frightened siblings that the whole thing is "just a show" (115). The snake in the ritual was dead at the outset and hidden in her clothes, not suddenly produced by Mrs. Gulubane and subdued by her magic. Yet all her customers, says Chanda, "'even people who know better,'" accept her practices. "'Nobody ways a word.... [N]obody wants to be at the end of her curse'" (114). Chanda's most trusted teacher tells his students that the entire business engaged in by spiritualists is a fraud.

This attitude has both past and present social contexts. It can be said to connect with the period when missionaries joined with colonial administrators in a joint effort to control indigenous populations. For Christian missionaries, the practice of debunking indigenous spirituality has been customary in relation to their own Christian conversion goals. As noted in the chapter on feminism in Africa (Chapter 2), traditional forms of spirituality remain a favorite subject on which children's novelists heap scorn. Neither Stratton nor other writers have combined the practices of medical and traditional practitioners in a united program to combat AIDS. But contemporary research shows the value of this approach.

Zambia began a health education campaign in 1986 with workshops that combined Western-style doctors and psychiatrists on the one hand, and traditional herbalists, spiritualists, and faith healers on the other. It was an interactive project that involved "a reciprocal relationship" between the groups. The mutually acknowledged success of this approach had its basis in "the mutual respect for one another's realm of activity" (Chirwa and Sivile, 333).[2] Mis-education stemming from Christian religionists, as well as indigenous spiritualists, was reduced and forestalled as healers from the different traditions worked through the attitudes that stigmatized afflicted persons.

Esther, Chanda's best friend, is an example of how destructive that stigma can be. They had been in school together until Esther ended her schooling to take up prostitution and thereby earn enough to recover her siblings—all parceled out among different relatives. Esther is housed with a Bible-thumping aunt and uncle who supposedly speak in tongues at their Gospel Church, but repeatedly beat Esther and call her a whore. Moreover, some of her beatings are by her sexual clients—a part of her life that Esther is trying to conceal from Chanda. Given all that has happened to Chanda, she has become a religious skeptic, and Esther is used in the novel to encourage her in this skepticism, as well as to foreshadow what could happen to Chanda if she loses both parents and is left with no financial support.

All these characters underscore Stratton's themes by exaggerating them. He writes more plausibly when depicting Chanda's surviving siblings: the preschooler, Soly, and the kindergartner, Iris. They display all the logic and anxiety of the very young, asking, for example, if Sara will be given away! (The AIDS-infected baby Sara is about to breathe her last breath as the story begins.) The many tragedies surrounding Iris toughen her and generate a talent for conniving, manipulative behavior. She is brilliantly adept at using the few resources in her survival kit. All told, Stratton has a finely tuned ear for early childhood words and deeds.

Historical Background: Colonialist Retentions and AIDS Vulnerability

The widening gap between "haves" and "have nots" has had an increasing impact upon the spread of AIDS. Colonial administrations introduced structural changes that have hindered African economic viability, as for example, reducing trade to only a few mineral and agricultural exports, a condition that has yet to be corrected. The struggle against poverty has led men and adolescent boys to seek jobs in mines and plantations, thus separating them from family life and negatively impacting their social behavior. And girls, widows, and divorced women are also forced into low-wage migrant jobs, a dilemma that leaves them particularly vulnerable to sexual exploitation (Schoepf, 22).

As will be noted in the discussion of *The Heaven Shop*, increasing globalization has increased an unfavorable trade balance. It has increased the monopolized ownership of land and mineral resources, it has increased an exorbitant foreign debt, and, in South Africa, it has adversely affected unemployment, which had a rate of over 26 percent in 2005 (Hunter-Gault, 58). With this number of unemployed workers, South Africa can attract only limited foreign investments, a condition that exacerbates poverty even further. Thus health and educational services are hampered and an increase in AIDS in one of the adverse consequences.

To deal with such circumstances, political leaders have a daunting task. Schoepf comments that they must commit themselves to the following priorities:

> Equitable access to public services and willingness to ... institute changes in power relations that determine how individuals interact with one another sexually and socially. Not least among the power relations that must be changed are inequalities of class, gender, generation, and ethnicity in local, national, and international arenas. (24)

The notion that interpersonal choices in themselves, or "that market capitalism by itself, without social programs, can create bright futures for the poor"—these are among the illusions that health workers must counter before AIDS and other ailments can be successfully challenged.

Chanda's Secrets is counterproductive because even the interpersonal choices are biased in the direction of mean-spiritedness. Chanda and her mother are an island of goodwill surrounded by people who choose to cheat, exploit, harass, attack, misinform, and generally abuse each other. It seems that Africa, more than AIDS per se, is under assault in this novel.

II. *The Heaven Shop*

Unlike Stratton, Deborah Ellis does not have a multi-dimensional quarrel with Africa. Yet in *The Heaven Shop* she does set Africa apart from other regions on the grounds that African culture and AIDS interact uniquely with each other. She puts on display the way families consistently deny that AIDS has been involved with someone's death. Without success, a grandmother tries to reduce such denials by vehemently addressing the congregation at one son's funeral: "'We think that if we don't say it [AIDS], it will go away, but it won't go away ... [I]f a lion came into our village and carried away our young, ... [we would] bang pots and yell, 'There is a lion in the village!' ... There is a lion in our village now. It is called AIDS'" (70). Only when the man's orphans are parceled out, do the people openly face their fears: "'You brought AIDS home to live with us?' Aunt Agnes exclaimed. 'How could you?'" (85). Ellis brings various myths to the surface, as when Aunt Agnes' children are told to "keep their distance." "'There's no need to worry unless you touch them or drink out of the same cup'" (85). Readers are informed about the myth that someone can be cured by intercourse with a virgin. This belief has entered into the life of a thirteen-year-old girl by way of her father, and as a result the girl becomes pregnant by intercourse with the father's friend. Both the girl and her baby become HIV-positive.

Ellis weaves AIDS education into her narrative in a fairly unobtrusive manner; however, she goes to great extremes when depicting the isolation of a present-day community in Malawi. The rural district where Binti, the protagonist, ends up with her grandmother is unable to understand how a person whose voice they hear on the radio can be present among them. To be *this* pre-industrial means that people in this village will never have heard about how telephones work, or radios, TVs, motion pictures, or phonograph recordings. Binti has been the principal child actor in a radio program in Malawi's largest city, and while living with her grandmother (Gogo), the villagers are told, "'That's my Binti, talking on the radio.' ... People applauded. They wanted to know how she could be on the radio and sitting with them in Mulanje at the same time" (142). Why make such a stretch if one is only trying to suggest that AIDS education is lacking in the region? Why focus on the high value placed on schooling by Malawians, and then think readers will believe that schoolteachers are apparently uninformed about radios, and so forth? Either that or they simply have little close contact with the people they serve.

The ease with which Ellis unfolds her story points to Ellis' skills and to how needless are these exaggerations.

Multiple Themes: Disease Prevention, Hunger, Greed

Another way Ellis overdraws her point is in her treatment of every relative except Gogo. Ellis makes them as greedy and abusive as the proverbial "wicked stepmother," even on the day that Binti and her siblings are grieving over their father's death. Family members have little on their mind except confiscating the property and savings, and gaining control over the children as involuntary laborers. Even the girls' clothes are seized. Understandably the author is underscoring the tragedy facing AIDS orphans. Kwasi, Binti's brother, will end up in jail. Junie, her older sister, will be rejected by her fiancé, lose her chance to graduate from high school, and end up in a brothel serving truck drivers. And further spin-offs from the main events (the AIDS deaths) include Binti's loss of her job as the child actor in the popular radio show, loss of her education at a good private school, Junie's subjection to molestation by customers in her aunt and uncle's bar, and Kwasi's loss of opportunities to follow his one passion: drawing portraits and wildlife scenes.

As soon as Binti and Junie move in with the relatives owning a restaurant and bar, readers have a glimpse of the public's ignorance of AIDS. (Ellis also tries to repair that ignorance in an informational "Author's Note.") The cousins, as well as their parents, are afraid to touch their new lodgers and one young cousin freaks out over such fears. Yet at this stage of their new circumstances, Junie and Binti are not experiencing near starvation. Binti learns the torment of hunger only after she runs away (at Junie's insistence) and begins a new life at the home of the destitute Gogo. Granny has turned her rural home into a home for babies and young children who are AIDS orphans, and her only means of support has been the money donated regularly by Binti's now deceased father. So when Binti arrives, hunger and exposure to the cold weather are serious hazards. Even one meal a day is hard to come by, and in some seasons the children search for roots and other bush plants to help sustain them.

In a different setting, hunger is again highlighted when Kwasi steals food from an uncle who is now using him as a worker in his fishing business. The uncle deprives him of adequate food and then calls in the police to jail him for his theft of food. But hunger is even harder to avoid in the prison since the guards simply unload pots of food and leave it to the prisoners to fight over who will actually obtain a meal.

Malawi's status as something less than a viable nation-state is on display throughout the novel. The public hospital has too few beds, too few nurses, and a non-existent program for informing families about AIDS and the true condition of the hospital's patients. The public prison does not allow cases like Kwasi's to come to trial for years. People taking in AIDS orphans (such as Binti's grandmother) have no way to keep going once a generous supporter (Binti's father) also dies as an AIDS victim. And hovering over all these problems is the state's inadequate AIDS education program and health care system. AIDS is depicted as the ultimate culprit. Binti's mother dies when Binti is very young, then her father dies when Binti is thirteen, and then Junie ends up HIV-positive since the truck drivers at the brothel do not like to use condoms and lower their payments if this becomes a requirement. A traveling AIDS educator is Junie's new love interest, but he is HIV-positive also. Granny has been able to exert enough pressure on her greedy fisherman-son so that charges against Kwasi have been dropped. But after he joins Binti at Granny's home and helps set up a coffin construction business, he falls for the thirteen-year-old who is living with grandmother and who is HIV-positive (along with her baby). No one except Binti and Kwasi can hope for a long life. And Grandmother dies suddenly. No cause is mentioned but it is easy to feel her exhaustion and her disappointment over the abuse suffered by her grandchildren at the hands of her remaining offspring.

AIDS Proliferation: Social and Economic Underpinnings

What readers of this novel will not be given a chance to understand is that interpersonal relations are not the whole problem. Additionally, as studies of AIDS in Africa have shown, knowledge of the disease is not enough to stem its increase. What needs to be known is the role of poverty and, in particular, the relation between poverty and gender. Poor women are not in a position to refuse risky sex, and the greater the level of poverty, the less economic help women receive from their partners. This condition is connected with an unfortunate increase in the number of a woman's multiple partners and an additional risk from AIDS (Schoepf, 247–249).[3]

Disease epidemics of all sorts occur at times of economic crisis, and since the mid-1970s, sub-Saharan Africa has had chronic economic problems: more debt, more poverty, more inequality between social classes. It is crucial to understand that international lending organizations have exacerbated these conditions because the economies in Africa have been distorted by exports of a limited number of products—exports not easily sold when world markets are unfavorable. Furthermore, international policies dealing with "structural adjustment" (conditions attached to debt and development policy) "have redistributed wealth upward to local rulers and outward to international capital" (Schoepf, 248). Structural Adjustment Programs have mandated "the removal of subsidies for education and health" (Steady, 92). The meagerness of health services in *The Heaven Shop* reflects the national budget cuts that have followed in the wake of ill-designed international programs and world market agendas.

The practices of multinational corporations, the World Trade Organization, the World Bank, and the International Monetary Fund (among other global entities) have led to what some are calling "the new market imperialism" (Steady, 13). According to the United Nations New Agenda for the Development of Africa, economic growth declined from 5.3 percent in 1997 to 2.0 percent in 2000. Both rates are below the United Nations minimum of 6.0 percent. Filomina Chioma Steady notes that this decline is particularly noticeable in the area of health, one reason that African women's organizations are treating opposition to the global political economy as a high priority.

At the end of the day, authors who wish to write novels about AIDS and other forms of devastation in Africa need to start with at least some interest in this uncontested reality: "Sub-Saharan Africa is the only region of the world where poverty has been steadily increasing during the last two decades" (Steady, 142).[4]

III. *Story for a Black Night*

Clayton Bess joins the authors already mentioned by featuring families with exceedingly cruel members. And in this case, decisions by a family member have fatal consequences. Added to this plotline are Bess' occasional commentaries about environmental protection[5] and his continuous commentary on religion. He sees foolishness in African-based spiritual traditions, and with equal fervor he pinpoints the foolishness in Christian traditions adopted by African populations. This material comes into the foreground as characters struggle with feelings of guilt about their behavior, and also feelings about how *somebody's* God has been guilty of evil. A narrative about a sometimes fatal disease—smallpox—works effectively to showcase these improvisations about guilt. Smallpox is only *sometimes* fatal, so do you behave as if the odds are so great that you commit what is, in essence, voluntary manslaughter? In other words, intentionally killing someone but doing so because of mitigating circumstances (because some dangerous person has made you desperate, for example)? All the adult characters argue about this in a very colloquial setting and manner. Although their philosophical struggles are convincing, they do not offset Bess' additional theme about Africa as a benighted land—a place steeped in "Dark Africa" beliefs and conditions.

One Family and Two Views of "God"

Momo, the ten-year-old who joins other family members in experiencing smallpox, is also the forty-year-old Momo of the frame story—the taleteller who is informing his son about family history. In the first three pages he reflects upon God (e.g., the electrical current is "lost tonight because it can't stand God" [2]; preachers only talk about white-man stuff [Western religion] and I know as much as they do [3]; before the construction of a blacktop road, "all around us [the bush] was clean like God put it down" [3]). Old Ma (Momo's blind grandmother) then enters the story and Bess switches to ideas about "evil spirits" (e.g., a leopard close to the house signals such a spirit [5]; Mommy Water is a spirit that captures babies and drowns them [7]; shutters must be firmly locked to keep out night spirits [8]; Momo is fearful because there is "no reason for person to be outside with dark spirit walking" [9]).

All this is the backdrop for Ma's banning the Bible and refusing to allow Momo to attend school. Ma "put up her Bible after Pa was killed [by a snake bite]" and tells her son that the Bible has "only brought confusion" (10–11). Readers first learn how Ma adamantly refuses to let Momo attend school until the "mission people" have pestered her enough to cause a change of heart. And then she is just as adamant about saving the life of a smallpox-infected baby who is abandoned at her house after the babe's mother and grandmother receive refuge for a night.

Ma explains to Old Ma that she must take the risk of infection in herself and her own children because the baby is so small and "without guilt" (30). Old Ma is certain that death has arrived with this child. Old Ma, according to Momo's mother, can "never know [Ma's reasoning]. You never had book [Bible]" (29). It seems that everyone in the capital city, Monrovia, and all the people in the nearby town, Kataka, understand Old Ma's position, for they have used force to drive out the smallpox-ridden family. Kataka has a Bible-exhorting population, and the Reverend's wife and Musa (Ma's sister) intermittently invoke the name of Jesus. Ma, says the wife, must be a terrible sinner to suffer so severely from smallpox, while Musa is loved by God because she does not become infected, even when she rescues Ma from drowning and helps her through a worst-case experience with the disease.

Musa finally confesses that she sent the diseased family to Ma's farm, and while Musa is begging for forgiveness, Ma has another change of heart: "Musa, if I was well, I would kill you" (83).

Trying to explain these fluctuating decisions to a ten-year-old, and trying to explain that all Christians are "civilized," is not easy. But finally the women proclaim that they cannot understand each other. Ma simply says to her son, "'Confusion, Momo, ain't it?'" (89).

Mandigoes are a Muslim people in the region who are abused by the Kataka Christians, but Bess gives them the last word. A "Mandingo woman looked in Ma's one good eye" and wept glad tears. "'Oh,' she said . . . , 'you must give me your heart'" (97).

In developing the book's cultural context, the author is sorting out the religious questions while presenting Liberia as a nation of extremes and literal-minded thinkers. Whether the folklore is about Mommy Water or about newly acquired stories from missionaries, Liberians seem incapable of interpreting narratives in symbolic terms. Given this intellectual limitation, "Darkest Africa" is an ever-present theme. Everything that is not instantly explainable (a leopard standing at the edge of the yard, for example) is an evil sign. In essence, this turns Africa into a self-spooked society as well as a "primitive" population. It belittles one of the most richly symbolic folk literatures in the world, a literature that blends common human routines with astute psychological insights. When African nations are treated as "developing," it is often said by book reviewers that they are in a state of "transition." Nancy C. Hammond claims that *Story for a Black Night* shows the "moral conflicts and confusion of a culture in transition" (398). But what the Bess novel shows is an Africa that exists intellectually in a timeless state and minus any moral anchor. "Tradition" leaves Momo's family in a no-win impasse where both formal education and traditional spirituality threaten more than support people.

Hazel Rochman, the author of the Afterword in the 2004 edition, is apparently well satisfied with Bess' view of an ethically ambivalent continent. She asks, "What is right and wrong? What would you have done?" Child readers may wonder why answers presented by the novelist are so limited. They have been told that the capital city, Monrovia, is a place where the villagers go regularly for canned milk, kerosene for their lamps, and other supplies. It would not have been unthinkable to find medical assistance in this metropolis. It would not have been unthinkable to build a separate, quarantined lodging place for the afflicted mother and child rather than drive them into the bush or send them without warning to Momo's family. After all, in just one day villagers have managed to send needed supplies to build a separate room for Momo and reduce his exposure to smallpox.

Alex Boyd's review points to the book's ironic title: "It not only connotes the death of a few innocent, superstitious and frightened individuals, it also symbolizes the death of an innocent and beautiful land and its culture" (32). Here the "Dark Africa" myth is lauded rather than treated with the severe criticism it deserves. Boyd explains precisely what this novel is telling us. In brief, he says smallpox brings the death of people and Christianity the death of "a way of life of an entire society" (32). In fact, Africa has been known for its ease in blending Muslim, Christian, and indigenous belief systems. Robert Baum writes that "despite nearly a thousand years of contact with Islam, and nearly five centuries of contact with Christianity, African religions continue to address the spiritual needs of their adherents." And, moreover, "they have also influenced the practice of Islam and Christianity in Africa" (85).

* * *

Moral choices make good subject matter for storytellers, but the truism still holds that novelists need acquaintance with their story's setting on a number of levels. They need reliable sources as they delve into places they would illuminate for young readers.[6] In the twentieth century, Bess' Liberia looks like a place without the benefit of viable institutions. A stint in Western-style schools is quickly given a causal relationship with a fatal snake bite. The older generation considers its brand of "black magic" as the necessary education to pass along to children. The family's relatives in a nearby town are under the influence of a Christian preacher, and they seem to garble his already questionable interpretation of Bible-based precepts about sin. Where is the council of elders or other problem-solving institutions? How are just laws created and enforced? What ethical traditions have been operating in their society? Do Peace Corps volunteers arrive in Africa with any appreciation of its intellectual and spiritual foundations?

Works Cited

Baum, Robert. 2005. "African Religions: An Interpretation." In *Africana: The Encyclopedia of the African and African American Experience*, vol. 2, 2nd ed., eds. Kwame Anthony Appiah and Henry Louis Gates, Jr., 82–86. Oxford, UK: Oxford UP.

Bess, Clayton. 1982, 2004. *Story for a Black Night*. Boston: Graphia.

Boyd, Alex. 1983. Review of *Story for a Black Night*. VOYA (Voices of Youth Advocates), (February): 32.

Cashmore, Ellis. 2005. "Cultural Racism." In *The Encyclopedia of Race and Ethnic Studies*, ed. Ellis Cashmore, 96–98. London: Routledge.

Chirwa, B. U. and E. Sivile. 1998. "Enlisting the Support of Traditional Healers in an AIDS Education Campaign in Zambia." In *Progress in Preventing AIDS?Dogma, Dissent and Innovation; Global Perspectives*, eds. David Buchanan and George Cernada, 327–334. Amityville, NY: Baywood.

Ellis, Deborah, 2004. *The Heaven Shop*. Toronto: Fitzhenry & Whiteside.

Hammond, Nancy C. 1982. Review of *Story for a Black Night*. Horn Book 58: 4 (August): 398.

Hunter-Gault, Charlayne. 2006. *New News Out of Africa: Uncovering Africa's Renaissance*. Oxford, UK: Oxford UP.

Schoepf, Brooke Grundfest. 1995. "Action-Research and Empowerment in Africa." In *Women Resisting Aids: Feminist Strategies of Empowerment*, eds. Beth E. Schneider and Nancy E. Stoller, 246–269. Philadelphia: Temple UP.

———. 2005. "Acquired Immunodeficiency Syndrome in Africa: An Interpretation." In *Africana: The Encyclopedia of the African and African American Experience*, vol. 2, 2nd ed., eds. Kwame Anthony Appiah and Henry Louis Gates, Jr., 21–25. Oxford, UK: Oxford UP.

Shohat, Ella and Robert Stam. 1994. *Unthinking Eurocentrism: Multiculturalism and the Media*. London: Routledge.

Steady, Filomina Chioma. 2006. *Women and Collective Action in Africa*. New York: Palgrave Macmillan.

Stecopoulos, Harilaos. 2007. "Putting an Old Africa on Our Map: British Imperial Legacies and Contemporary US Culture." In *Exceptional State: Contemporary U.S. Culture and the New Imperialism*, eds. Ashley Dawson and Malini Johar Schueller, 221–247. Durham, NC: Duke UP.

Stratton, Allan. 2004. *Chanda's Secrets*. Toronto: Annick Press.

Chapter Ten
When the West Talks to Itself: Ethnocentricity in Nancy Farmer's "African" Novels[1]

> Colonialism is ethnocentrism armed, institutionalized, and gone global.
> —Ella Shohat and Robert Stam (16)

> [B]etter than the cannon, [schools produced by imperialists] made a conquest permanent. The cannon forces the body and the school fascinates the soul.
> —Cheikh Hamidou Kane (qtd. in Ngũgĩ, 9)

"Dark Continent" mythologies are throwbacks that continue to define Africa in the lives of Western schoolchildren. Nancy Farmer's novels, although strongly applauded in the West, illustrate this dilemma. They enjoy wide institutional support in Western book circles but offer few unbiased impressions of the region Farmer has chosen as subject matter. They illustrate how present-day fiction has a direct antecedent in colonialist popular culture. One could say Farmer exemplifies "the West talking to itself" (to quote Emmanuel Chiwome's quip about imperialist writers ["Foreword," vii]). Her portrayals of Africa in *The Ear, the Eye, and the Arm* (1994) and *A Girl Named Disaster* (1996) evoke memories of such Western crowd–pleasers as H. Rider Haggard's *King Solomon's Mines* (1885), Edgar Rice Burroughs' *Tarzan of the Apes* (1912), and similar nineteenth- and twentieth-century novels and films.[2]

Farmer's connection with pop cult predecessors is especially noticeable in her references to slavery and cannibalism as practiced in modern times. In

The Ear ..., she depicts slave-trading as an ongoing activity in the year 2194 in an imagined African nation (307). In *A Girl Named Disaster*, she uses her young protagonist to comment upon modern Mozambique as the possible home of cannibals. One must wonder how this eleven-year-old acquired such an outlandish fear of her neighbors. While cannibalism has been a stock ingredient in Western pulp fiction, this child character has had little contact with the West. Such irrational tale-telling, however, is not new, and Chiwome makes the point that imperial responses to Africa—that is, "Dark Continent" and "noble savage" myth-making—"tell us more about European mythology and ethnocentrism than about the African culture" (vi). Similarly Ella Shohat and Robert Stam comment, "the West organizes knowledge in ways flattering to the Eurocentric imagination" (14).

"Knowledge" in Farmer's novels flows through contradictory channels. On the one hand, glossaries, appendices, and bibliographies have been added to reinforce a sense of historical accuracy. On the other hand, the stories themselves lead in the opposite direction. The educational supplements are presumably useful as a way to counter ethnocentric biases, and thus *A Girl Named Disaster* has fourteen pages of factual reference material, including a fifty-title book list. In *The Ear* ... Farmer includes ten pages of definitions and cultural commentary, but her fictional narrative is largely at odds with the historical realities of the Shona linguistic group.[3] She describes, for example, "a terrible fate" for the child protagonists who are suspected of witchcraft and are being threatened with involuntary, lifelong residency in a traditionally organized Shona community:

> [Y]ou'll wish you died. You'll get food the goats wouldn't touch and the nastiest chores. But worst of all, people will hate you. They'll look at you with loathing for the rest of your days. It's a terrible fate. (159)

This notion about hateful people is a theme Farmer expands upon repeatedly. In fact Shona religious beliefs (with their basis in spiritualism) are portrayed as sadistic, and the group's social and civic structures are depicted as dysfunctional at best, malicious at worst. Put simply, the non-fiction material (intended to guide readers to more complete knowledge) runs counter to the novel and its distortions of cultural and social reality.

Before examining the two books in detail, it is worth mentioning some basic elements of culture formation. For example, a group's collective response to history and natural phenomena is reflected in its values and problem-solving strategies. The outcome includes physical, mental, and emotional endeavors that are typically relevant, evolving, dynamic, and not reducible to monolithic interpretations (Chiwome, vi). Farmer's cultural portraits could not be farther removed from this description of collective behavior.

Envisioning a Failed State: *The Ear, the Eye, and the Arm*

One ironic feature of this novel is the way Farmer's considerable imaginative gifts have been put to such misuse. Without doubt her creativity is impressive and well-suited to science fiction novel-writing. In this story she reverses the rags-to-riches formula, placing the pampered heroes in Dickensian predicaments. She sets up these latter-day Oliver Twists to face fearsome dangers and astounding technological wonders. The children reside in Zimbabwe's capital city, Harare, but we meet them in two politically resonant settings—the urban environment and a pre-colonial Shona society that exists in complete isolation within the city's borders. Both the ancient and futuristic landscapes are richly detailed. The world of 2194 is replete with highly advanced robots, antigrav pads (for landing flying vehicles), holoscreens (for viewing things three-dimensionally), triple-hardened titanium–molybdenum razor wire (for breaking house locks), and a variety of weapons (nirvana guns, soul stealers, etc.). Besides devising so many engaging contraptions, the author finds the means for introducing her perspective on social and political problems. Farmer's portrait of Zimbabwe implies that after two hundred additional years, we can expect this nation to exist in a state of utter chaos. Anarchy, criminality, privileges for officialdom, poverty for the homeless, and horrific levels of ecological neglect—these have become the norm. What underlies such an unrelenting picture of misery? What creates a perspective that is so focused on negative prospects and so oblivious to the impact of colonialism and neo-colonialism in Africa?[4]

Farmer's urban setting is in contrast to the agrarian, pre-colonial community that the author calls Resthaven. At first this traditional village looks as if it may be contrived as a foil for the futuristic scenes. Actually its pastoral aura relies upon descriptions of animals and luxuriant vegetation. The human inhabitants are the means Farmer uses to comment upon Africa minus European contact. Her interpretations touch upon marriage, child-rearing practices, medical remedies, religious ceremonies, and the alleged oppression of women (to name just a few "lessons" embedded in the Resthaven chapters). As the story unfolds, the children of the nation's security chief, Kuda (aged 4), Rita (aged 11), and Tendai (aged 13), are escaping from kidnappers. They beg for entry at the Resthaven gates, and from that point we see what a hellish set of rules and customs the Shona people have devised for themselves. Malevolent witch doctors and spirit mediums are busily manipulating ancestor worship and witchcraft accusations to intimidate the people. There is no effective government exercised by the chief or council of elders. Instead, community officials participate in the spirit medium's agenda of "pure hate" (153).

This narrative segment revolves around Rita and Tendai. Rita is our window on the Shona woman's backbreaking workload and on the machinations of a midwife. (Specifically, the midwife intends to murder the female twin born to the youngest wife: a fourteen-year-old.) We see the way witchcraft is used as a political tool and the way various witch-testing potions produce agonizing illness. We see the women engaged in sadistic practices (e.g., Rita's chest is burned by peanuts pulled from the fire [137], and the newborn female is having ashes shoved into her mouth when Rita intervenes [157]). Through Tendai we observe the ritualistic inter-clan fighting of the boys (135), the indolent lifestyle of the men, and the suspicion leveled at anyone not conversant with Shona folktales and proverbs. All told, this Resthaven subplot is perhaps the most paradoxical aspect of the book. On the one hand it expresses the author's apparent abhorrence of Shona customs, while at the same time it presents an elaborately woven set of images pertaining to Shona culture. The question, however, remains: How can Farmer (who lists African culture and history among her interests) offer such a distorted portrayal of cultural and social history? (*Something About the Author*, 56).[5]

Even a serious consideration of Shona art forms (e.g., praise poetry, proverbs, and folktales) could have steered her toward a different perspective. As it is, through Farmer's very selective examples, we see these aesthetic creations as largely a support system for spiritualism, or in the case of praise poetry, a device for mischievous manipulation. The Mellower, the praise poet who serves the Chief of Security, recites panegyric monologues on demand, thereby tranquilizing this official and his wife into a trance-like peace. In this way the Mellower can trick the minister and help his children escape from their safe but imprisoning compound. Once outside, the children fall into the hands of the She Elephant, a huge, drunken matron who sells children into slavery or else puts them to work in her underground waste dump. Three human mutants, the Ear, the Eye, and the Arm, enter the tale as detectives, employing their misshapen but efficient ears, eyes, and limbs in locating the children. They also indulge in the self-gratifying pastime of praise poems, but recognize the poems' enervating intoxication.

All this misrepresents Shona lyric poetry, but it follows a consistent pattern in the novel: that is, Farmer appropriates cultural materials and then uses them as a basis for sensationalizing the plot. The reality of lyric praise poetry includes its integration into daily Shona experience. Praise songs can be clan praises, personal praises (as in courtship), and praises that are formal salutes to rulers (Owomoyela, 44). Actually "every person has a role which entails poetry performance. . . . [It has] a symbiotic relationship" with corporate life (Chiwome, *Critical History* . . . ,17). Farmer mimics praise singing in the character she names the Mellower (an English-descended character with a *shave* embedded in him—i.e., a wandering spirit who can inhabit other identities).[6]

In the domestic sphere, a division of labor is equated with sexism, and Rita becomes the mouthpiece for a Westernized feminism:

"It's all right for you," said Rita tearfully. "You're a *boy*. You get to lie around listening to stories. I have to scrub the floor, wash clothes, sweep the courtyard, and—and—air out the babies' bedding. It's so horrible." (126)

Referring to the Shona diet: "'Our ancestors ate [fried mice], but our ancestors' *wives* had to kill them. You should have heard their little squeaks'" (126). Farmer sums up the division of labor: "Tribal law was perfectly clear on that point: boys and girls had different duties, and unfortunately, the nastiest ones fell on the girls" (127). One could just as easily make a list of male responsibilities and claim they represent "nastiness" and the exploitation of men. According to Oyekan Owomoyela, women had "full participation on a par with men, although in most cases genders operated as exclusive groups with discrete functions" (101). With the advent of European incursions, this equality was disrupted since Europeans confiscated the best lands and parceled out the rest to men. Women lost the full control of their own plots of land and suffered a reduction in status, self-esteem, and the wealth they were accustomed to using "as they saw fit" (101).

Women's prospects vis-à-vis marriage and child-bearing are another part of the skewed feminist subtext. Since the chief's first wife, Myanda, bore no children, "the Spirit Medium said she might be a secret witch. He said witches eat their own babies on the sly" (127). Myanda is forced into a phony witchcraft confession as a way to demonstrate remorse and thereby save herself from execution:

> Myanda writhed in agony ... "Yes! Yes! I am a witch! ... I rode hyenas after dark! I made *chidoma*, bogeymen, out of dead bodies. I caused Chipo to have twins! Augh! Augh!" Myanda scurried on hands and knees into the bushes. (168)

Given the many horrors of Resthaven (the place symbolizing traditional Africa), one must wonder why the Chief of Security does not intervene. Farmer explains this puzzle by having him describe Resthaven's "emotional appeal." It represents, he says, "the Heart of Africa." It is like Mecca for Muslims, Jerusalem for Jews, and Ayodhya for Hindus (148). But how could Africa's "heart" be anything but afflictive and deformed if Resthaven is its representative? This lapse in logic remains unexplained. However, Chinua Achebe's comment on Western xenophobia offers a clue: "[O]ne might indeed say [there is] the need in Western psychology to set Africa up as a foil to Europe, as a place of negations ... in comparison with which Europe's own state of spiritual grace will be manifest" (2–3). As for African spiritualism (and especially its "Medium Culture"), the novel's climax again introduces it as a ghastly way of life. By following the detective work of the Ear, the Eye, and the Arm, the reader meets the gangs that function as the primary villains, particularly "The

Masks." Gang members are possessed by demonic spirits, wear spirit-empowered masks, and devise a plan to murder Tendai in the hope that they can release his spirit as a messenger from one spirit world to another. The intent of this scheme (later aborted) is to gain more tyrannical power for the gang. Additionally, the Masks are in collaboration with the neighboring nation that practices slave-trading (the Gondwanna nation [307]). After a series of wildly phantasmagoric scenes, both the Gondwanna conspirators and the Masks are defeated, the Chief of Security adopts better parenting practices, the Mellower is marginalized, and the Arm gains a degree of normalcy when he adopts the girl twin rescued from Resthaven.

The story's sheer quantity of political and cultural insinuations is extraordinary. These insinuations are not introduced simply as products of imagination. Farmer herself insists that she is basing some material on documentary evidence (e.g., a British newspaper) and tells readers that present-day slavery on the part of Africans is a reality. In essence she is associating what she believes to be slave-trading during the Sudanese civil war with early forms of slavery as schoolchildren would superficially learn about them. Specifically Farmer cites the *Sudan Democratic Gazette* (March, 1993), which relates how children from sixty destroyed Nubian villages were distributed as slaves to fourteen Arab towns in the northern Sudan (308). This report does not provide readers with any understanding of slavery as practiced in different time frames, on different continents, or as connected with wartime measures. By positioning slavery as the work of modern Africans, the novelist misleads readers and capitalizes on the child's incomplete knowledge of this subject.

Is all this "a marvelous odyssey," a "rich tapestry," "a witty projection of the future," as *Kirkus Reviews* claims? (554). Can skewed history be justified when it serves an author's futuristic fantasy? Anne Deifendeiger, writing for the *Horn Book Magazine*, calls this work an "impeccable creation of the futuristic society" (597). She praises the "multiple sociopolitical aspects that parallel or are extensions of modern problems" (597–598). But in drawing that conclusion, she seems to accept as valid Farmer's interpretation of "problems."[7] In any case, with *The Ear*... dubbed "impeccable," Farmer pushed on with her next imperialistic novel.

Cultural Conflict and Distortion in *A Girl Named Disaster*

As in the Resthaven section of *The Ear, the Eye, and the Arm*, this novel includes a traditional community whose customs produce largely negative consequences. To be precise, Farmer uses her text to set up two explicit polarities. She depicts a clash between Christianity and a traditional belief system, and then she contrasts Western science with alleged African superstition. Even the few redeeming features that come into view—for example, folktales—maintain the focus upon spiritualism, although African stories are by no means confined to narratives about the supernatural.

In forcefully condemning spiritualism, Farmer makes her religionists either frauds or fools, and depicts an entire community as too irrational and too tradition-bound to oppose a malevolent *muvuki* (witch doctor). Eleven-year-old Nhamo is both the clan's and the witch doctor's victim as they attempt to appease an evil spirit that is producing a cholera epidemic. The various traditionalists line up against the child's protectors (Europeans, Christians, and a grandmother whose Western contacts suggest a potential means of escape). Highlighted specifically is a Portuguese trading post owner—a humane, generous, brave, friendly, child-centered colonizer. But since his attempts to save Nhamo fail, Grandmother urges the child to locate nuns in Zimbabwe and seek out her long-lost father. Western connections are vital to the plan (e.g., Nhamo's mother had attended a Catholic school, and her marriage to a Catholic means that Nhamo can claim Catholicism and challenge the authority of the witch doctor.) The "doctor" has presumably murdered his son as a means for gaining the boy's spirit-power. He allows only one form of compensation for a death caused by Nhamo's father: Nhamo must marry the slain man's brother and give her first son the aggrieved spirit's name. Trickery activates this scheme. That is, the witch doctor learns the family history and feigns the powers of a seer as he speaks of the family's past. Meanwhile Aunt Chipo fakes a fit, becoming "possessed" at an opportune moment. There is no sign of input from clan elders, no sign of communal organization and government, no process for arriving at just settlements. Grandmother can foresee only tragedy: Nhamo will "not last a year" in this marriage (85). Either her malicious husband will beat her to death or his three older wives will poison her.

After escaping by boat, camping out with island-marooned baboons, and finally reaching Zimbabwe, she simply finds more unfriendly (read: non-Westernized) Africans. She views the Mozambican fishermen on the beach as possible cannibals (216). And after coming ashore, the women she meets believe she may be a witch. This is no small matter since readers have already learned about the torturing of witches (e.g., sticks are used to poke out their eyes [35]). While Nhamo does escape to Zimbabwe, such scenes only reinforce spiritist beliefs as dangerous.

But she stumbles eventually upon a scientific laboratory and here the novel shifts to a commentary on Western science vis-à-vis African voodoo. The child begins her Western education among Shona, Matabele, and Tonga lab employees, and one Afrikaner doctor. Baba Joseph, an elderly lab worker, is used to highlight the contrast between so-called Western rationality and African backwardness. His followers belong to a sect that amalgamates Christian and traditional beliefs (the Vapostori sect), and although such an amalgamation is common in Zimbabwe, the Vapostoris are characterized as absurd and dangerous to their own well-being. They walk on hot coals, perform "weird music" (259), speak in tongues, and engage in ceremonies to exorcise demons. Baba Joseph says he recognizes a demon in Nhamo, and this is when Christian incantations (e.g., "I call on you false gods of Africa") are pitted against the traditional beliefs (260). In their state of religious confusion, the Vapostoris fall, stumble, throw themselves off a cliff, and are about to do worse damage to themselves when rescued by the Afrikaner doctor and an African colleague. The African doctor tries to explain where the problem lies with the Vapostoris: in Africa, the child's early lessons about ancestor worship and spiritualism remain with the child, mingling unsuccessfully with the teachings of Christianity (264–265).

A portrait of urban dysfunction concludes the novel. Nhamo is received reluctantly by her uncle's family, a group of nouveau riche snobs who made their fortune in a British-owned chrome-mining company. All they do is quarrel, drink, and abuse the son born to wife number two. At this point Farmer begins her extensive indictment of the Zimbabwean liberation movement. She mocks the war of independence as an event ungrounded in conviction, a struggle that is really just a matter of switching from one "fashion" to another. During the British period, the Murenga family has switched its name to Lloyd (the name of the chrome mine industrialist). The family has switched religions, becoming "Methodists when it suit[ed] them" (280). They refrained from polygamous marriages only as long as necessary. They treated great-grandfather as a "senile old peasant" (280), but when the insurgents began to win, the "senile old peasant" suddenly switched to "revered elder." A second wife again became permissible, and "it became unfashionable to have a white name" (281). "What wonderful luck!" observed the great-grandfather. "Lloyd-the-lackey turned into Murenga-the-revolutionary overnight. Oh he was first in line for the victory parades . . . " (281).

Since the great-grandfather is the one Murenga family member who befriends Nhamo, and since he is presented as more reasonable than the others, his lampooning of the national liberation movement serves to efficiently discredit that historical event. Great-grandfather is the voice of pure scorn when it comes to Black self-determination. Earlier in the novel Frelimo (the insurgent organization that came to power in Mozambique in 1974) received similar treatment. It was characterized as essentially foolish, an army with gun-toting women in pants, combatants "swaggering around like men," and soldiers setting off flares with no purpose but to scare people (48). Since the Portuguese trader was given a major role in trying to rescue Nhamo, it is not surprising that the novelist trivializes and mocks the war against imperialistic Portugal. Among the cultural weapons of the imperialist, writes Ngũgĩ wa Thiong'o, is the annihilation of "a people's belief in their . . . heritage of struggle" (3).

Even in devising a title, Farmer misuses an important tradition: the naming of children. Specific customs differ among Shona groups, but their naming practices express a positive intent; for example, children receive the names of an admired relative, or important events, or names expressive of good expectations for the child (Masasire, 47–48; Owomoyela, 113–114). When Farmer names her protagonist "Nhamo," meaning literally "disaster," "calamity," "misfortune," she is not taking account of such practices (Dale, 154; Hannan, 461). In the same vein, choosing "Nhamo" as a nickname is unconvincing since it is unlikely that a family would fasten on a child a constant reminder of her bereavement (loss of father and mother). In contrast to such imaginings, people in an extended Shona homestead typically take an interest in the children and provide practical child care as well.

All told, whether the subject is domestic life, politics, economics, or religion, Farmer manages to discredit African self-reliance and malign indigenous cultural practices.[8] Is this just a matter of adhering to the requirements of art? That *A Girl Named Disaster* depends upon the conventions of the adventure story is a "given." Accordingly the hero is beaten, bitten, scratched, stung, poisoned, shot at, starved, and otherwise tormented. Moreover, the wilderness setting goes a long way in making this mayhem persuasive. The white supremacy theme, however—the way Farmer is constantly structuring her readership's views of others—is not compelled by genre. By systematically treating African communities as alien to modern, viable, organized societies, Farmer implies an invidious distinction between European and African populations. Across centuries, that distinction has been repeated, as seen in Western literature and in the practice of Western literary criticism.

Haggard, Burroughs, and Farmer: A Century of Xenophobia

A century after H. Rider Haggard's *King Solomon's Mines*, Edgar Rice Burroughs' *Tarzan of the Apes*, and a continuing stream of imperialistic tales, Farmer produced her "African" novels. She took advantage of similar techniques and themes, using, for example, a prose style that is frequently characteristic of pulp fiction. This style is not hard to trace if we consider how easy it would be to exchange one "beastly" African for another in the following passages:

> [A captured French soldier watches his captors:] The bestial faces, daubed with color—the huge mouths and flabby hanging lips—the yellow teeth, sharp filed—the rolling demon eyes—the shining naked bodies—the cruel spears. Surely no such creatures really existed upon earth. . . ." (228)
>
> *Tarzan of the Apes*

> [O]ut of the masses of the warriors strange and awful figures came running towards us . . . (162). Quicker and quicker [one figure] danced, till she lashed herself into such a frenzy of excitement that the foam flew in flecks from her gnashing jaws, her eyes seemed to start from her head, and her flesh to quiver visibly.

Suddenly she stopped dead, and stiffened all over, like a pointer dog when he scents game ... (163–164).

King Solomon's Mines

He had a hard, bitter face, and his eyes were so bloodshot they were almost red. His clawlike hand grasped a walking stick carved into the shape of a serpent ... (153). "Eh!" shouted the Spirit Medium ... His arms jerked back and forth, and his feet smacked the ground, raising puffs of dust. "Eh! Eh! Eh!" He seemed to be on puppet strings. He lunged forward in grotesque spurts around the clearing. His head wobbled on his skinny neck, and his eyes rolled up until only the whites were showing (164–165).

The Ear, the Eye, and the Arm

In addition to such similar characterizations, statements related to local customs have often been similar. For example, Farmer's distortions of the division of labor are mentioned above, and here is Burroughs' take on that subject: "He noticed that the women alone worked. Nowhere was there evidence of a man tilling the fields or performing any of the homely duties of the village" (97). Whether writers are commenting upon employment, government, or family matters, they are apt to misrepresent complex social systems if they isolate one small piece of that system and give readers nothing more to go on. A bride price system, for example, is not conceived as a process for "forced marriages" when it functions to benefit the group's social and economic relations. It is not typically perceived as "forced" when brides and grooms generally agree about the good offices of their relatives in serving as marriage brokers. As for the legal system, grievances do not remain unresolved. Systematic rules for adjudication, including hearings and procedures for appealing decisions—these were not absent in pre-colonial Africa. "[I]n the end," writes Owomoyela, "traditional African life was organized to ensure the security, safety, and well-being of every human being" (111). Failing to recognize important "organizing" factors in an unfamiliar community, storytellers may spin their tale from a superficial base. Or their xenophobia may be ideological. "An ideology," writes Daniel Iwerks, "represents the fictions individuals create to allow them to 'mis'- interpret reality to their liking" (72).

In any case, colonialist ideologies in literature have had an enormous scope and duration. Their history is examined in studies such as Jan Nederveen Pieterse's *White on Black: Images of Africa and Blacks in Western Popular Culture*, Patrick Brantlinger's *Rule of Darkness: British Literature and Imperialism, 1830–1914*, and Jeffrey Richards' *Imperialism and Juvenile Literature*.[9] Typical misconceptions about Africa are identified:

- Africans are incapable of establishing functional, democratic governments.
- African nations do not become viable unless there is sustained pressure and influence from outside.
- African traditional religions are destructive to human life (a condition stemming from involvement with spiritualism).
- The polygamous family structure inhibits the achievement of amicable relationships and their promise of happiness.
- Africans try to imitate Western culture but only end up looking foolish.
- African orature is made of minor, shrilly didactic verbal forms.

In *Decolonizing the Mind*, Ngũgĩ observes that the colonized are induced to "see their past as one wasteland of non-achievement" (3). That "wasteland" myth remains largely unchallenged in the children's book establishment. But when young people *are* allowed a valid African literature, they will perhaps recognize the mock African imagery the West conjures for itself.[9]

Works Cited

Achebe, Chinua. 1989. *Hopes and Impediments: Selected Essays*. New York: Doubleday.
Brantlinger, Patrick. 1988. *Rule of Darkness: British Literature and Imperialism, 1830–1914*. Ithaca, NY: Cornell UP.
Burroughs, Edgar Rice. 1912. *Tarzan of the Apes*. New York: Grosset & Dunlap.
Chiwome, Emmanuel M. 1996. *A Critical History of Shona Poetry*. Harare: University of Zimbabwe Publications.
Chiwome, Emmanuel M. 1996. "Foreword." *Introduction to Shona Culture*. By Solomon Mutswairo, Emmanuel Chiwome, Nhira Edgar Mberi, Albert Masasire, and Munashe Furusa, v-viii. Kadoma, Zimbabwe: Juta Zimbabwe.
Dale, D. 1981. *Duramazwi: A Basic Shona-English Dictionary*. Gwelo: Zimbabwe: Mambo Press in association with The Literature Bureau.
Deifendeiger, Anne. 1994. Review of *The Ear, the Eye, and the Arm* by Nancy Farmer. Horn Book 70 (September-October): 597–598.
Farmer, Nancy. 1996. *A Girl Named Disaster*. New York: Orchard Books.
Farmer, Nancy. 1994. *The Ear, the Eye, and the Arm*. New York: Orchard Books.
Gelfand, Michael. 1962. *Shona Religion*. Cape Town: Juta & Company, Limited.
Haggard, H. Rider. 1989. *King Solomon's Mines*. Oxford: Oxford UP (World Classics). Originally published in 1885.
Hannan, M. 1984. *Standard Shona Dictionary*, Rev. ed. Harare and Bulawayo, Zimbabwe: The College Press in conjunction with The Literature Bureau.
Iwerks, Daniel. 1995. "Ideology and Eurocentricism in Tarzan of the Apes." In *Investigating the Unliterary: Six Essays on Burrough's* Tarzan of the Apes. Ed. Richard J. Utz, ed. 69–90. Regensburg: Verlag Ulrich Martzinek.
Kirkus Reviews. 1994. Review of *The Ear, the Eye, and the Arm* by Nancy Farmer. 62 (April. 15): 554.
Masasire, Albert. 1996. "Kinship and Marriage." In *Introduction to Shona Culture*, ed. Solomon Mangwiro Mutswairo, et al., 40–50. Kadoma, Zimbabwe: Juta Zimbabwe.
Mutswairo, Solomon Mangwiro. 1996. "The Mbire Hypothesis." In *Introduction to Shona Culture*, ed. Solomon Mangwiro Mutswairo, et al.,1–15. Kadoma, Zimbabwe: Juta Zimbabwe.
Ngũgĩ wa Thiong'o. 1986. *Decolonizing the Mind: The Politics of Language in African Literature*. London: James Currey; Nairobi: Heinemann Kenya; Portsmouth, N.H.: Heinemann.

Owomoyela, Oyekan. 2002. *Culture and Customs of Zimbabwe.* Westport, Ct: Greenwood Press.

Parravona, Martha. 1996. Review of *A Girl Named Disaster* by Nancy Farmer. *Horn Book Magazine* 72 (November): 734–735.

Pieterse, Jan Nederveen. 1992. *White on Black: Images of Africa and Blacks in Western Popular Culture.* New Haven and London: Yale UP.

Richards, Jeffrey, ed. 1989. *Imperialism and Juvenile Literature.* Manchester: Manchester UP.

Shohat, Ella and Robert Stam. 1994. *Unthinking Eurocentrism: Multiculturalism and the Media.* London: Routledge.

Something About the Author. 2002. "Nancy Farmer," v. 117. Detroit: Gale Group: 56–59.

Sutton, Roger. 1994. Review of *The Ear, the Eye, and the Arm* by Nancy Farmer. *The Bulletin of the Center for Children's Books*, 47 (March): 220.

Chapter Eleven
Child Soldiers and Survivors in *Chanda's Wars*

[My study of child soldiers] demonstrates the inability of governmental and international programs to deal with the serious problems of poverty and under-development that are at the origin of child soldiering and children's victimization by war.

—Alcinda Honwana (164)

Unfathomable violence is placed before the reader of Allan Stratton's *Chanda's Wars* (2008). And many sadistic actions referred to in the novel have been similarly reported in academic studies of child soldiers. Years of research by Alcinda Honwana have shown that most children were coerced into active wartime participation. As young soldiers they were themselves first brutalized to the point of submission and then forced to brutalize other civilians. Stratton faithfully works this pattern into *Chanda's Wars*, yet his novel misrepresents the wartime exploitation of children. Chanda is the appealing protagonist from *Chanda's Secrets* (Stratton's novel about AIDS from 2004), and in the new work she barely survives an international conflict that includes the kidnapping of her young brother and sister. In modern African wars, children as young as six years have been abducted, and when they were too young to be frontline combatants they became servants of combatants in a variety of ways. But there is a secondary story threaded through the novel, one that broadly indicts Africa in relation to traditional beliefs and customs, governmental malfeasance, and child abuse at the hands of close family members. Chanda and others are suffering as a result of such dysfunctions and cultural bankruptcy *before* they are presented to readers as the traumatized victims of war.

Modern History and the Vulnerability of Children

The increase in child soldiering in modern times stems in part from the way conflicts can now be defined as "irregular." That is, they lack a well-defined state sponsorship. Civil wars put children in a more vulnerable position, but beyond the internal dimensions of modern warfare, many young people face conditions that will start them on the path to child soldiering. Extreme poverty leads to the dissolution of communities, to erratic migrations, and to no options for children except to become "street" children in cities, or join gangs, or become members of local militia groups. These makeshift solutions stave off starvation, but still leave children severely victimized: deprived of education, jobs, health care, and acceptable prospects for the future. In the militia groups, recruits are sometimes forced to kill another child (even a brother or sister); girls are forced to become "wives" of soldiers; and younger girls are made to run errands and carry the loot obtained from raids. Not surprisingly, modern wars have been compared to organized crime.

Other underlying forces behind extraordinary violence in "new wars" include the practice of mutilation, the extreme rivalry over obtaining and trading valuable minerals (e.g., diamonds), ideological fervor and loyalty to a leader, and "assistance" supplied by mercenaries, professional strategists, global business and media establishments, and neighboring states (e.g., the Apartheid regime in South Africa systematically destabilized Angola and Mozambique). Also modern technology has played a part in child soldiering since lightweight weapons, grenades, and landmines are all easy for a child to handle.

Statistics about child soldiers in Africa include data from Mozambique (at least 10,000 child soldiers) and Angola (36% of children in 1995 had accompanied or supported soldiers). Other participants in "new wars" included Sierra Leone, Liberia, Republic of Congo, Rwanda, Burundi, Uganda, and Algeria. And worldwide, children have played a significant role in the Chinese Cultural Revolution (1966–1969), the conflicts in Northern Ireland, Sri Lanka, Bosnia, Palestine, Kashmir, Afghanistan, Peru, Nicaragua, Colombia, El Salvador, and so many other nations that the unprecedented number of child soldiers has been called "a defining feature of our times" (Honwana, 27).[1]

Chanda and Local Customs

As the novel opens, Chanda is experiencing nightmares that are not entirely related to her mother's death from AIDS. A neighbor therefore urges her to contact a traditional healer. In his first novel, Stratton put much emphasis on the wrongheaded practices of spiritist healers, and now he introduces the same subject as he begins his new book. "[She's] a fake," says Chanda while dismissing the idea of talking to Mrs. Gulubane, a local "spirit doctor" (8). The neighbor views the spiritist as an interpreter of dreams, and in relation to child soldiers traumatized by war, academic studies have had much to say in support of such traditional healing practices. Amadu Sesay and Wale Ismail note that African culture in general is a necessary element in the rehabilitation of child soldiers, and it is especially important to employ the skills of traditional healers. This recommendation is based on these healers' grasp of the specificities of the culture and upon a centuries-long record of healing mental health problems (168). Similarly, Honwana writes that "the use of indigenous approaches to healing is necessary in order to address people's perceptions and understanding of their [children's] afflictions" (163). Expanding on this point about children in wars, Irae Baptista Lundin notes that "African culture is replete with rituals of reconciliations, in which dances, songs and other collective actions help to heal abused and afflicted souls, [and] these are playing a role in the process of healing and reintegrating those very young men and women ..." (2). For successful intervention programs on behalf of ex–child soldiers, Honwana urges the international community "to go beyond Western psychotherapy and universalizing notions of childhood" (163). On the contrary, in *Chanda's Wars* the novelist uses the narrative to channel his Eurocentric biases about African ritual and religion.

Stratton makes intermittent jabs at African spirituality,[2] but he spins off his whole plot from his objection to African marriage customs. Chanda's mother was victimized by these practices, and now Chanda and her siblings are pulled into the ongoing war because like her mother, Chanda refuses to accept a marriage "package." This matrimonial scheme would rob her of her land (the inheritance from her late mother) and also deprive her of the future she chooses for herself (a college education and career). Her grandparents, aunts, and uncles are depicted as virtual thieves vis-à-vis Chanda's belongings, and as this plotline unfolds, we meet the man whom her mother had once been instructed to marry—a man who has become a chronic wife beater and child abuser.

The Plot

Prior to witnessing the action occurring in the war zone, readers follow Chanda and her young siblings to the cattle outpost where her late mother's family members have lived for generations. A neighbor believes that Chanda's nightmares may have some connection with a feud resulting from her mother's elopement with a man of her own choice. At first Chanda is too overcome with grief and bitterness to accept this suggestion. After all, her mother had been placed to die in an abandoned outpost hut, and only Chanda's intervention and some help from a nearby clinic had enabled her to return her dying mother to her home in the city. There she lives her last days among her devoted children. Nonetheless, Chanda finally concludes that her mother would want a family reconciliation, and initially Chanda is relieved to discover that her relatives are not as bad as she had believed. That is, they are remorseful about the ill treatment of the dying AIDS victim and they express a genuine affection for Chanda and her young brother and sister (Soly and Iris). All is well until a family palaver includes a request that Chanda marry the neighbor's son and transfer all rights to her urban house and land to the family (supposedly a transfer of property that would constitute her dowry). She will then live out her life at the cattle outpost and its adjacent village. Chanda's own plan, and the one her mother worked to achieve for her, included a secondary education, a scholarship, a career as a lawyer or doctor, and the creation of a settlement house for AIDS victims. After telling off her relatives and making preparations to leave, rebel soldiers from the neighboring nation attack her family, burn her grandfather alive, capture and stone to death one aunt, abduct Soly and Iris, torch the village, and engage in other hit-and-run operations nearby.

During the assault, Chanda has been on her way to visit for the last time the abandoned hut where her late mother was left to die. Luckily the young man she has rejected as a husband has found her there and hides her from the vicious rebel commandant. The rag-tag army has camped at the deserted outpost in order to terrorize and brand the latest group of child recruits. Chanda goes with Nelson (the undesirable but soon desirable "love interest") as they search for Soly, Iris, and nine-year-old Pako (Nelson's youngest brother). We watch the fate of Pako in particular since he suffers the most: first from beatings by his father and two older brothers, then from unspeakable violence at the hands of the rebel leader: amputations of a victim's hands, murders by stoning and kicking a victim, a family burned alive in their home, and the fatal shooting of Pako's own brothers when the commandant so orders. After finally escaping to a safe place with Nelson, he kills himself rather than embark on the healing process that Nelson is desperately trying to arrange for him.

Stratton clearly takes the side of African children, but his Western perspective turns up repeatedly in ways that debase African society. It would seem that African children must reside anywhere but in Africa since their relatives are either dangerously abusive or dangerously passive in the midst of such abuse. Throughout the story African culture and social and political policies are described as intolerable. Stratton's Africa is an intellectual and moral wasteland. His accusations target communally planned marriages, "spirit doctors," domestic violence, and government officials who tell the public lies to protect their own possession of "limos and mansions" (55). When presented as the total African world, such a scenario works as an implied justification for

Western interference in Africa. With the exception of one school teacher and one schoolmate (in addition to her mother), Chanda is surrounded by foolish or obnoxious people in the first "Chanda" novel, and by a similar cast (with the exception of the "love interest") in the second novel. A few short-lived reformations occur in *Chanda's Wars* (e.g., one of the "bad" aunts befriends little sister), and a friendly safari guide and storekeeper have been added as minor characters. But these bright spots do not outweigh the corrupt, inhumane armies in both warring nations, the relatives who are mainly interested in exploiting Chanda, and the sadistic practices that Stratton treats as the norm rather than the exception.

As noted above, the history of modern wars includes an unprecedented scale of brutality. And considering the frequent use of child soldiers, Stratton's interest in this theme is understandable. But at the same time what responsibility does this choice entail? What might Stratton have written if he had placed some value on the many contemporary studies of indigenous African populations? Alcinda Honwana writes that a great need is "in reinforcing norms and value systems for child protection based on indigenous local worldviews and meaning systems" (47). An "indigenous worldview" is what Stratton downgrades in his "Chanda" novels.

The war-scape is his focus. But it is worth noting that in the actual Africa, it is often *hunger* that leads children to beg for food among rebel and government combatants, and this results in being seized for involuntary military service. Here is a line of cause and effect that storytellers have yet to probe.

Treaties and Other Transnational Influences

International law addresses the child soldier problem in the UN Convention on the Rights of the Child (1989), the Organization of African Unity's Charter on the Rights and Welfare of the Child (1990), the International Criminal Court's Rome Statute (1998), and the International Labor Organization's Convention on the Worst Forms of Child Labor (1999), among other legal initiatives. *Chanda's Wars* is sometimes in line with the spirit of these treaties, all of which repudiate the enlistment of young people under the age of either sixteen or eighteen for use in armed conflicts.[3] But other aspects of the novel contradict the international mandates, as when Stratton disregards Article 29 of the UN Convention, which requires respect for the child's cultural identity and values. Also this Article mandates respect for the national values of the country where the child is living, the country from which he or she may originate, and the civilizations different from his or her own (UN Convention, 13). In other words, the daily life of a child has crucial importance; it directly impinges upon the safety of the child or, conversely, the likelihood that a child will be swept into a child army.

Article 30 states another law that Stratton has disregarded—namely, that where there are persons of indigenous origin, "a child ... who is indigenous shall not be denied the rights, in community with other members of his or her group, to enjoy his or her own culture, to profess and practice his or her own religion, or to use his or her own language" (UN Convention, 13–14). As noted above, the novelist castigates traditional religions, healing practices, and marriage customs without taking the trouble to supply context or examine the way "rights" can sometimes cancel each other out. In Article 42, signatories are bound by its provisions to "make the principles and provisions of the Convention widely known ... to adults and children alike" (UN Convention, 17), but this point has apparently been less than successful in implementation. In any case, Stratton's novel has nothing positive to say about African indigenes, much less any awareness of their "rights." And Stratton's position is at odds with the scholarly works on child soldiers that show how traditional societies are the key to preventing child vulnerability and to succeeding with a child's rehabilitation. Sesay and Ismail have urged "government[s] and communities to reinforce the traditional societal norms that had broken down as a result of the horrific atrocities that were committed during the war and which had seriously undermined traditional value systems in the country" (155). Canada, to its credit, signed the 1989 UN Convention along with every other nation except two: Somalia and the United States.

With regard to other aspects of war, the novelist explains the intransigence of the warring parties by noting that neither nation wanted an end to hostilities. On the rebel side, the leader would be killed if captured; on the government side, the government doesn't want peace because foreign funds would be canceled—funds for fighting terrorists (55). Actually the government uses the funds to support its own members' extravagant lifestyles. In short, foreign money fuels the war, but more important to local officials is the way cash is at hand to line their own pockets. Stratton's point about such wartime graft is well taken, but as mentioned on an earlier page, specific to the civil wars in southern Africa is the destabilization of Angola, Mozambique, and other states by the Apartheid regime (Máusse, 6). A reader's understanding is incomplete without this knowledge. It is incomplete without knowledge of the mercenary forces that splintered off from South Africa's "Special Forces" following the 1994 election—forces central to the conflicts and the use of thousands of child soldier combatants in Sierra Leone and Liberia. Understanding is incomplete if young people do not know about the land mines and lightweight guns being trafficked throughout the region by a variety of nations. And perhaps most important, local wars of the sort Stratton alludes to have become examples of the "privatisation of violence"—the process that involves the massive looting of minerals, the use of external military experts, the ill-informed reportage from non-African media, and the targeting of civilians as a matter of *theory* as well as practice (Honwana, 32–34).[4]

The novelist provides a long list of sources, including interviews with officials and NGO volunteers, but there is not much evidence that he actually utilized those sources. Perhaps the informants were less than forthright, or unfamiliar with how writers for teenagers might need their assistance. Either way, children have remained disserved.

In *Voices of Youth Advocates* (*VOYA*), however, this novel is called a "masterpiece." Amy Fiske focuses her attention on Chanda as a young woman with "courage and strength . . . tenderness and vulnerability" (534). This is a persuasive description, but Fiske is ignoring Stratton's profile of fictionalized African nations. The critic speaks of how the chief characters will succeed because "beauty will win," even in "unlikely situations." Yet the two warring nations in Stratton's portrayal are anything but beautiful, and their grotesqueness is treated as a likely, not an unlikely, condition. The Fiske critique must, therefore, be again referring to the appealing Chanda, who can be expected to survive despite the cruelty, corruption, and malfunctioning of African nations. Fiske continues her commentary by commending the author for a story "ripped-from-the-headlines," and herein resides a clue to the problem. If authors and critics keep abreast of African affairs by way of the Western press, then we cannot expect much from them. Opportunities to responsibly depict Africa will continue to be squandered.

* * *

Two political points run through Stratton's story as he makes Chanda an observer and potential captive in a rebel army. He shows the most grisly aspects of war when depicting a marauding militia from a neighboring country. And simultaneously he reveals the government of the defending nation as steeped in corruption and self-serving maneuvers that will preserve the officials' privileged lifestyles. These institutional attacks against one's own population look less violent than actual destructions of lives, but there is no real security under extreme government malfeasance. In the novel it is Chanda's home government that is warned of the upcoming massacre in the town where her relatives live, yet the officials take no preventive action because they are unsure about what will transpire and "they don't want to be blamed" (214). Thus great loss of life occurs (including people being burned to death) where this may have been avoided. In the end then, no African government is revealed to readers as just (or even less than dangerous), and Chanda and Nelson will live through their teen years in threatening, risk-filled surroundings. We see them at Chanda's house, planning to become a couple after Chanda fulfills some of her dreams about life as an educated woman. But readers are given only a Western colonialist interpretation of how a twenty-first-century Africa operates—how it is ungovernable if self-governed. Like unnecessary wars, this perspective is an invidious, unnecessary mistake.

Works Cited

Convention on the Rights of the Child. 1989. U.N. document A/RES/44/25 (12 December 1989). http://www.cirp.org/library/ethics/UN-convention

Fiske, Amy. 2008. Review of *Chanda's Wars* by Allan Stratton. *VOYA (Voices of Youth Advocates)* 30: 6 (February): 533–534.

Honwana, Alcinda. 2006. *Child Soldiers in Africa*. Philadelphia: University of Pennsylvania Press.

Lundin, Irae Baptista. 1999. "Overview." In *Child Soldiers in Southern Africa*, ed. Elizabeth Bennett, 1–3. Halfway House, South Africa: Institute for Security Studies.

Máuse, Miguel A. 1999. "The Social Reintegration of the Child Involved in Armed Conflict in Mozambique." In *Child Soldiers in Southern Africa*, ed. Elizabeth Bennett, 5–41. Halfway House, South Africa: Institute for Security Studies.

Sesay, Amadu and Wale Ismail. 2003. *Civil Wars, Child Soldiers and Post Conflict Peace Building in West Africa*. Obadan, Nigeria: College Press.

Stratton, Allan. 2008. *Chanda's Wars*. New York: HarperTeen.

Part III
Rewarding the Best

Chapter Twelve
Out of Bounds and the Legacy of South African Child Martyrs

[African literature] is written out of the emotional, intellectual and physical experience of an African people, fashioned by their cultures. The writer's sensibility must be ... defined by African life that is committed to African soil. ... [A]s whites native to Africa have never, as a group, shared the African's indigenous culture, we need to observe the culture that they *do* practice.
—Ezekiel Mphahlele (13)

A great deal of the "people's revolution" ... was led by or involved [Black] children under eighteen years.... [They] were operating under their own wisdom and intuitions, against an oppressive regime.
—Daniel Nina (45)

Beverley Naidoo is a White woman native to Africa—one whose experience has not been defined by an African cultural tradition, but *has* been "committed to African soil." In *Out of Bounds: Seven Stories of Conflict and Hope* (2001), we glimpse the Apartheid ideology embraced by most South African Whites, and we see the author's anti-Apartheid perspective, a political stance that landed her under house arrest at the age of twenty-one and then in exile beginning in 1965. Had Naidoo been typical of South African White children, she would have remained "under the umbrella of the state and institutions of socialization such as the church." She would have grown up "driven by the need to defend the nation from an imminent 'communist attack'" (Nina, 44).[1]

Historical veracity is a distinguishing feature of the *Out of Bounds* collection, but most extraordinary is the psychological dimension. This allows readers to become effortlessly engaged with the child characters. Unmistakably, Apartheid created unique problems in a child's development. As a philosophy and way of life, it was morally contradictory, and placed children in situations where there were no winning options. Naidoo's collection illustrates the way this happens. It pinpoints numerous means by which an Apartheid-ruled society socialized its youthful population.

The author's treatment of place is an important feature in the most effective stories. Mphahlele has noted: "An aesthetic begins with the very dust you kick around," with "all the benevolence and tyranny you get from it" (15). No formula will succeed in stirring up such "dust," but firsthand experience contributes to a writer's sensibilities in relation to place. We have selected five stories that illustrate this point. They are all grounded not only in Naidoo's vantage point as a protester within South Africa, but also in the role children increasingly played in the anti-Apartheid resistance movement. From her home in exile (i.e., London), Naidoo learned of the government's 1976 massacre of 104 Soweto students under sixteen years of age. In this chapter we will consider this incident as part of the historical background for the *Out of Bounds* collection. But first a look at the stories.

"The Dare"

Wide class disparities are consciously felt and acted upon by four White children in "The Dare." Brutal punishments and White-over-Black control are connected with their world, but both the lower- and upper-class protagonists take their race-based superiority for granted. Their differences in economic status, however, have become increasingly troubling. Children apparently have a sixth sense about their own self-respect, and Naidoo indicates how they will fight hard and ingeniously to defend it. The cast includes Veronica (an upper-class urban child) and three Afrikaner children whose small farm serves as a "bed and breakfast" hideaway for the rich (Veronica's parents). Having reached the upper primary school grades, the less well-off children now begin to observe closely the unfairness embedded in their working-class lives. Consequently they devise a simple scheme to retaliate: they dare Veronica to steal a poinsettia blossom from the neighboring farm (a posh orange-growing plantation with a mean-spirited owner).

Veronica's exaggerated fear of the plantation owner is entirely credible, given a child's inexperience in the world and given the way the rich farmer has been demonized by the poor farmer's offspring. Additionally, Veronica has become alarmed by secretly watching the man beat a young Black child accused of stealing. Her stomach heaved as the "boy's cries pierced her ears" (15), but when her own theft results in a mere pat on the head (the rich man has mistaken her for his neighbor's child), she rejoices in being one-up on her playmates. In fact, she will now press her advantage by ripping off *four* poinsettia blossoms. She will even consider stealing *oranges*!

Without any direct references to race and class privilege, Naidoo sketches scenes that enable us to experience children as children, while also seeing Apartheid as "apartness," as the total separation of Whites from non-Whites. We watch what Veronica does after being warned that she must *never* enter the living quarters of the maid. This servant has spent months creating a quilt for her bed, and Veronica will give her no peace unless she is allowed to see the beautiful quilt in its final location. In this incident, we see a child's development being wrenched in opposite directions: she is duty-bound to maintain her separateness from the maid, but her sense of reason puts her mind to work in contriving ways to counter this separateness.

Naidoo is subtle in creating a story that is essentially issue-oriented, but still lets the differences among the children emerge through characterization—especially through their developing class-based rivalry. Veronica's lower-class counterpart, Marika, opens the story by showing off her latest trophy—a snake (very poisonous!) floating in the green liquid used for corpses. Marika's accounts of bravery have become more and more dramatic during Veronica's intermittent visits. Now she joins her brothers in the unfriendly dare—a game with only unpleasant results: that is, punishment from a cruel neighbor or exclusion from all the interesting escapades of the "bed and breakfast" children.

Readers will observe the fractured relations of sensitive children when their unequal economic position suddenly dawns on them. And at the same time, these children relish their alleged superiority over indigenous Africans. Apartheid allows no doubts on this score.

"One Day, Lily, One Day"

Again a friendship is unsustainable under Apartheid. This time "best friends" become enemies when their parents end up on opposite sides of government policy. Lily and Caroline had been sharing a double desk since their first days in school. They had been dubbed Snow White and Rose Red by their Grade One teacher. But Lily's father is a doctor who befriends and treats Black patients, invites them to political meetings at his house, and ends up being repeatedly arrested. Caroline's parents are shocked out of their wits. They believe the government's claims that Blacks are communists, or at least far Left in outlook—people who in all probability are terrorists. Still, the parents do not openly split the friends apart. Instead, Caroline gradually absorbs her parents' and teacher's perspectives and selects a new "best friend." She's had enough of Lily when she hears the school radio reporting that "The natives are coming to attack us. They're on their way now" (60). To keep her safe,

Caroline's mother picks up Lily at school and drives her to her own home, but Lily hardly feels protected when Caroline questions her angrily: "The natives are dangerous. How come you don't know?" (64).

Street demonstrations and an official state of emergency are occurring offstage in this story, but a young child's emotional and mental turmoil is persuasively revealing itself. How can Lily believe that "natives are dangerous" when so many are her parents' friends? How can Lily believe the police when they have shot Busi, the child of her Black nanny's cousin? Why was it that only Lily's father had been willing to rescue Busi from a dangerous fever? Why is Lily left with fewer and fewer White friends at school, but given no opportunity to make friends with Black children? Why are Lily's parents, due to their active political agenda, willing to end up in jail and risk leaving Lily and her brother abandoned? Lily asks her mother, "Don't we matter?" (70). Mom's reply is accurate, but hardly comforting: "But what about Uncle Max's children? [Uncle Max is Lily's special Black friend.] And all the other children in this country—like Busi? Don't they matter too?" (70). Why is Lily in the emotionally wrenching position of hearing Blacks bad-mouthed at school, while she is left searching (unsuccessfully) for some way to reply?

Caroline's confusion contrasts with Lily's, but illustrates how a child in an Apartheid-supporting family can be deeply disturbed by an anti-Apartheid family. Carolyn sees Uncle Max inside Lily's house and is convinced that a thief has broken into the building. And like her mother, Caroline does not believe a Black servant should be allowed to accompany Lily home from school. Like her mother, Caroline sees more and more reason to believe the government's "protective" measures, since surely innocent people are not locked in prison for months (the way Lily's father is repeatedly punished). And given the pro-Apartheid propaganda all around her, it is not surprising that Caroline is totally unstrung by the blaring radio message: "The natives are coming . . ." (60).

Naidoo's depiction of Caroline corresponds with what psychiatrist Robert Coles discovered in his many interviews with South African children, which began in 1974. Twelve-year-old Petrus would probably have been as unnerved as Caroline in hearing that the "natives are coming." He tells Coles that "there are millions of them in those countries to our north. . . . They want to take away what we have here, . . . they want to walk in and take it all away" (188). Moreover, in the townships "they're very bad; . . . they cut each other up" (187).

In order to collect such youthful Afrikaner impressions, as well as the ideas of Black children, Coles needed to visit families in the segregated White and Black neighborhoods. He managed this despite the laws that made it illegal for a small white group to enter Soweto or other townships. While such Apartheid laws were designed to prevent unfavorable publicity, as it turned out, it was conversations with White children in Coles' case studies that exposed racism in Apartheid school and family settings. His child respondents were candid and especially open in reporting the fearsome warnings given by their parents about "the natives."

"One Day, Lily, One Day" does not exaggerate the likelihood that Lily's parents will have frequent run-ins with the "security forces." Robert Coles says that he "fear[s] he can't explain fully how we managed to do it [avoid being arrested]" (16).

"The Typewriter"

Children in this story are essentially proxy "soldiers," not unlike another type of quasi-soldier: that is, local police officers who were really a paramilitary force. No officially declared civil war existed in South Africa, but confrontations in the urban districts were important to the momentum leading to Apartheid's overthrow. Since Apartheid touched every conceivable sector of the community, it is not surprising that local issues (e.g., Afrikaans being mandated as the language in half of the secondary school classes) sparked school boycotts and murderous retaliations by the police. The subtitle for "The Typewriter" is simply "1976," the year when more than one hundred Soweto students were gunned down by the government.[2]

Nandi is eleven years old and is babysitting her siblings when high school marchers come past her Soweto house. They carry banners with the slogans "Down with Bantu education!" and "Down with white rule!" "Bantu education" was the official designation for curricula offered to indigenous Africans (73). The young marchers are trying to attend the funeral of two classmates that the police had killed the week before. Tear gas, a tank, and swarms of police halt their march while the police shoot and kill three more students. Since Esther (Nandi's cousin) is one of the protesters, the plot centers on her activities and those of her guardian-grandmother: Khulu.

The wounded Esther wakes Nandi in the middle of the night and asks her to find the typewriter used in producing leaflets. She has hidden it in Khulu's kitchen and wants it destroyed before it leads the police to Khulu and to the punishment her grandmother can expect at the hands of the "security forces." In the end, Esther escapes capture, but Khulu is caught as she disregards her granddaughter's request about destroying the typewriter and tries, instead, to hide it in a White woman's garage. She tells Nandi that Esther and the other protesting students will need it at some future time. In this plot twist Khulu is defined by Naidoo as another "marcher" on behalf of freedom. She has been one for most of her sixty-eight years. The connection between Nandi, Esther, Khulu, and Nandi's mother is close and is clearly grounded in their anti-Apartheid solidarity. We see the extent of grandmother's activism when a newspaper announces eight months later that a grandmother has been convicted for refusing to testify against Esther's friends, against two classmates charged with "sedition and terrorism." Moreover, further charges against

Khulu may result from her possession of the weapon the government most fears: Esther's typewriter (94–95).³

The matter-of-fact treatment of each scene, as suggested above, is characteristic of Naidoo's style. She illustrates that for storytellers "less is more." She stops short of giving readers the grisly details about Soweto, or editorializing about the four strong women, young and old, who are central to this narrative. Even the police are largely offstage, except for one who impudently swipes a stalk of bananas from the fruit basket balanced on Khulu's head. (Khulu is a fruit vendor.) For an explicit treatment of the theme, we are offered only the song Nandi and other protesters sing:

> We are the young people,
> We will not be broken!
> Come with your cannons,
> Come with your guns!
> We demand freedom
> And say
> "Away with slavery,
> In our land of Africa!" (75)⁴

"The Gun"

"Homeland" injustice and deprivation provide this story with its principal plotline. Thirteen percent of South Africa had been set aside as reserves (i.e., "homelands") for Blacks, but in 1959 this policy was fine-tuned in the Promotion of Bantu Self-Government Act—a means by which anyone who was not clearly White could be technically transformed into a "foreigner." This Bantustan plan was sometimes called "Grand Apartheid," based as it was on the idea that "there was no African majority in South Africa" (Terreblanche, 321). The government reasoned that numerous indigenous ethnic groups were really "Bantu," not South African, and thus their citizenship should be exercised exclusively in the "homelands." For Apartheid officialdom, the beauty of this system included the fact that now Blacks could be deported without the right of legal appeal. Also, the influx of Black Africans into the cities could be more efficiently controlled, as could the way "homelands" could be turned into labor reservoirs for the benefit of Whites.

At the outset, the Black protagonists in "The Gun" have a fragile but workable means of making a living. The father of fifteen-year-old Esi works as a tracker and security guard on the large country estate of a White man who likes to hunt. The townspeople hate this Black African—this one-person police force—who is keeping them from poaching on the estate, a practice they engage in only out of sheer necessity. In general, people on the reserves suffer from malnutrition, stark poverty, and little chance of subsisting on overcrowded, denuded land (Terreblanche, 325). Esi joins his aunt's household in the city in order to attend school, but he becomes so weak and so ill from malnutrition that his father brings him home again to the hunter's estate. He will teach his son to be his assistant and learn to track both game and poachers.

This is, at least, a survival plan, but it falls apart when the rich hunter decides to let his neighbor's relative live permanently and take charge on the estate. This new manager is an openly outrageous racist, but Esi and his family endure the abuse until the young bigot decides to go hunting and bring Esi along as his guide and tracker. When the man accidentally shoots himself in the foot, Esi takes away his gun. Then he heads for the border to join those in the resistance movement who are stationed in neighboring countries.

This tale is persuasive in revealing how people can exercise much patience in the face of maltreatment, yet a breaking point can be almost instantaneous when an escape route suddenly opens. Again, Naidoo's style is low-keyed. Explanations do not encumber the unfolding plot and yet survival strategies (no matter how bad the conditions) become entirely convincing. Emotional tension builds gradually as a family tries to hold together, while Apartheid is allowing few prospects for success. Esi has discovered that although his father's struggle to sustain family life in the face of unreasonable bosses seemed reasonable to him at the outset, there came a point of no return. And for an adolescent in an exceedingly devoted, self-sacrificing family, the moment of separation does not come easily.

The economic backdrop for this story is suggested by historian Allister Sparks when he notes that the "entire black population, wherever they lived, became economically dependent on the cities" (49), since migrant labor policies reduced Black families to inadequate subsistent levels. In Naidoo's story, most of the Black men work in mines—a job that keeps them far from their families and pays so little that the miners are unable to contribute financial support. The Land Act of 1935 allowed thirteen percent of the space for seventy-five percent of the population and this could only result in overcrowding, land erosion, rigid control of employment and housing, and the end of Black commercial farming (Sparks, 48–49). Gregory Maddox also makes this point, noting that "the demand for labor in diamond and gold mines, as well as Afrikaner farms, led to a policy of strangling potential peasant production in order to keep labor costs down" (xiv). Women were left to grow food on inadequate land and thus forced to move their families to "the same land their ancestors had, but now as squatters on white-owned farms with an uncertain tenure and subject to heavy labor demands" (xv).[5] At the end of the day, Blacks were "supposed to stay in their own little tribal 'homelands,' which were one day supposed to become independent, leaving the greater part of the country as the white man's land" (Sparks, 21). Everyone knew, of course, that to expect some future Bantustan independence was to harbor an illusion. The South African economy depended on Black labor, and from the standpoint of the

White minority, the more flexible and underpaid was the migrant labor force, the better!

"Out of Bounds"

In the book's final story, Naidoo utilizes the catastrophic floods of the year 2000 as a plot device, and on every page finds ways to illustrate the continuing struggle against "apartness." Now we see an Indian family, still within their own separate community, but economically better off than Africans in an adjacent squatter camp. Twelve-year-old Rohan no longer attends his previous school since "squatter" children are now enrolled there. His family has built a high wall around their hilltop home, and practically everything they own is carefully locked up. They seldom drive at night. They will not share water with the squatters nor buy products from their poverty-stricken neighbors. They teach their children: "If we start buying from these people, we'll be encouraging them! That's not the message we want them to get now, is it?" (150). Rohan's family and neighbors take it upon themselves to secure their privileged lifestyle, while hoping that the government will create a "safety net" for the Black underclass. Refugees from other African nations have heightened the scarcities, even beyond what the more affluent South Africans have endured while the post-Apartheid government builds a more equitable social system.

In his parents' absence, Rohan gives water to a boy whose mother is in the throes of childbirth, and he helps carry the water to the camp. He never asks the boy his name, but the midwife has called him Solani and Rohan knows this is the boy who has left a beautifully crafted wire car by Rohan's gate as a token of gratitude. Naidoo tells readers a little about the craft of sculpturing wire, and also about the difficulty in earning a fair price or even finding a commercial outlet for Solani's finely crafted objects. The nearby mall keeps guards at the gates to fend off young artists of his class.

Naidoo has not portrayed Rohan as miraculously shedding his life-long socialization in relation to class privilege,[6] but the devastating floods in southern Africa at the turn of the century enable her to insert scenes from TV newscasts about Mozambique. Thus Rohan sees the risks people take (even people in the South African army) when emergencies leave people stranded. He sees a mother and newborn being lifted from a tree by a South African helicopter. This same aircraft, Rohan reasons, may have been used to bomb African National Congress freedom fighters that were opposing Apartheid and receiving sanctuary in Mozambique.

South Africa's Child Martyrs

The young people who crossed borders to fight Apartheid were not the kind of desperate teenagers we encountered in the Stratton novels about Chanda.

And they were different from the child soldiers we have already touched on in this book. These young people did not participate in great numbers in the ANC anti-Apartheid rebellion until they saw unmistakably the writing on the wall in Soweto in 1976. The child martyrs of Soweto were schoolchildren with the right sensibilities. That is, they recognized the deep meaning embedded in the new school rule that in half of their classes they would be taught in the Afrikaans language. Through this rule their identity would be so unforgivably attacked that to acquiesce meant that no future was left for them. They had suffered terrible injustices through forced home removals, the separation of their parents through anti-miscegenation laws, and the dispersion of family members through labor laws geared solely to enrich White South Africans. But now they would be coerced into speaking the language of the perpetrators of these insufferable afflictions. Moreover, as in Soweto, they would be killed if they took their objections into the streets.

Thus Soweto inadvertently started a movement across the whole South African landscape. Young people boycotted and demonstrated in what was essentially an unending time frame. In other words, they were unlike adults who could go on strike, yet would be quickly brought back into line when the government reduced them and their families to starvation. Although the Black adult work force was *needed* by the White minority population to sustain the nation's economy and its own privileges, it was also Whites who had all the necessary *weapons* to control Black Africans inside the country. But we speak here of adult Black Africans. With amazing wisdom and foresight, the children saw their chance and took it. They waged war on Apartheid and "the line of command rested with the children themselves" (Nina, 44).

The "transformation of South Africa from an undemocratic and oppressive society into one that is democratic and participative"—this was the history-making event in which children participated. And they operated outside the regulation of the state, and "in many cases of the family itself" (Nina, 44). This participation lasted from 1976 to the election of Nelson Mandela in 1994 and took a great toll on children. They made a wide-ranging sacrifice not only due to government repression, but also in terms of inner wounds such as alienation and the effects of a life basically denied both a childhood and its customary patterns of development.

The overthrow of Apartheid occurred on many spontaneous, makeshift "battlefields" that victimized children even as it made them liberationist heroes. In the end, the children experienced, on many levels, the extreme suffering of martyrdom.

* * *

Summaries of Apartheid laws beginning in 1948, the year the Afrikaner National Party took charge, are included at the end of Naidoo's book. Most of the stories touch on laws restricting marriage, job opportunities, living spaces, and school attendance, and also on the resistance movement that slowly gained strength through student boycotts and other strategies. This factual background material is historically important, and is accompanied by Naidoo's fictional profiles of privileged White children who defended the Apartheid regime (as in the story "One Day, Lily, One Day"). The history of these White children is not included in most of the literature dealing with the years 1974 through 1994, but their early socialization is part of what influences South Africa.

Naidoo looks closely at socialization and usually manages to avoid sermon-like interruptions, no matter what the temptation might be. Characterization is uppermost and credible except in those stories (e.g., "The Noose") in which too many Apartheid laws are introduced with too much frequency. When this happens, readers may come away with the impression that they have been observing an argument rather than a life.

With so much psychological and fact-based detail offered to the reader, it would be hard to doubt Naidoo's genuine familiarity with both the conditions and personalities she describes. She knows well Apartheid's traumatic effects. She knows the "very dust you kick around." She illumines a history unique to the African continent's "child soldiers"—that is, the young fought *one another* as the result of the racial differences that the state regulated for its own unjust purposes. Over centuries, and stemming from no fault of their own, many South African children had come to assume that contrasting, disparate White and Black interests were normative. From the first imperialist incursion, a chasm among children had been constructed upon the myths that treated "race" as unmistakably significant.

Research in the field of genetics has long since debunked the notion that humans can be meaningfully classified in relation to distinct races. "On average, 99.9 percent of the genetic features of humans are the same; and of the remaining percentage that accounts for variation, differences *within* groups are larger than *between* groups" (Bangura, 3, emphasis added). Nonetheless, "race" continues to adversely affect social relations and political progress. We let that which is most trivial, in scientific terms, become the most widespread as a source of prejudice and mischief-making.

In the world of books, *Out of Bounds* rests upon actual science. It casts light on the tragedies that beset children when their caregivers let purely imagined distinctions rule their lives.

Works Cited

Bangura, Yusef, with Thomas Ansorg and Anita Tombez. 2002. "UNRISD Conference News: Racism and Public Policy" (International Conference Report, September 3–5, 2001, Durban, South Africa). *The Black Scholar* 32: 3–4 (Fall/Winter): 2–25.

Coles, Robert. 1986. *The Political Life of Children*. Boston: The Atlantic Monthly Press.

Maddox, Gregory. 1993. "Introduction." In *The Colonial Epoch in Africa*, vol. 2, ed. Gregory Maddox, xi–xvi. New York: Garland.

Mphahlele, Ezekial. 1976. "The African Critic Today: Toward a Definition." In *Reading Black: Essays in the Criticism of Africa, Caribbean, and Black American Literature,* ed. Houston A. Baker, Jr., 13–19. Philadelphia: University of Pennsylvania.

Naidoo, Beverley. 2001, 2003. *Out of Bounds: Seven Stories of Conflict and Hope.* London: Puffin Books; New York: HarperCollins.

Nina, Daniel. 1999. "Children Involved in South Africa's Wars: After Soweto 1976." In *Child Soldiers in Southern Africa,* ed. Elizabeth Bennett, 43–86. Halfway House, South Africa: Institute for Security Studies.

Sparks, Allister. 2003. *Beyond the Miracle: Inside the New South Africa.* London: Profile Books.

Terreblanche, Sampie. 2002. *A History of Inequality in South Africa, 1652–2002.* Pietermaritzburg, South Africa: University of Natal Press

Epilogue

The [United Nations] General Assembly, Recalling its previous resolutions, especially... those of the Commission on Human Rights... reaffirm[s] that children's rights require special protection and call for continuous improvement of the situation of children all over the world, as well as for their development and education in conditions of peace and security.
—**Convention on the Rights of the Child (1989)**

Descriptions of what are in the best interests of children are not in short supply. The twenty-two-page Convention on the Rights of the Child (1989) is a detailed list of what we can consider to be the bare minimum of what children and young adults deserve. But caregivers in continuous contact with the young—for example, parents, teachers, and librarians—tend to accept whatever is dished out about Africa in children's literature. After all, authors, publishers, and disseminators of books are part of a service-oriented profession. Their goals are tied to quality book creation and selection. Yet when derived from Western sources, children's fiction about Africa has generally disserved children. And the evaluation of works of fiction by literary critics has similarly disserved them. The parameters of our critical inquiries have been noticeably narrow and Eurocentric. Admittedly, children's books have always been situated in a national context, but books we have critiqued in this book show the need to begin looking closely and deliberately at the international context.

To begin addressing this need, we might take account of the difference between social service and social change. Meaningful change is not apt to spring forth spontaneously in Europe and North America given the involvement of these regions in imperialism—in programs that increase the unequal treatment of those in "disadvantaged" regions. Paul Kivel puts the issue bluntly: "Do our efforts to provide human services maintain or even strengthen social inequality?" (129). We can learn about equity and inequity in the Convention on the Rights of the Child and in other international documents. The need is to harness our child-related occupations to social justice for children on every continent.

Many of us are connected with groups or organizations with which we are regularly in touch. It would not be hard for us to highlight in professional circles questions that Kivel poses as he contrasts social service and social change:

> What are the historical *roots* of the work that you do? . . . Who actually *benefits* from the work that you do? Are there ways in which . . . you have come to enforce the status quo or train young people for their role in it? (137, emphasis added)

In responding to the first question, we could turn to a number of children's literature studies (many listed in the Selected Bibliography) that uncover connections between literature, white supremacy, and Western-based imperialism. This background material is important in any study of contemporary fiction about Africa. Patterns that emerge in new and old novels suggest what needs doing in our daily round if we are to replace disservice with service. The second question—who benefits?—is not in the least ambiguous to those professing multicultural ideals. Serving one group as a means to entertain one child population at the expense of another—this is the injustice that multiculturalism was born to challenge. Kivel's third question—how much do we promote the status quo?—relates to the whole children's book establishment. Do our reviews, prizes, and celebratory conferences only echo what poorly informed authors and disinterested publishers have said about Africa and Africans?

These questions offer good starting points for social and cultural historians as well as children's literature activists. Succeeding the Black Revolution in the United States in the 1950s and 1960s, the "N" word finally disappeared from children's literature, but novels about Africa are replete with cultural racism.[1] Unfamiliar or unappreciated cultural elements become stand-ins for supposed biological inferiority. Whatever aggravates feelings of aversion toward a group casts shadows of doubt on that group's human legitimacy. To study American social history, this type of racism must be understood because it illustrates how similar battles against social rejection and political repression are faced by both Africans and African Americans. And in response a Pan-African movement has preceded and continues to shape African and African American reformist initiatives in every cultural field—children's literature included. Pan-Africanism is a thread running through all Black history because, as Michael Williams stresses, the liberation of both African and Diasporan people has been hugely inhibited. It has faced "the manipulations and intransigence of imperialist domination, especially in its neo-colonial phase of development" (180). We argue that children's novels about Africa continually contribute to that intransigence. They blithely prepare each new generation in the West for fear of the "Dark Continent," as well as for the anti-social actions that fear engenders. Certainly Western domination and expansionism receive encouragement from the many children's novels that bad-mouth African traditions—that complain about supposed environmental irresponsibility, abuse of women and animals, and political dysfunction in African states.

Taking a broad view, Williams sees hope stemming from the vigorous efforts that were taken to end Apartheid in South Africa. However, he might well be disappointed if he took up the study of children's novels originating in the Apartheid and post-Apartheid children's book establishment.[2] Any international and Pan-African hopes he might entertain are severely challenged in the White-over-Black propaganda in cultural productions directed at the young.[3]

Children's literature practitioners have typically been enthralled by the idea of "universalism," even when they were hearing and repeating only a "monumental Western monologue" (Osundare, 206). Despite well-meaning objectives, universal ideals do not come into play when authors seek to flatten out events in the world (as when a character in one novel admits Apartheid's genocide and then dilutes its meaning by explaining to the young how *every* country has things to be ashamed of).

In the works of neo-imperialist fiction critiqued in this book, the novelists' distortions of Africa call for deliberately thorough rebuttals. Such refutations constitute a Pan-African endeavor—an effort to challenge the ahistorical treatment of Black experience across the globe. The more these counterarguments find their way into children's book criticism, the closer we will come to attaining social justice and the realization of children's rights.

Works Cited

Cashmore, Ellis. 2005. "Cultural Racism." In *The Encyclopedia of Race and Ethnic Studies*, ed. Ellis Cashmore, 96–98. New York: Routledge.

Convention on the Rights of the Child. 1989. U.N. document A/RES/44/25 (December 12). http://www.cirp.org/library/ethics/UN-convention/

Kivel, Paul. "Social Service or Social Change?" In *The Revolution Will Not Be Funded: Beyond the Non-Profit Industrial Complex*, ed. by INCITE! Women of Color Against Violence, 129–149. Cambridge, MA: South End Press.

Osundare, Nyi. 1994. "How Post-Colonial Is African Literature?" *Matatu* 12: 203–216.

Williams, Michael. 1998. "The Pan-African Movement." In *Africana Studies: A Survey of Africa and the African Diaspora*, 2nd ed., ed. by Mario Azevedo, 169–181. Durham, NC: Carolina Academic Press.

Notes

Notes to the Introduction

1 "The White Man's Burden" is a poem written by Rudyard Kipling in response to the conquest of the Philippines by the United States. It appeared in *McClure's Magazine* in 1899 and persuaded many Americans that British imperialism was a benevolent enterprise, a mission well worth copying.
2 Kenyan novelist and playwright Ngũgĩ wa Thiong'o has written frequently about education and comments about the era following nominal colonialism: "During the neo-colonial stage of imperialism education and culture play an even more important role as instruments of domination and oppression.... Since the petit-bourgeoisie grew up accepting the world-view of the imperialist bourgeoisie, it will drive the youth even more vigorously into educational factories producing the same world-view" (*Barrel of the Pen*, 97).
3 An English teacher in Iowa, Nick Spencer, shared with his eighth-grade students an incident in Cameroon as a way to imply that rational thinking means *White* thinking. He tells them about his "houseboy," Ipanda, who killed a poisonous snake in Spencer's house, and although others in the community wanted to expel it, "they considered it impossible, [believing] it was a guardian, an immortal spirit, of my house, a product of *my* magic." Spencer told them the incident changed Ipanda's life forever: "'Ipanda became a white man.' 'A white man?' 'Yes,' I assure them. 'In every way that mattered to the villagers, he became a white man.'" That is, Ipanda "left his village, ... graduated from the University of Cameroon, ... and became a lawyer for his nation's Supreme Court" (Spencer, 37). Spencer chooses "whiteness" as a convenient shorthand when asserting ethnocentric ideas about "progress" versus "backwardness" in Africa.
4 In *Writing Against Neocolonialism*, Ngũgĩ clarifies his use of gender-based pronouns: "The terms 'he' and 'his' . . . are not used to denote the 'maleness' of a person. It should be read to indicate an individual person, whether male or female" (20).

152 • Neo-Imperialism in Children's Literature About Africa

5 We want to mention at the outset how important has been the work of Nancy J. Schmidt over more than a quarter of a century. Schmidt is an African Studies Area specialist at the Indiana University Library and in 1975 began alerting children's literature workers to the character and importance of children's books about Africa. (See *Children's Books on Africa and Their Authors: An Annotated Bibliography* [Africana, 1975]; the *Supplement* for *Children's Books on Africa* in 1979; and *Children's Fiction About Africa in English* [Conch Magazine Limited, 1981]).

6 Fourny and Ha draw upon Raymond Williams' definitions of culture by noting its eighteenth-century meaning as synonymous with "civilization," and its modern meanings as (1) a process of intellectual and artistic development; (2) a way of life for a people (the anthropological definition); (3) the activities connected with music, painting, etc. The meanings revolving around art are often perceived as elitist, and therefore in sharp contrast with culture viewed as the life of a people or group (Fourny and Ha, 2).

7 Professor Steady cites AAWORD (Association of African Women for Research and Development) and DAWN (Development Alternatives for Women in a New Era) as offering alternatives to the undemocratic proclivities of IMF (the International Monetary Fund), WTO (The World Trade Organization), and the World Bank. Members of women's organizations have, in her view, taken a more egalitarian approach, and have understood the neo-colonialism that underlies much corporate globalization (174).

8 George Orwell observed that popular films and fiction can be the "worst" and still the "most important": " . . . the worst books are often the most important because . . . read earliest in life. It is probable that many people who would consider themselves . . . 'advanced' are actually carrying through life an imaginative background which they acquired in childhood . . . ." (qtd. in Richards, 2).

9 Chris Tiffin and Alan Lawson have commented on how children see the "ground plan of the universe"—the layout of immutable race hierarchies—in colonialist children's fiction. And when children internalize their own subjection by means of such literature, that is when "the true work of colonial textuality is done" (4).

Notes to Chapter 1

1 For an overview of the centuries-old "stunted children" motif, see Chapter 15 ("Are They Children?") in Basil Davidson's *Awakening Africa*.

2 In his meticulous study, *The Scramble for Africa:1876–1912*, Thomas Pakenham concludes with a "post-colonial" comment: "Giant European and North American companies continue to dominate the economies of fledgling African states. The new word for this is neo-colonialism. It

is much the same as informal empire: the invisible empire of trade and influence that had preceded the Scramble" (680). A former Tanzanian Minister of Economic Affairs and Development Planning, A. M. Babu, recognized a similar phenomenon and stated that "As long as we continue ... to produce for the so-called world market which was founded on the hard rock of slavery and colonialism, our economies will remain colonial." His observation here is as pertinent today as in the 1970s, namely, that "Any development will be entirely incidental, leaving the vast majority of the population wholly uninvolved in the economic activity" (284). (See A.M. Baba in Walter Rodney's *How Europe Underdeveloped Africa*.)

3 Much of the distress over Black education seems clearly tied to class-based anxieties. For example, "Negroes sneer at the idea of work"; "they feel that manual labor is beneath them" (Howard Odum, 1910); "We have thousands of negro men and women roving the streets looking impudent and avoiding work" (John Ambrose Price, 1907); "The negro teacher," said Alabama Governor William Dorsey Jelks, "has taught the beauty of idleness and the decency of theft, or has, at least, made no impression to the contrary ... " (qtd. in Newby, 177, 178).

4 For information about this Muslim sharia law and others that are child-related, see Fatima L. Adamu's address at a 2005 Nigerian conference on women's rights and sharia. (http://www.peacewomen.org/new/Nigeria/April05/Rights.html)*

5 Historically, anthropology has had a problematic relationship with African Studies. This is because it "emerged as a help mate" for European colonizers—an academic discipline aiding in the study of those African communities that the colonizers were administering. This was to neglect the central aspects of colonialism and instead to concentrate on a so-called clash of cultures. A careful study of societies was called for, but as Iheanyi Samuel-Mbaekwe comments, there was "a more or less conscious desire on the part of these anthropologists to avoid questioning the very foundations (and ideology) of the society to which they belong, the society of the colonial power" (37).

6 Francis Galton was a cousin of Charles Darwin and established the Eugenics Education Society in London in 1908.

7 This phrase is borrowed from John M. MacKenzie's introductory comments to Jeffrey Richards' *Imperialism and Juvenile Literature* (1989).

Notes to Chapter 2

1 In studying and revisiting African proverbs, we have found these collections helpful: *African Proverbs* collected by Lady Kofo Ademola (Pocket Gifts, An imprint of Bookcraft Ltd., Ibadan, Nigeria, 2000) and *The A-Z of African Proverbs* collected by Jan Knappert (Karnak House, 1989).

2. White supremacy in the American women's movement is entrenched. "It is not simply a matter of ideology, ideas, stereotypes, images, and/or misguided perceptions. It is about power and control, be it in terms of money, construction of ideology, or control over organizational agenda" (Russo, 306). This situation still defies correction. Speaking about White women at feminist events, Cherríe Moraga comments that "so often the women seem to feel no loss, no lack, no absence when women of color are not involved; therefore there is little desire to change the situation" (33).
3. Another type of modern practitioner is the Zionist faith healer who combines a type of Pentecostal Christianity with traditional beliefs. According to Enid Gort, "they espouse prophesy, speaking in tongues, ecstatic dancing, and the laying on of hands." And like a traditional diviner, they believe that dreams are a divine channel for needed inspiration (Gort, 300–301).
4. For the role that faith healers have been having in the rehabilitation of child soldiers and especially with regard to helping them through postwar mental problems, see *Civil Wars, Child Soldiers, and Post Conflict Peace Building in West Africa* by Amadu Sesay and Wale Ismail (2003) and *Child Soldiers in Africa* by Alcinda Honwana (2006).
5. In what is called "eco-racism," some international institutions have capitalized on the environmental preservation issue with deals that ostensibly aid in the maintenance of national parks and other areas marked for conservation. For example, Ghana entered into such a plan with the Development Coalition/Smithsonian Institute at the cost of US $250,000, but the plan was neither environmentally nor economically advantageous to Ghana (Okediran, 254).
6. In addition to improved water and agricultural policies, African communities need protection from the Western industrial pollution practices that endanger health in poor countries. Large companies enjoy tax breaks and the lax enforcement of environmental regulations, thus making poor and disadvantaged regions easy targets for dangerous levels of pollution. At least 64 studies have "demonstrated that race is the most potent variable determining where people live, where industries are located, and where environmental law enforcement is lax" (Bangura, 18–19, 21).

Notes to Chapter 3

1. Another glaring example of institutional racism is the re-segregation of the American public schools. In 2004, more than 70 percent of Black students attended segregated schools, and on all fronts those schools were sub-standard: below standard in building safety, student health, curriculum, and class size. Also "tracking" arrangements were racist in

their racial disproportionality—that is, the lowest social and economic groups were placed on the lowest track, although this type of discrimination has been ruled unconstitutional. (See Anne Wheelock's *Crossing the Tracks* and John I. Goodlad's *A Place Called School.*)
2. To win the Batchelder Award, an American publisher must publish the "most outstanding of those books originally published in a foreign language in a foreign country and subsequently published in English in the United States during the preceding year" (Batchelder Award Terms and Criteria).
3. See John Newsinger's "Lord Greystoke and Darkest Africa: The Politics of the Tarzan Stories" for an analysis of racism in the Tarzan novels.
4. Parents' Choice was founded in 1978 to evaluate toys, children's books, and other media, and to prepare study guides for parents and other kinds of products that can help them make informed decisions.
5. KidsPOD ("Kids Protecting Our Diversity") is the work of writers, artists, teachers, and musicians committed to combating prejudice. It publishes online its own reviews of children's books.
6. Brenda Randolph is the first recipient of the Francois Manchuelle Award sponsored by the Association of African Studies Programs. This award (honoring an Africanist who lost his life in the TWA-800 plane crash in 1996) promotes innovative work in African Studies at undergraduate and K–12 levels. Randolph has edited the online database Africa Access for a dozen years and has made it a critical voice in relation to books about Africa for children and young adults.
7. Chronologies of historical events, lengthy bibliographies, author's notes, and references to an author's on-the-spot journal entries are among the devices authors and publishers use to convince readers of a work's authenticity. They can be found in many of the novels discussed in this book. They would be a positive feature were it not for the way they contradict what the novel contains.

Notes to Chapter 4

1. As noted in Chapter 2, Islamic scholars Sada, Adamu and Ahmad have summarized various Islamic sharia laws pertaining to the rights of women. Equal education for women is one example. Another is the rule that girls be protected from harassment and assault. Also noted is the danger that a young girl can experience from pedophiles and others when girl-child marriages are practiced (Sada, Adamu, and Ahmad, 9–13).
2. This exploitation of wildlife for recreational purposes is one link between conservation and imperialism. But studies on conservation show another—namely, "the recognition of environmental degradation in oceanic islands subjected to the needs of European empires

[e.g., St. Helena, Mauritius, and islands belonging to India]" (MacKenzie, 3).

3 *Our Secret, Siri Aang* won the Henry Bergh Book Prize sponsored by the ASPCA (American Society for the Prevention of Cruelty to Animals). It was honored for its promotion of compassionate treatment of animals.

4 Kessler's emphasis on anesthetics is somewhat misleading, since today circumcision can be performed with the aid of antibiotics, tranquilizers, and pain killers, and people performing the procedure are being professionally trained with the help of government-sponsored programs.

Notes to Chapter 5

1 The term "Darkest Africa" is an invention of the nineteenth century and could express either "geographical ignorance" or "cultural arrogance." It also indicates the aura of what Western travelers were selectively reporting from Africa—namely, accounts of things most repellent to the West (e.g., lavish, high-spirited festivals, body decorations, polygamy, etc.) Indicators of a *shared* humanity were thoroughly submerged (Curtin, 9, 23).

2 This quotation is from an address by Maurice Evans delivered at the South African "Durban Native Affairs Reform Club" in 1912. Evans proclaimed the need to "protect, assist, control, study to give the black man in our midst, not an individual opportunity but a racial opportunity." South Africa was not unique in vigorously promoting race-oriented pseudo-science in the twentieth century, as the German Third Reich and the British and American eugenics movements bear witness. In these movements, as in Evan's case, racial inferiority was deemed essentially inevitable through the inheritance of "inferior" (and frequently African-associated) characteristics.

3 International record-keeping on the current existence of slavery contradicts Allende's blithe introduction of "Pygmy" slaves in her plot. According to the monitors of the slave trade, in the Central African Republic, there has been no evidence of persons trafficked to, from, within, or through the country.

4 Reviewers making the magical realism connection include Nancy Zachary in *VOYA*. She writes, "Magic realism is blended throughout in a richly detailed narrative about tribal customs, good versus evil, the harmony between the real world and the spirits, and the necessary coexistence of animals and humans" (141). Paula Rohrlick's review in *Kliatt* (May, 2005) mentions that "[T]his tense tale has . . . lots of action and excitement along with elements of magical realism." *Kirkus Reviews* finds the young protagonists' totemic animal spirits "rather baffling even within the context of Allende's magic realism" (467).

5 In 2004, Allende was inducted into the American Academy of Arts and Sciences.

Notes to Chapter 6

1 Clitoridectomy/excision, the practice in most of West Africa, involves the partial or complete removal of the clitoris and labia minora. Infibulation is another form of circumcision in which the clitoris and labia minora are cut and the edges of the vulva are sewn together. It has been practiced in parts of Africa and Asia, and in Europe it was practiced until early in the nineteenth century. (See Hanny Lightfoot-Klein's *Prisoners of Ritual*.)
2 It is worth noting that for thousands of years, the Sande and Poro societies (the latter created for young men) were serious, thoroughly developed educational institutions offering *equal* educational opportunities for boys and girls. These learning facilities had honor students, school principals, and other well-planned structural elements. The idea that *no* education would be offered to girls was an idea transported to Africa by the colonizing West.
3 For a discussion of *Papa Tembo* in relation to Joseph Conrad's *Heart of Darkness*, see Mawuena Kossi Logan's "Labor Party Reforms Versus Imperial Literary Practices."

Notes to Chapter 7

1 *Many Stones* received ecstatic praise within children's book circles. It was a National Book Award finalist and a *Los Angeles Times* Book Prize finalist in 2000. It was rewarded a Michael L. Printz Honor Book citation in 2001. The American Library Association added it to its "Best Books for Young Adults" list. The important journal for librarians, *Booklist*, made it an "Editors' Choice" selection, and the *School Library Journal* included it in the "Best Books of the Year" list in 2000. Critics liked its emotional elements, its reconciliation theme, and its breathless pace. When Africa is mentioned, it is referred to as a country with a "savage past" (see the Rochman review cited in Chapter 7). However, critics are silent about the degree to which Carolyn Coman depicts Africa with a "savage" present. This dimension of the work cuts off the possibility of offering the novel to Africans. And if Africans cannot read it, who among the world's population of children *can* benefit from all this misinformation? An emotional trip for Western teenagers is hardly a worthwhile trade-off.
2 When Margaret Thatcher was Prime Minister of the United Kingdom, she voiced how natural it would be for people in Britain to reject some non-Brits: "The British character has done so much for democracy, for law and order and so much throughout the world that, if there was any

fear that it might be swamped, people are going to react and be hostile to those coming in" (qtd. in Cashmore, 96). She made sure that Asians desiring to enter Britain after Hong Kong was returned to China would qualify only if they were doctors, lawyers, Ph.D.s, and so forth.
3. Under the new South African constitution and with the supervision of a special commission, lands taken from Africans since 1913 could be restored to them (Thompson, 250–251).

Notes to Chapter 8

1. According to some scholarly studies of the San, it would be difficult to find anyone in this group with a purely San heritage.
2. In 1869, Francis Galton put forth his eugenics theories in *Hereditary Genius*, including the idea that heredity determined differences in moral, mental, and physical traits. Galton was Charles Darwin's cousin and the association of eugenics with Darwin's theory of evolution added force to eugenic theorizing (Stepan, 113–114).
3. Negotiations were under way in 2003 between the Council for Scientific and Industrial Research and the South African San Council due to the alleged theft and patenting of a hunger- and thirst-suppressing formula based on a succulent *(Hoodia gordonia)* that the San people have used for generations. The American Pharma-Companies were the appropriators of this traditional science (Holmann, 15).
4. In 1839, Samuel Morton proclaimed in *Crania Americana* that American Indians and Negroes had such a small cranial capacity that they were doomed to either extermination or enslavement. In *The Descent of Man* (1871), Charles Darwin was explicit in noting the way native peoples would become extinct as the natural result of evolution. George Chatteron Hill commented on the way every "superior race" had been engaged in the elimination of "inferior races" (*Heredity and Selection*, 1907). In 1927, anthropologist George H. L.-F. Pitt-Rivers wrote in *The Clash of Cultures* that the "Native Problem" stemmed from the *survival* of races that should have been "exterminated by the 'blessings of civilization.'" (See Ellis Cashmore's *Encyclopedia of Race and Ethnic Studies* [2005] for these references and many more examples.)
5. Jan Christian Smuts was of Boer descent and held the post of South African Prime Minister from 1919 to 1924 and 1939 to 1948. He was in the upper echelon of the British war councilors in World War II and was active in organizing the United Nations. In the 1930s he contributed articles and speeches about the supposed inevitability of "Bushman" extinction (e.g., in a speech in 1932 for the South African Association for the Advancement of Science).
6. Beverley Naidoo broke new ground in South African children's fiction with her short novel geared for beginning readers, *Journey to Jo'burg*

(1984). Its sequel *Chain of Fire* (1989) is a novel for older readers and a much more substantial work in relation to character development and in terms of its historical content dealing with forced removals of Blacks to the so-called Homelands. Beginning in 2000 she turned her attention to novels about Africans in exile in Britain. We cover her collection of short stories (*Out of Bounds: Seven Stories of Conflict and Hope*, 2001) in Chapter 12.

Notes to Chapter 9

1. In Chapter 10 ("When the West Talks to Itself"), excerpts from Edgar Rice Burroughs' *Tarzan of the Apes*, H. Rider Haggard's *King Solomon's Mines*, and Nancy Farmer's *The Ear, the Eye, and the Arm* show the similarity among nineteenth- and twentieth-century portrayals of "witch doctors."
2. Among many findings in a set of workshops in Zambia is a record of the increase in those attributing AIDS to HIV (75% in contrast to only 33.3% when examined earlier) and a reduction for participants believing that AIDS was God's punishment (5% in contrast to an earlier 24.2%) (see Chirwa and Sivile, 330).
3. The feminization of poverty in Africa adds to the AIDS problem and has been attributed to the employment structure inherited from the colonial period. Without patrons or specialized job skills, urban men as well as women survive through work in the informal sector where job security and income are inadequate. Without waged employment, many men are too poor to start families since the informal sector is overcrowded. Women's activities in this sector (e.g., domestic service, sewing, market gardening, midwifery, smuggling, and prostitution) are so unprofitable that women seek occasional partners, multiple partners, or both, as a means to survive. All this impacts the spread of AIDS (Schoepf, 248–249).
4. The Association of African Women for Research and Development has emphasized the neo-colonial nature of research on women and the negative impact of debt burdens and such policies as privatization. It has been noted that the World Bank, the International Monetary Fund, and the General Agreements on Tariffs and Trade (all founded in 1944) are agencies of the United Nations, but "unlike the U.N. General Assembly, they do not function on the principle of "one country, one vote" but on the basis of "one dollar, one vote" (Steady, 168–169).
5. "'Damn the coal-tar,'" says the adult storyteller, Momo. He complains that the car noise and traffic frighten the birds. "'Now bird is gone just as leopard is gone, following deer and monkey, since people came to be too plenty'" (5, 6).

6 The anti-African assumptions in Bess' novel are all the more unfortunate because he is unusually gifted as a writer of colloquial dialogue and poetic description. Here are a few samples from his refreshing prose style: "I looked around at Ma and Old Ma to see them scary too of leopard coming to weep at our house" (6); "Cold hand took hold of my heart . . . and made fist?"(19); "Next weeks walked by like turtle in sand" (72).

Notes to Chapter 10

1 This chapter by Donnarae MacCann was first published in volume 3 of *Sankofa: A Journal of African Children's and Young Adult Literature* (2004). It is reprinted here in a slightly revised form.

2 The two additional "African" novels by Farmer are *Do You Know Me* (1993) and *The Warm Place* (1995). In the former, stereotypic characterizations dominate the work, from the "backward" uncle whose mentality is that of a child, to the snobbish uncle who becomes absurdly elitist in his government job. *The Warm Place* (1995) features only anthropomorphic African animals and their relationship with an African American child.

3 The name "Shona," writes Solomon Mangwiro Mutswairo, was imposed from outside and "then applied to the multiplicity of the so-called Shona dialects in Zimbabwe," and in neighboring states (1).

4 Ella Shohat and Robert Stam offer this definition of neo-colonialism: "a conjuncture in which direct political and military control [as typical in colonialism] has given way to abstract, semi-direct . . . forms of control . . ." (17).

5 Nancy Farmer, a native of Arizona, worked in the Peace Corps in India and spent seventeen years in Africa as a chemist, lab technician, entomologist, and freelance writer. She cites Roald Dahl, J. R. R. Tolkien, and C. S. Lewis among the authors she studied vis-à-vis novel-writing (*Something About the Author* [57]). Ironically, although Farmer has written three politically charged novels about Africa, she says of politics that she has "none whatsoever" (SATA, 56).

6 Michael Gelfand notes that a *shave* is often described according to its main function. The basic belief is that a wandering spirit ("wandering" because denied certain burial rites) selects a medium through which it can speak (84, 166).

7 Roger Sutton, writing for *The Bulletin of the Center for Children's Books*, seems to agree with Deifendeiger about *The Ear, the Eye, and the Arm*. He comments: "Farmer has wisely considered what the passage of two centuries might bring"—e.g., "grimy street life, high-rise glamor, and a simultaneous vision of apocalypse . . . and [a] fundamentalist paradise (where the 'old ways' are preserved . . .)" (220).

8 Writing in the *Horn Book*, Martha Parravano does not see the social and cultural material in *A Girl Named Disaster* as distorted. She commends Farmer for "fascinating, minute detail" and for teaching readers "an amazing amount about . . . Shona culture and Zimbabwean politics" (734–735). In this assessment, misinformation is mistaken for "detail."

9 The ongoing history of colonialist literature can be traced in a number of additional works: Kathryn Castle's *Brittania's Children: Reading Colonialism Through Children's Books and Magazines*; Dorothy Hammond and Alta Jablow's *The Africa That Never Was*; G. D. Killam's *Africa in English Fiction, 1874–1939*; and Mawuena Kossi Logan's *Narrating Africa: George Henty and the Fiction of Empire*.

Notes to Chapter 11

1 Children in earlier centuries were active combatants. In 1212 they were persuaded to believe that by joining the Children's Crusades, Jerusalem would be delivered by God into their hands. Boys were recruited to serve in the Middle Ages as squires for knights and to replace an injured or dead knight on the battlefield. In Britain under Admiral Nelson, boys of fifteen years served as cabin boys and in dangerous jobs handling explosives. Napoleon removed twelve-year-olds from lower-class families and turned them into soldiers.

2 Stratton interrupts his narrative repeatedly to tell readers how Africans believe in magic. One example is his account of how people believed a hollowed-out pumpkin had been used by a spirit doctor to spy on a rival spirit doctor by flying over his house. But the rival cast a spell on the pumpkin, bringing it to the ground, and that led to a broken leg in the first spirit doctor (an accident from falling off a ladder, he said, but to the African community this was unlikely since "the timing [was] considered suspicious," [76]). Chanda becomes a target of suspicion and is driven away when a shopkeeper finds two owls in the eaves of his shop. He screams at her: "'It's you that brought this. Things were fine before you came. Now there's bandits. Owls. Death'" (178–179). Some nearby soldiers observe her as if "I'm a witch." Child soldier recruits are fair game for "spiritual" tricks with skulls, monkey skins, and so forth—talismans that terrorize.

3 For six years UN negotiators debated the minimum age they felt was suitable for child recruits, and they decided in 2000 on eighteen as the minimum age. But the United States, United Kingdom, and Australia vigorously protested since this interfered with their access to young boys for enrollment in military schools. Thus an optional protocol was added to the Convention on the Rights of the Child allowing for what they called *voluntary recruitment*, which made sixteen years

the minimum that would be permitted for "voluntary noncombatant recruits" (Honwana, 36).

4 By referring to civilian casualties as a *theoretical* feature in "irregular" wars, Honwana is speaking of a methodology for warfare that makes women, children, the elderly, and the domestic animal population fair game for targeted destruction (34–35). She mentions that over 90% of casualties in "new wars" have been civilians. At the same time, traditional wars had already removed the line between civilian and military targets with the bombing of London in World War II by the Germans, the bombing of Dresden by the Allied forces, and the nuclear bombing of Hiroshima and Nagasaki by the Americans.

Notes to Chapter 12

1 In the note on her "timeline" for 1950, Naidoo describes The Suppression of Communism Act this way: "People are listed as 'communists' if they actively fight against apartheid. They can be banned from meeting other people, confined to a particular area, or banished to a faraway place" (171).

2 Naidoo's outline of important events includes this statement about 1976: "Thousands of black secondary school students in Soweto protest when the government says half their lessons will, from now on, be taught in Afrikaans. Police open fire, killing children. Anger explodes across the country. Hundreds of young people are killed in demonstrations and many more thousands are thrown into jail. Many young people escape from the country, some to train with MK" (173–174). (MK stands for the ANC's Umkhonto we Sizwe [Spear of the Nation]—one of several liberation armies that was engaged in traditional battle tactics against the South African armed forces.)

3 The protest tradition that was so greatly enlarged after the police's unprovoked murder of schoolchildren grew further over time and the state retaliated in kind. The government called for two states of emergency between 1983 and 1990 in its effort to contain young resisters in the townships.

4 South Africa is unusual in being a nation where children were the victims of a brutal regime, and at the same time played a leadership role in overthrowing it. This was less true when the ban on anti-Apartheid organizations was lifted in 1990 and the exiled population could return to South Africa. However, at the time when Apartheid (the National Party) had full control over discriminatory law-making and law-enforcing, there were almost no windows of opportunity for opposition by adults. Factory workers could not sustain a protest since their wages (if not their jobs and lives) were at stake. Only their meager wages protected their families from starvation.

5 According to a conference conducted by the UN Research Institute for Social Development in 2001, land inequalities in South Africa are still enormous: 60,000 White farmers own 85 million hectares, while 12 million Blacks subsist on 17.1 million, and only 5% of that 17.1 million is arable (Bangura, 9).
6 Average income for Indian-headed families is R71,000 in contrast to R23,000 for African-headed families. Thus Rohan enjoys many small luxuries that Solani will never be able to imagine in his childhood. Both families, however, are far below the income level for White-headed families: that is, R103,000 (Bangura, 20).

Notes to the Epilogue

1 Cultural racism is defined by Ellis Cashmore as "a conceit: a way of disguising racist thought and behavior by phrasing it in a way that precludes reference to biological or psychological differences" (Cashmore, 96).
2 Not only novels, but also professional critiques of novels about South Africa often lend support to white supremacy. Therefore we added a footnote in the Bibliography of our 2001 book *Apartheid and Racism in South African Children's Literature, 1985–1995* to explain why we did not include in our list some well-known works by South African children's literature specialists. Novels we criticized in our book as racist were works praised in Elwyn Jenkins' *Children of the Sun: Selected Writers and Themes in South African Children's Literature* (Johannesburg: Ravan Press, 1993); Jay Heale's *From the Bushveld to Biko: The Growth of South African Children's Literature in English from 1907 to 1992 Traced through 110 Notable Books* (Grabouw, South Africa: Bookchat, 1996); Jay Heale's *South African Authors & Illustrators* (Grabouw, South Africa: Bookchat, 1994); Shirley Davies's *Reading Roundabout: A Review of South African Children's Literature* (Pietermaritzburg, South Africa: Shuter & Shooter, 1992).
3 Nyi Osundare notes that "names commit; which is why the Yoruba say that it is only mad people who do not mind the names they are called, or who refuse to see the difference between the names they choose to bear and the ones the world prefers to call them by" (204).

Selected Bibliography

Social, Political, Historical Studies

Abu-Sahlieh, Sami A. Aldeeb. 2006. "Male and Female Circumcision: The Myth of the Difference." In *Female Circumcision: Multicultural Perspectives*, ed. Rogaia Mustafa Abusharaf, 47–72. Philadelphia: Pennsylvania University Press.

Appiah, Kwame Anthony and Henry Louis Gates, Jr. 2005. *Africana: The Encyclopedia of the African and African American Experience*. Oxford, UK: Oxford UP.

Bell, Terry with Dumisa Buhle Ntsebeza. 2001, 2003. *Unfinished Business: South Africa Apartheid & Truth*. Observatory 7935, South Africa: RedWorks; London: Verso.

Biko, Steve. 1987. *I Write What I Like*. London: Heinemann. (Originally published 1978)

Curtin, Philip D. 1964. *The Image of Africa: British Ideas and Action, 1780–1850*. Madison: University of Wisconsin Press.

Davidson, Basil. 1955. *The African Awakening*. London: Jonathan Cape.

Davidson, Basil. 1994. *Modern Africa: Social and Political History*, 3rd ed. London: Longman.

Dubow, Saul. 1995. *Scientific Racism in Modern South Africa*. Cambridge, UK: Cambridge UP.

Fredrickson, George M. 1981. *White Supremacy: A Comparative Study in American and South African History*. New York: Oxford UP.

Fredrickson, George M. 1995. *Black Liberation: A Comparative History of Black Ideologies in the United States and South Africa*. New York: Oxford UP.

Fyfe, Christopher. 1992. "Race, empire and the historians." *Race & Class* 33:2: 15–30.

Godlewska, Anne and Neil Smith, eds. 1994. *Geography and Empire*. Cambridge, MA: Blackwell.

Guelke, Adrian. 2005. *Rethinking the Rise and Fall of Apartheid: South Africa and World Politics*. Basingstoke, Hampshire, UK: Palgrave Macmillan.

Hirson, Baruch. 1979. *Year of Fire, Year of Ash: The Soweto Revolt: Roots of a Revolution?* London: Zed Press.

Hunter-Gault, Charlayne. 2006. *New News Out of Africa: Uncovering Africa's Renaissance*. New York: Oxford UP.

Iliffe, John. 1995. *Africans: The History of a Continent*. Cambridge, UK: Cambridge UP.

Le May, G. H. L. 1994. *The Afrikaners: An Historical Interpretation*. Oxford, UK: Blackwell.

MacKenzie, John M. 1990. *Imperialism and the Natural World*. Manchester, UK: Manchester UP.

Marx, Anthony W. 1992. *Lessons of Struggle: South African Internal Opposition, 1960–1990*. New York: Oxford UP.

Meredith, Martin. 2007. *Diamonds, Gold, and War: The British, the Boers, and the Making of South Africa*. New York: Public Affairs.

Mermelstein, David, ed. 1987. *The Anti-Apartheid Reader: The Struggle Against White Racist Rule in South Africa*. New York: Grove Press.

Mikell, Gwendolyn, ed. 1997. *African Feminism: The Politics of Survival in Sub-Saharan Africa*. Philadelphia: University of Pennsylvania Press.

Murray, Nancy. 1997. "Somewhere Over the Rainbow: A Journey to the New South Africa." *Race and Class* 38:3: 1–24.

Ngeokovane, Cecil. 1989. *Demons of Apartheid: A Moral and Ethical Analysis of the N.G.K., N.P. and Broederbond's Justification of Apartheid.* Cape Town, South Africa: Skotaville.

Nnaemeka, Obioma, ed. 1998. *Sisterhood, Feminisms & Power: From Africa to the Diaspora.* Trenton, NJ: Africa World Press.

Okediran, Adefolake Y. 1998. "Bonds That Bind, Bondages That Burden—Women and Environmental Sustainability in Africa." In *Gender Perceptions and Development in Africa: A Socio-Cultural Approach,* ed. Mary E. Modupe Kolawole, 243–259. Lagos, Nigeria: Arrabon Academic.

Olusi, Omolara. 1998. "Socio-Cultural, Economic and Environmental Determinants of African Women's Poverty and Disempowerment: The Nigerian Example." In *Gender Perceptions and Development in Africa: A Socio-Cultural Approach,* ed. Mary E. Modupe Kolawole, 261–284. Lagos, Nigeria: Arrabon Academic.

Onwubu, Chukwuemeka. 1990. "The Intellectual Foundations of Racism." In *Black Studies: Theory, Method, & Cultural Perspectives,* ed. Talmadge Anderson, 77–88. Pullman: Washington State UP.

Pakenham, Thomas. 1991. *The Scramble for Africa: 1876–1912.* London: Weidenfeld and Nicolson.

Rich, Paul. 1993. "Race, Science, and the Legitimization of White Supremacy in South Africa, 1902–1940." In *Colonialism and Nationalism in Africa: A Four Volume Anthology of Scholarly Articles,* eds. Gregory Maddox and Timothy K. Welliver, 81–102. New York: Garland.

Rodney, Walter. 1982. *How Europe Underdeveloped Africa.* Washington, DC: Howard UP.

Samuel-Mbaekwe, Iheanyi J. 1993. "Colonialism and Social Structure." In *Colonialism and Nationalism in Africa: A Four Volume Anthology of Scholarly Articles,* eds. Gregory Maddox and Timothy K. Welliver, 33–47. New York: Garland.

Schoepf, Brooke Grundfest. 1995. "Action-Research and Empowerment in Africa." In *Women Resisting AIDS: Feminist Strategies for Empowerment,* eds., Beth E. Schneider and Nancy E. Stoller, 246–269. Philadelphia: Temple UP.

Schutte, Gerard. 1995. *What Racists Believe: Race Relations in South Africa and the United States.* Thousand Oaks, CA: Sage.

Steady, Filomina Chioma. 2006. *Women and Collective Action in Africa: Development, Democratization, and Empowerment, with Special Focus on Sierra Leone.* New York: Palgrave Macmillan.

Sparks, Allister. 2003. *Beyond the Miracle: Inside the New South Africa.* London: Profile Books.

Stepan, Nancy. 1982. *The Idea of Race in Science: Great Britain 1800–1960.* London: Macmillan.

Terreblanche, Sampie. 2002. *A History of Inequality in South Africa, 1652–2002.* Pietermaritzburg, South Africa: University of Natal Press.

Thompson, Leonard. 1985. *The Political Mythology of Apartheid.* New Haven, CT: Yale UP.

Thompson, Leonard. 1995. *A History of South Africa,* rev. ed. New Haven, CT: Yale UP.

Literary and Cultural Studies

Achebe, Chinua. 1989. *Hopes and Impediments: Selected Essays.* New York: Doubleday.

Ahmad, Aijaz. 1995. "The Politics of Literary Postcoloniality." *Race and Class* 36:3: 1–20.

Brantlinger, Patrick. 1988. *The Rule of Darkness: British Literature and Imperialism, 1830–1914.* Ithaca, NY: Cornell UP.

Cashmore, Ellis, ed. 2005. *Encyclopedia of Race and Ethnic Studies.* London and New York: Routledge.

Dabydeen, David, ed. 1985. *The Black Presence in English Literature.* Manchester, UK: Manchester UP.

Davis, Geoffrey and Holger G. Ehling. 1994. "On a Knife Edge: Interview with Dennis Brutus." *Matatu* 11: 101–110.

English, James F. 2005. *The Economy of Prestige: Prizes, Awards, and the Circulation of Cultural Value.* Cambridge, MA: Harvard UP.

February, V. A. 1981. *Mind Your Colour: The "Coloured" Stereotype in South African Literature.* London: Kegan Paul.

Fourny, Jean-François and Marie-Paule Ha. 1997. "Introduction: The History of an Idea." *Research in African Literatures* 28:4 (Winter): 1–7.

Frankenberg, Ruth and Lata Mani. 1993. "Crosscurrents, Crosstalk: Race, "Postcoloniality" and the Politics of Location." *Cultural Studies* 7:2 (May): 292–310.

Hammond, Dorothy and Alta Jablow. 1970. *The Africa That Never Was.* New York: Twayne.

Katz, Wendy R. 1987. *Rider Haggard and the Fiction of Empire: A Critical Study of British Imperial Fiction.* New York: Cambridge UP.

Killam, G. D. 1968. *Africa in English Fiction, 1874–1939.* Ibadan, Nigeria: Ibadan UP.
MacKenzie, John M. 1986. *Imperialism and Popular Culture.* Manchester, UK: Manchester UP.
McClintock, Anne. 1992. "The Angel of Progress: Pitfalls of the Term 'Post-Colonial.'" *Social Text* 31/32: 84–98.
Morrison, Toni. 1992, 1993. *Playing in the Dark: Whiteness and the Literary Imagination.* Cambridge, MA: Harvard UP; New York: Vintage Books.
Mphahlele, Es'kia. 2002. *Es'kia: Education, African Humanism & Culture, Social Consciousness, Literary Appreciation.* Cape Town: Kwela Books.
Mphahlele, Ezekiel. 1976. "The African Critic Today: Toward A Definition." In *Essays in the Criticism of Caribbean and Black American Literature,* ed. Houston Baker, Jr, 13–19 Ithaca, NY: Cornell UP.
Newsinger, John. 1986. "Lord Greystoke and Darkest Africa: The Politics of the Tarzan Stories." *Race & Class* 28:2 (Autumn): 59–71.
Ngũgĩ, wa Thiong'o. 1986. *Decolonizing the Mind: The Politics of Language in African Literature.* Portsmouth, NH; Heinemann; London: James Currey.
Ngũgĩ, wa Thiong'o. 1993. *Moving the Centre: The Struggle for Cultural Freedoms.* Portsmouth, NH: Heinemann; London: James Durrey.
Nnaemeka, Obioma. 1995. "Feminism, Rebellious Women, and Cultural Boundaries: Rereading Flora Nwapa and Her Compatriots." *Research in African Literatures* 26:2: 80–113.
Ogbaa, Kalu. 1981. "An Interview with Chinua Achebe." *Research in African Literatures* 12:1 (Spring): 1–13.
Okonkwo, Chidi. 1999. *Decolonization Agonistics in Postcolonial Fiction.* New York: St. Martin's Press.
Osundare, Nyi. 1994. "How Post-Colonial is African Literature?" *Matatu* 12: 203–216.
Peck, Richard. 1997. *A Morbid Fascination: White Prose and Politics in Apartheid South Africa.* Westport, CT: Greenwood Press.
Pieterse, Jan Nederveen. 1992. *White on Black: Images of Africa and Blacks in Western Popular Culture.* New Haven, CT: Yale UP.
Press, Karen. 1990. *Towards a Revolutionary Artistic Practice in South Africa.* Cape Town, South Africa: University of Cape Town, Centre for African Studies.
Said, Edward W. 1993. *Culture and Imperialism.* New York: Knopf.
Samin, Richard. 1997. "Interview: Richard Samin with Es'kia Mphahlele." *Research in African Literatures* 28:4: 182–200.
Sheckels, Theodore F., Jr. 1996. *The Lion on the Freeway: A Thematic Introduction to Contemporary South African Literature in English.* New York: Peter Lang.
Shohat, Ella and Robert Stam. 1995. *Unthinking Eurocentrism: Multiculturalism and the Media.* London: Routledge.
Smith, Linda Ruhiwai. 2002. *Decolonizing Methodologies: Research and Indigenous Peoples.* London: Zed Books.
Stecopoulos, Harilaos. 2007. "Putting an Old Africa on Our Map: British Imperial Legacies and Contemporary US Culture." In *Exceptional State: Contemporary U.S. Culture and the New Imperialism,* eds. Ashley Dawson and Malini Johar Schueller, 221–227. Durham, NC: Duke UP.
Strongman, Luke. 2002. *The Booker Prize and the Legacy of Empire.* Amsterdam: Rodopi.
Tiffin, Chris and Alan Lawson. 1994. *De-Scribing Empire: Post-Colonialism and Textuality.* London: Routledge.

Childhood Studies: Social, Political, Literary

Asante-Darko, Kwaku. 2002. "Towards a Post-Colonial Children's Literature for Black Africa." *Mots Pluriels* 22 (September): 1–9.
Attikpoé, Kodjo. 2006. "African Images in Current German Fiction for Children and Young Adults: A Denial of African Culture." *Sankofa: A Journal of African Children's and Young Adult Literature* 5: 62–70.
Bennett, Elizabeth, ed. 1999. *Child Soldiers in Southern Africa* (ISS monograph series, no. 37). Halfway House, South Africa: Institute for Security Studies.
Burman, Sandra and Pamela Reynolds, eds. 1986. *Growing Up in a Divided Society: The Contexts of Childhood in South Africa.* Johannesburg: Ravan Press.
Castle, Kathryn. 1996. *Britannia's Children: Reading Colonialism Through Children's Books and Magazines.* Manchester, UK: Manchester UP.
Coles, Robert. 1986. *The Political Life of Children.* Boston: Atlantic Monthly Press.

Guy, Arnold. 1980. *Held Fast for England: G. A. Henty, Imperialist Boys' Writer*. London: Hamish Hamilton.
Honwana, Alcinda. 2006. *Child Soldiers in Africa*. Philadelphia: University of Pennsylvania Press.
James, Louis. 1973. "Tom Brown's Imperialist Sons." *Victorian Studies* 17:1 (September): 89–99.
Journal of African Children's and Youth Literature (JACYL). Ed. Osayimwense Osa. Virginia State University, Chesterfield, VA 23831.
Khorana, Meena. 1988. "Apartheid in South African Children's Fiction." *Children's Literature Association Quarterly* 13:2: 52–56.
Khorana, Meena, ed. 1998. *Critical Perspectives on Postcolonial African Children's and Young Adult Literature*. Westport, CT: Greenwood Press.
Kidd, Kenneth. 2007. "Prizing Children's Literature: The Case of Newbery Gold." *Children's Literature* 35: 166–190.
Klobah, Mahoumbah. 2005. "Sowing the Seeds of Knowledge in Children's Literature: Sociocultural Values in J. O. de Graft Hanson's *The Golden Oware Counters*." *Children's Literature Association Quarterly* 30:2 (Summer): 152–163.
Logan, Mawuena. 1994/1995. "Pushing the Imperial/Colonial Agenda: G. A. Henty's *The Young Colonists*." *Journal of African Children's and Youth Literature* 6: 29–42.
Logan, Mawuena Kossi. 1999. *Narrating Africa: George Henty and the Fiction of Empire*. New York: Garland.
Logan, Mawuena Kossi. 2001. "Labour Party Reforms Versus Imperialist Literary Practice." *The Lion and the Unicorn* 25:3 (September): 391–411.
MacCann, Donnarae. 1998, 2001. *White Supremacy in Children's Literature: Characterizations of African Americans, 1830–1900*. New York: Garland; New York: Routledge.
MacCann, Donnarae. 2005. "The Sturdy Fabric of Cultural Imperialism: Tracing Its Patterns in Contemporary Children's Novels." *Children's Literature* 33: 186–209.
MacCann, Donnarae and Yulisa Amadu Maddy. 2001. *Apartheid and Racism in South African Children's Literature, 1985–1995*. New York: Routledge.
Maddy, Yulisa Amadu and Donnarae MacCann. 1996. *African Images in Juvenile Literature: Commentaries on Neocolonialist Fiction*. Jefferson, NC: McFarland.
Maddy, Yulisa Amadu and Donnarae MacCann. 1998. "Ambivalent Signals in South African Young Adult Novels." *Bookbird: World of Children's Books* 36:1 (Spring): 27–32.
Mangan, J. A. 1988. *"Benefits Bestowed?" Education and British Imperialism*. Manchester, UK: Manchester UP.
Osa, Osayimwense. 1995. *African Children's and Youth Literature*. New York: Twayne.
Petzold, Jochen. 2005. "Children's Literature After Apartheid: Examining 'Hidden Histories' of South Africa's Past." *Children's Literature Association Quarterly* 30:2 (Summer): 140–151.
Reynolds, Pamela. 1989. *Childhood in Crossroads: Cognition and Society in South Africa*. Cape Town, South Africa: David Philip.
Richards, Jeffrey, ed. 1989. *Imperialism and Juvenile Literature*. Manchester, UK: Manchester UP.
Sankofa: A Journal of African Children's and Young Adult Literature. Ed. Meena Khorana. Morgan State University, Baltimore, Maryland 21239.
Schmidt, Nancy J. 1981. *Children's Fiction About Africa in English*. Owerri, Nigeria: Conch Magazine.
Sesay, Amadu, ed. 2003. *Civil Wars, Child Soldiers and Post Conflict Peace Building in West Africa*. Ibadan, Nigeria: College Press.
Sharra, Steve. 2001. "*The Baboon King*: Institutionalizing Anti-African Bias in Children's Literature." *Children's Literature Association Quarterly* 26:2 (Summer): 96–99.
Smith, Katharine Capshaw. 2004. *Children's Literature of the Harlem Renaissance*. Bloomington: Indiana UP.
Spidle, Jake W. 1975. "Victorian Juvenilia and the Image of the Black African." *Journal of Popular Culture* 9:1 (Summer): 51–64.

Index

Achebe, Chinua, 13
African Images in Juvenile Literature: Commentaries on Neocolonialist Fiction, 3
African independence mocked, 120
African National Congress (ANC), 83, 85, 89
African Studies Association, 34
Africans "dying out," 91–100
Africans on exhibit, 92–95, 97–99
Aidoo, Ama Ata, 18
AIDS; *see* health problems
Aina, Olabisi, 21
Ajeemah and His Son, 18
Aka groups (Central African Republic)
  Bantu links with, 59–60
  colonial religion and white supremacy, 57–58, 61
  domestic life, 58
  forestry specialization, 59
  French colonial rule, 59–60
  "Pygmy" label, 58
  religion mocked, 58–59
  speech and appearance demeaned, 58
  Western "saviors," 56
Allende, Isabel, 16, 21, 25, 55–63
  novel
    Forest of the Pygmies, 55–63
American Library Association, 31
American Society for the Prevention of Cruelty to Animals (ASPCA), 33–34
Anglo-Boer War (1899–1902), 96
Angola, 130
Apartheid and anti-Apartheid issues
  anti-Apartheid activism in "The Typewriter," 139–140
  class disparities in "The Dare," 136–137
  destabilizing Southern Africa, 30
  exile in "The Gun," 140–142
  Indian family in "Out of Bounds," 142
  martyrdom of children, 142–144
  migrant workers, 141–142
  parent friction in "One Day, Lily, One Day," 137–139
  socialization of children, 135–136
Apartheid and Racism in South African Children's Literature, 1985–1995, 3
Apple, Michael, 30
Asante-Darko, Kwaku, 13

Babatunde, E, 49
The Baboon King, 32
Bantu groups (Central African Republic)
  Aka groups, ties with, 59–60
  caricatures: drunks, henchmen, 58–59
Bess, Clayton, 101, 109–112
  novel
    Story for a Black Night, 109–112
book critics
  anti-African fiction applauded, 3, 11, 34, 88, 118, 131, 156n, 157n, 160n, 161n
  "Dark Africa" myth promoted, 13–14, 31
  internationalist goals, 31–32
  nationalism, 30–31
  studies of South African children's literature, 163n
Brantlinger, Patrick, 122
Bregin, Elana, 91–99

short story
  "Ella's Dunes," 91–99
Brown v. Board of Education, 18
Burroughs, Edgar Rice, 113, 121, 122
Bushman; *see* San groups (South Africa)
By Sheer Pluck: A Tale of the Ashanti War, 14

Cameroon, 151n
Campbell, Eric, 65–66, 70–77
  novel
    Papa Tembo, 70–77
Carmichael, Stokely, 29
Cashmore, Ellis, 2, 87
Castle, Kathryn, 14
Central African Republic
  setting for *Forest of the Pygmies*, 57–64
Césaire, Aimé, 16
Chain of Fire, 18
Chanda's Secrets, 25, 101–106, 125
Chanda's Wars, 25, 125–131
child martyrs
  anti-Apartheid movement leaders, 143, 162n
  child supporters of Apartheid, 144
  psychological impact on leaders, 143–144
  Soweto uprising and massacre, 143, 162n
child soldiering
  abductions, 125, 128
  government complicity, 126, 131
  historical roots, 161
  indigenous rights, 130
  international examples, 126
  light weight weaponry, 126
  neighboring states, involvement of, 126, 130
  poverty-related roots, 125–126, 129
  prostitution, 126
  treaties that protect children
    International Criminal Court's Rome Statute, 129
    International LaborOrganization's Convention on Worst Forms of Child Labor, 129
    Organization of African Unity's Charter on the Rights and Welfare of the Child, 129
    UN Convention on the Rights of the Child, 129, 131, 147
children; *see also* child martyrs, child soldiering
"captive audience" status, 8
child-animal bonding, 46–48, 71–72
child culture, 7
  hegemonic indoctrination of, 5, 56, 147, 152n
  miseducation of ethnic groups,
    Aka, 55–64
    Bantu, 55–64
    Berber, 39–46
    Kikuyu, 32
    Maasai, 46–54, 71–78
    San, 91–100
    Shona, 115–118
    Zulu, 85–90
  social control of, 7
  social responsibility toward, 62–63, 147–149
  socialization of, 1, 4, 6–7, 31, 152n
Children's Africana Book Award (CABA), 34–35
Children's Literature Association, 33
circumcision; *see* genital cutting
City of the Beasts, 55
class issues,
  disparities in "The Dare," 136–137,
  educational dimensions, 2–3, 153n
  racial connections, 27
  schoolbooks and class disparities, 7, 35, 85–89, 136–137, 142
colonialism
  definitions, 1–2, 160n
  epochal in scale, 2
  foundations of, 15–16
  literary prizes implicated, 35
  neo-colonial interventions, 30
  neo-colonialism, comparison with, 152–153n
  polygamy, opposition to, 25
  resistance to, 8
  traditional practices, campaigns against, 50
Coman, Carolyn, 79–85
  novel
    Many Stones, 79–85
Conrad, Joseph, 69
conservation; *see* environmental issues
criminality
  Apartheid government crimes
    assassinations, 81
    human rights repressions, 83
    kidnapping, 82
    torture, 81
    unmarked graves, 82
  bribery, 86

car-jacking, 79
drugs, influence of, 84
international crime syndicates, 79
international smuggling (gold, ivory, diamonds), 84
poaching, 86
police discrimination against Blacks 84, 85
"primitivism" and crime linked, 75
unemployment, influence of, 85
weapons, availability of, 88
cultural imperialism; see cultural racism
cultural racism
　colonialist connections, 6
　contemporary forms, 87, 148–149
　definition of, 163n
　segregation of races, 3, 85–89, 96–97, 138
　"universalism" contradicted, 149
culture
　"cultural schizophrenia" charged, 6
　cultural practices outlawed, 76
　culture formation, 114
　definitions, 152n
　economic dimensions, 4
　group naming practices, 120–121
　"high culture," 5
　political connections, 2–3, 4, 7, 29, 76, 120, 151n
Curtin, Philip D., 13

"The Dare," 136–137
"Darkest Africa"
　African character maligned, 13–15
　children, influence on, 13–15, 16, 18, 19, 96–99
　definitions, 14, 156n
　European connections with, 15, 16
　pandemics, connections with, 101–102
　"White man's burden," 1, 13, 56, 151n
Davidson, Basil, 55
De Klerk, F.W., 83
Deborah Ellis, 101, 106–109
　novels
　　The Heaven Shop, 106–109
Doctor Dolittle's Zoo, 14

The Ear, the Eye, and the Arm, 18, 21, 25, 113–118, 122
education
　African American education opposed, 17–18
　African subject matter outlawed, 76

"Dark Africa" myth supported, 13–15
European invasions celebrated, 14
hostile educational settings, 4, 86–87, 94–95
inequality supported, 1, 7, 67
Maasai schooling, 76
San schooling, 94–95
school boycotts, South Africa, 162n
social control, 6–7
systemic racism, 30–31, 97
"warrior" schooling, 50, 52–53
"Ella's Dunes," 91–99
English, James F., 32, 35
environmental issues
　back-to-nature romanticism, 71
　child-animal bonding, 46–48, 71–72
　colonialist interference, 71–78
　colonialist mismanagement, 73
　ecology in novels, 113–118, 70–77, 113–118
　environmental laws ignored/violated, 50, 52, 73, 74, 154n 155–156n
　ivory trade, 71
　Maasai conservation policies, 73
　neo-colonialist projects, 71–78, 154n
essentialism, 5–6
ethnic and language based groups
　Aka, 16, 55–64
　Bantu, 55–64
　Berber, 17, 39–46
　Hausa, 42
　Hutu, 36
　Khoikhoi, 97
　Kikuyu, 32
　Maasai, 17, 33, 46–54 (Kenyan), 71–78 (Tanzanian)
　San, 91–100
　Shona, 115–118
　Tutsi, 36
　Zulu, 85–90
Eurocentricity, 58, 65–66, 70, 113–123, 147, 157–158n

Farmer, Nancy, 113–123
　novels
　　The Ear, the Eye, and the Arm, 113–118, 122
　　A Girl Named Disaster, 118–121
Feagin, Joe, 81, 82
feminism; see also traditional practices
　African activism, 22, 23, 152n

education for girls, 42, 43, 50, 157n
globalization, connections with, 6, 27, 159n
history shaping theory, 21
international development programs
　African resources undervalued, 27
　Cold War connections, 26
　family life, impact on, 26–27
　International Monetary Fund, 26
　loans in Western foreign policy, 26–27, 159n
　jobs in informal sector, 159n
　Western and African versions of, 21, 23, 39
　white supremacy combined with liberationist themes, 56–57, 154n
　women and Islamic laws, 22–23
Ferreira, Anton, 79–80, 85–89
　novel
　　Zulu Dog, 85–89
fiction; *see* literature
Forest of the Pygmies, 16, 21, 25, 55–63

"gatekeepers;" *see* book critics
genocide, 35, 96
A Girl Named Disaster, 17, 21, 25, 113–114, 118–121
"The Gun," 140–142

Haggard, H. Rider, 69, 113, 121–122
Hamilton, Charles V., 29
Hari, Johann, 1
health problems
　AIDS
　　denials, public and private, 103, 104, 106
　　fraudulent druggists and morticians, 103–104
　　global economics, 105, 108–109
　　hospitals unprepared, 107–108
　　orphan prostitution, exploitation, 104, 106–108
　　poverty connections, 101, 104, 105, 108, 159n
　　religious involvement, 104, 159n
　　women vulnerable, 101, 103, 105, 108
　circumcision, risk of, 66–67
　smallpox
　　family conflicts, 109–110
　　quarantine law, 111
　　religious and theoretical arguments, 109–110

The Heaven Shop, 101, 106–109
Hegel, Georg Wilhelm Friedrich, 15
Henty, George A., 14, 18, 69
history; *see* social history
Honwana, Alcinda, 125, 127, 129
Horowitz, Irving Louis, 91
Hunter-Gault, Charlayne, 79, 84
hybridity, 3, 93

Imperialism and Juvenile Literature, 122
imperialism
　African resistance, 3, 8
　aims of, 2–3
　child development thwarted in, 1, 6
　different from neo-imperialism, 2
　"habit of mind," 2
　violence inherent in, 63
　"White man's burden," 1, 13, 56, 151n
inequality, 1, 2. 3. 5, 96, 97, 105, 163n
Inkatha Freedom Party (IFP), 89
institutional racism; *see* racism

Kane, Cheikh Hamidou, 113
Kenya, 23, 32, 46–54, 56
Kessler, Cristina, 39, 46–54, 65–70
　novels
　　No Condition is Permanent, 65–70
　　Our Secret, Siri Aang, 46–54
Khorana, Meena, 35
Kidd, Kenneth, 5, 30
KidsPOD, 34
King Solomon's Mines, 113, 121–122
Kingdom of the Golden Dragon, 55

land issues
　appropriations and restitution, 3, 14, 56, 95–96
　erosion, 141
　indigenous farming destroyed, 141–142
　inequalities in contemporary South Africa, 163n
　Land Act of 1935, 141
　women farm laborers, 141–142
Liberia, 33, 109–112, 130
Libya, 22, 40–46
literary prizes
　art as "nontemporal," 35
　bureaucratic influences, 35
　colonialist involvement, 35
　commercial influences, 32
　racial connections, 30–34

literature; *see also* book critics, literary prizes
  aesthetics of fiction, 7–8, 136, 144
  history, connections with, 7–8, 135, 136, 143–144
  imperialist dimensions, 3–4, 16, 31–34
  inequalities condoned, 1–4, 29–30
  "magical realism," 60–62
  Maasai creation myth, 51–52
  pulp fiction retentions, 4, 32, 36, 113, 121–122
  Shona lyric poetry, 116
  theories, 4–7
  universalist assumptions, 2, 5
  Western-derived subject matter, 31–34
Lofting, Hugh, 14
Logan, Mawuena Kossi, 63

MacKenzie, John, 2, 65
Madhubuti, Haki, 63
Malawi, 106–109
Mandela, Nelson, 80, 82, 83, 84, 87, 143
Many Stones, 79–85
McClintock, Anne, 25
Memories of Sun: Stories of Africa and America, 91
Mohanty, Chandra, 39, 41, 70
Mozambique, 114, 120, 130
Mphahlele, Ezekiel (Es'kia), 7–8, 135, 136
multiculturalism
  Batchelder Award, connections with, 31–33
  definition of, 5
  ideals unfulfilled, 3, 5
  misrepresentations in literature, 31–34
  political component, 5
Naidoo, Beverley, 8, 18, 35, 99, 135–144, 158–159n, 162n
  short stories
    Out of Bounds: Seven Stories of Conflict and Hope, 135–144
Nazism and "eugenics," 18
Nina, Daniel, 135
neo-colonialism; *see* colonialism
neo-imperialism; *see* imperialism
Ngũgĩ wa Thiong'o, 2–3, 4, 7, 76, 120, 123, 151n
Nigeria, 23, 27, 45, 49, 71
Nkrumah, Kwame, 55
Nnaemeka, Obioma, 8, 39, 45–46, 65

No Condition is Permanent, 21, 24, 65–70

"One Day, Lily, One Day," 137–139
Our Secret, Siri Aang, 17, 21, 22, 33, 39, 46–54
"Out of Bounds," 142
Out of Bounds: Seven Stories of Conflict and Hope, 135–144
Over a Thousand Hills I Walk with You, 35

Pan-African Movement, 148–149
Papa Tembo, 18, 25, 65–66, 70–77
Parents' Choice, 34
paternalism, 29, 30, 88
Paul Kivel, 147–148
Peace Corps, 33, 66, 160n
Pearson's Magazine, 72
Pieterse, Jan Nederveen, 13, 98, 122
political issues; *see also* criminality
  AIDS and official neglect, 102–108
  Anti-Apartheid movement, children in, 135, 141–144, 161n
  child soldiers, recruitment of, 125, 161–162n
  child soldiering, international scope, 126
  civil service corruption in education, 86–87
  corruption in prison systems, 75, 83, 107
  crimes against humanity, 82
  cultural practices outlawed, 76
  culture and oppressive rule, 151n
  democracy deemed impossible in Africa, 123, 131
  environmental laws violated, 50, 52, 73, 74, 155–156n
  globalization, unfair practices, 105, 108–109, 152–153n, 154n, 158n
  "Jim Crow" policies (US), 31
  land distribution, 88, 95–96, 163n
  militia groups, 126, 130
  peace agreements as undesirable, 130
  post-Apartheid governance inept, 86, 88
  treaties and child protection, 129–130, 147
  vigilante methods in policing, 74
  wars against civilians, 125–131, 161n
  wealth distribution, 108–109, 163n
popular culture; *see* literature

174 • Critical Approaches to Food in Children's Literature

Poro Society (Sierra Leone), 23, 24, 68–69, 157n
prizes; *see* literary prizes
proverbs (African), vii, 21, 23, 67, 69
pulp fiction; *see* literature
racism; *see also* cultural racism
   eugenics/white supremacy, 17–18, 156n
   individual racism, definition of, 29
   institutional
      connection with awards
         Batchelder Award, 31–33
         Bergh Award, 33–34
         Newbery Award, 30
         Phoenix Award, 30
      definition of, 29
      political-economic containment of Blacks, 30
   poverty-race interconnections, 27
   "reverse racism," 81–82
   science of biology, connections with, 17–18
   segregation, 3, 85–89, 96–97, 138
   Western legal system circumvented, 30
   zoos, people/animal connected, 97–99
Randolph, Brenda, 35–36
Richards, Jeffrey, 1, 122
Robben Island prison, 80, 82, 83
Rule of Darkness: British Literature and Imperialism, 1830–1914, 122
Rwanda, 35, 57

Said, Edward, 2
Samuel-Mbaekwe, Iheanye, 2, 15, 153n
Sande Society (Sierra Leone), 23, 68–69, 70, 157n
San groups (South Africa)
   Afrikaner history, role in, 96–97, 99
   appearance, 93, 96
   begging for survival, 92
   "doomed race" stereotype, 91–99, 158n
   drunkard stereotype, 92
   color-consciousness, 94,
   land losses, 92, 94, 95, 99
   lifestyles, 93, 94
   political activism, 95
   public exhibitions, 91–95, 97–99
   schooling, 94–95
Sankofa: A Journal of African Children's and Young Adult Literature, 35

Schmidt, Nancy J., 152n
Schoepf, Brooke Grundfest, 101
schooling; *see* education
The Science of Society, 16
The Shadows of Ghadames, 17, 21, 22, 25, 39–46, 54
Sharra, Steve, 32
Shohat, Ella, 101, 113
short-statured people, 16, 55–64; *see also* Aka groups, San groups
Sierra Leone, 23, 24, 66–70, 130
slavery, 14, 15, 18, 21, 113–114, 116
smallpox; *see* health problems
Smuts, Jan, 91, 92, 96
social change, 147–149
Social Darwinism and "survival of the fittest," 16–17
social history
   child leaders/activists, 142–144
   diversified situations and histories, 55
   ethnocentrism encoded, 39
   "Jim Crow" politics (US), 31
   literary prizes, connections with, 32, 35
   theoretical import, 6–7
social responsibility, 62–63, 147–149
Somalia, 74
South Africa, 31, 34, 79–100, 130, 135–144
South African Association for the Advancement of Science, 96–97
Soviet Union, 26
Soyinka, Wole, 30
spiritist healers; *see* traditional practices
Stam, Robert, 101, 113
Steady, Filomina Chioma, 6, 24, 27
stereotypes applied to indigenous Africans
   "black magic," 67
   brutish, animalistic, 58
   drunkenness, 91, 116
   "exotic," 4
   extinct (doomed), 91–100
   fanatical, 43
   immoral, 14–15
   infantile, 14
   murderous, 14
   over-weight, 43, 57, 68
   "primitive," 5, 13, 46, 67, 69, 75, 119
   "savage," 3, 14
   "stunted children," 13
   tribalistic, 35, 50
   unclean, 67, 71, 76

untamed, 15
"warrior-like," 50, 52–52
witchcraft (voodoo) practitioners, 14, 25–26, 59, 67, 76, 103
Stolz, Joëlle, 39–46, 54
novel
   The Shadows of Ghadames, 39–46, 54
Story for a Black Night, 33, 101, 109–112
Stratton, Allan, 101–106, 125–131
novels
   Chanda's Secrets, 101–106
   Chanda's Wars, 125–131
Sunday Reading for the Young, 58
Swaziland, 26

Tanzania, 71–78
Tarzan of the Apes, 32, 113, 121
'Tarzan" stereotypes, 32
terminology
   "Dark Continent" label, 15–16
   essentialism, definition of, 5–6
   ethnic names and labels
      capitalization, uses of, xiii
      colonial origins, connotations, xiii
   eugenics, definition of, 17–18, 158n
   evolutionist theory, 17
   multiculturalism, definition of, 5
   "survival of the fittest," 16
traditional practices
   ancestor worship, 61, 115
   bride price system, 122
   coming-of-age initiations, 23–24, 49–50, 68–69
   education, employment, domestic duties, interdependence of, 22
   genital cutting (circumcision)
      fertility connections, 23
      health problems, 66
      male and female, 49–50
      modern medicine, use of, 24, 49, 68
      religious implications, 49
   group loyalty, 22–23
   healing, traditional forms

      contemporary practices/ advantages, 26
      "growth industry," 26
      pulp fiction, connections with, 25
      "witch doctors," 25, 43, 75–76, 87, 117–120, 161n
   hunting ceremonies, 75–76
   marriage and polygamy, 22, 24–25, 41, 43, 44–45, 127, 128
   motherhood, valorization of, 45–46
   orphans, care of, 22
   "science" (Western) versus African beliefs, 119–120
   "secret" societies, 23–24
   sharia (Islamic) laws, 22, 155n
   "warrior" schooling, 50, 52–53
Transvaal Leader, 96
Troyna, Barry, 2
Truth and Reconciliation Commission (TRC), 80–83, 85
Tutu, Bishop Desmond, 83
"The Typewriter," 139–140

United Nations Convention on the Rights of the Child, 129–130, 147, 161–162n

Verwoerd, Hendrik, 85

"White man's burden," 1, 13, 56, 151n
White on Black: Images of Africa and Blacks in Western Popular Culture, 122
white supremacy; *see also* racism
   American women's movement, entrenchment in, 154n
   Blacks as "natural" subordinates, 16, 58, 65–66
   inequalities deemed inherent, 1–4
   "liberal" pretensions, 56, 62–63, 65–66
   persistence of, 2, 4, 14–18, 65

Zambia, 104, 159n
Zimbabwe, 115, 119–120
Zulu Dog, 85–89